Governance for the Environment

THE FONDAZIONE ENI ENRICO MATTEI (FEEM) SERIES ON ECONOMICS, THE ENVIRONMENT AND SUSTAINABLE DEVELOPMENT

Series Editor: Carlo Carraro, *University of Venice, Venice and Fondazione Eni Enrico Mattei (FEEM), Milan, Italy*

Editorial Board

FEEM is a nonprofit, nonpartisan research institution devoted to the study of sustainable development and global governance. Founded by the Eni group, officially recognized by the President of the Italian Republic in 1989, and in full operation since 1990, FEEM has grown to become a leading research centre, providing timely and objective analysis on a wide range of environmental, energy and global economic issues.

FEEM's mission is to improve – through the rigor of its research – the credibility and quality of decision-making in public and private spheres. This goal is achieved by creating an international and multidisciplinary network of researchers working on several innovative projects, by providing and promoting training in specialized areas of research, by disseminating research results through a wide range of outreach activities, and by delivering directly to policy makers via participation in various institutional fora.

The Fondazione Eni Enrico Mattei (FEEM) Series on Economics, the Environment and Sustainable Development publishes leading-edge research findings providing an authoritative and up-to-date source of information in all aspects of sustainable development. FEEM research outputs are the results of a sound and acknowledged co-operation between its internal staff and a worldwide network of outstanding researchers and practitioners. A Scientific Advisory Board of distinguished academics ensures the quality of the publications.

This series serves as an outlet for the main results of FEEM's research programmes in the areas of economics, the environment and sustainable development.

Titles in the series include:

Governance for the Environment

A Comparative Analysis of Environmental Policy Integration

Edited by

Alessandra Goria
Fondazione Eni Enrico Mattei, Italy

Alessandra Sgobbi
*Fondazione Eni Enrico Mattei, Italy
and European Commission – EuropeAid Cooperation Office,
Belgium*

Ingmar von Homeyer
Ecologic Institute, Germany

THE FONDAZIONE ENI ENRICO MATTEI (FEEM) SERIES ON
ECONOMICS, THE ENVIRONMENT AND SUSTAINABLE
DEVELOPMENT

Edward Elgar
Cheltenham, UK • Northampton, MA, USA

Published by
Edward Elgar Publishing Limited
The Lypiatts
15 Lansdown Road
Cheltenham
Glos GL50 2JA
UK

Edward Elgar Publishing, Inc.
William Pratt House
9 Dewey Court
Northampton
Massachusetts 01060
USA

A catalogue record for this book
is available from the British Library

Library of Congress Control Number: 2009938411

ISBN 978 1 84844 410 2

Printed and bound by MPG Books Group, UK

Contents

Figures

Tables

Contributors

Michela Catenacci, Fondazione Eni Enrico Mattei, Italy

Frank J. Convery, University College Dublin, Ireland

Bruno Dente, Politecnico di Milano, Italy

Alessandra Goria, Fondazione Eni Enrico Mattei, Italy

Kenneth Hanf, Department of Political Science, Pompeu Fabra University, Barcelona, Spain

Andrew Jordan, Centre for Social and Economic Research on the Global Environment, School of Environmental Sciences, University of East Anglia, Norwich, UK

Keti Medarova-Bergström, Central European University, Hungary

Josu Mezo, Faculty of Environmental Sciences, University of Castilla-La Mancha, Toledo, Spain

Carolina Pacchi, Dipartimento di Architettura e Pianificazione, Politecnico di Milano, Italy

Adam Paulsen, Ecologic – Institute for International and European Environmental Policy, Germany

Duncan Russel, Department of Politics, University of Exeter, UK

Philipp Schepelmann, Wuppertal Institute for Climate, Environment and Energy, Germany

Alessandra Sgobbi, Fondazione Eni Enrico Mattei, Italy and European Commission – EuropeAid Cooperation Office, Belgium

Tamara Steger, Central European University, Hungary

Georgios Terizakis, City of Hannover/Metropolitan Region Hannover Braunschweig Göttingen, Germany

Ingmar von Homeyer, Ecologic – Institute for International and European Environmental Policy, Germany

Davide Zanoni, Avanzi – Idee, Ricerche, Progetti per la Sostenibilità, Italy

Foreword

Carlo Carraro

Environmental protection is very often a public good, that is the benefits from a better environment can be captured by all the members of a given community (global, regional or local), and not only by those who contribute to protect nature or improve environmental quality. This makes it difficult to design effective environmental policies. Free-riding incentives and very asymmetric preferences for environmental protection dominate the decision process and weaken policy decisions.

Governing the global environment is a notoriously complex diplomatic task, and the lack of appropriate supra-national institutions contributes to this complexity. But governing national or local environments is not any simpler, even in the presence of well-designed and effective governing institutions.

The solution to the governance problem can be found in the integration of environmental policies with other global, regional or local policies. Environmental problems are likely to affect many dimensions of economic and social life, and can therefore be addressed by a number of integrated economic and social policies, rather than by specific environmental measures.

This volume addresses the above policy issues in a very detailed and effective manner. It is part of the output of the EPIGOV project that brought together scholars from eighteen universities and research institutes across Europe in an effort to synthesise and examine research and policy analyses on environmental policy integration. The project convened researchers belonging to a broad range of disciplines, including political sciences, economics, law and land use planning, and working with various methodological approaches. Three conferences were held under the auspices of the project and were used to compare and summarise the main findings of the research work.

This book focuses on the modes of governance associated with relevant measures to protect the environment at the national, regional and local levels. Its chapters provide a comprehensive assessment of the progress achieved in integrating the environmental dimension into national, regional and local policies. The book also compares different experiences with a view to identifying modes of governance which tend to be more or less conducive to environmental policy integration.

This book is the product of the outstanding work of the three editors in cooperation with all the partners of the EPIGOV network. FEEM (Fondazione Eni Enrico Mattei) provided secretarial and administrative support and organized the whole process leading to the publication. The analyses, results and experiences presented in this book can be very valuable to scholars and policymakers in the attempt to identify institutions and measures to protect the environment.

Carlo Carraro
Director of Research
Fondazione Eni Enrico Mattei

Introduction

Alessandra Goria, Ingmar von Homeyer and Alessandra Sgobbi

The integration of environmental concerns into other policy areas is widely recognised as a key element to achieve sustainable development. It also represents a challenge for the environmental community, requiring not only a new approach to policy making but also changes in existing policies and their implementation. More importantly, however, the cross-cutting nature of environmental policy integration (EPI) does not easily fit in with traditional practices and conceptions of hierarchical governance based on (nation) state authority, sectoral differentiation, and command-and-control type instruments. It is therefore not surprising that measures to promote EPI frequently seem to rely on different modes of governance, such as voluntary, procedural, information, learning and market-based instruments. To complicate matters further, EPI often entails different approaches depending on the level of governance – and may thus call for specific processes and instruments. Indeed, efforts to achieve and improve EPI are currently being made at local/regional, national, European and global levels of governance, and are not limited to the public sphere, but often take place within the private sector. Furthermore, measures at different levels may affect each other, thereby improving or weakening EPI and sustainable development. Indeed, the inter-linkages between the different levels and modes of governance are emerging as a central challenge in the area of EPI and are increasingly analysed and discussed in the literature.

This book examines existing research on environmental policy integration at three levels of policy-making: at the national level, both in relation to strategic and sectoral decision-making; at the regional level, where both supra-national and sub-national regional entities are discussed; and finally at the local level, where strategies available to municipalities or individuals for furthering environmental policy integration are presented. New and innovative approaches to the study of EPI at these levels of governance are also proposed. The chapters are a collection of selected research papers presented and discussed at the conference 'Integrating the environment into national, regional and local policies: current practices and future directions'.[1]

The conference was the second in a series of three thematic conferences, each of which focussed on the theory and practice of EPI at particular levels of governance as well as on more conceptual questions relating to modes of governance and multi-level governance. The three conferences were held under the auspices of the project Environmental Policy Integration and Multi-Level Governance (EPIGOV).[2] EPIGOV brought together researchers working on EPI from eighteen universities and research institutes across Europe in an effort to synthesise and analyse existing findings from a multi-level governance perspective. The EPIGOV project comprised research associated with a broad range of disciplines, including political sciences, economics, law, and land use planning, and with various methodological approaches. Reflecting this diversity, work was not based on a common analytical framework. However, papers were required to refer – either positively or critically – to a set of concepts discussed and set out in the EPIGOV Common Framework (Homeyer, 2006).

Reflecting different views of governance, definitions abound. For example, governance has been described from a more state-centric perspective as a 'continuous political process of setting explicit goals for society and intervening in it in order to achieve these goals' (Jachtenfuchs and Kohler-Koch, 2004: 99) or as 'conceptual or theoretical representation of co-ordination of social systems' (Pierre, 2000: 3) from a society-centric point of view. Given that EPIGOV focused mainly on the integration of environmental concerns into policies, the project was more concerned with the political processes emphasised by a state-centric definition of governance than with 'spontaneous' or 'bottom-up' environmental integration by societal actors. Nonetheless, research adopting a more society-centred perspective may also be relevant in so far as relevant environmental integration efforts affect policy-making and/or state-actors play an important role in the respective networks.

Although, due to its focus on policies, the very concept of EPI gravitates more to a state- than to a society-centric perspective, it is interesting to note that EPI appears to be mostly pursued on the basis of various so called 'new' modes of governance, such as communicative governance, voluntarism, market-based governance or targeting (Homeyer, 2007). These modes of governance are often associated with a relatively strong involvement of non-state actors in policy-making. On the one hand, this is not surprising if one considers that aspects of 'traditional' governance, in particular the sectoralisation of policy-making, are often identified as key reasons for the need to pursue EPI in the first place. Starting in the 1980s, it became increasingly apparent that 'sectoral' environmental policies were not adequate to deal with problems which were rooted in the functioning of other sectors. Cross-cutting, persistent environmental problems – such as the loss of biodiversity or climate change – call for an integrated approach to decision-making and strong collaborative efforts among different state and non-state actors (cf. Jänicke). This poses a challenge to the traditional system of sectoral governance. On the other hand, other aspects of 'traditional' governance, in particular hierarchical decision-making, are, if anything, much less clearly linked to the causes underlying the need to pursue EPI. In fact, there are frequent calls in the literature for more political leadership and more hierarchical intervention to increase the effectiveness of EPI measures. Today EPI is widely recognised as a critical environmental policy objective as well as a concept which has become central to sustainable development. This applies, in particular, to the EU and its Member States. For example, EPI has been anchored in the EU Treaties. Article 6 TEC states that

> environmental protection requirements must be integrated into the definition and implementation of [...] Community policies and activities [...], in particular with a view to promoting sustainable development.

This book thus focuses on EPI and the modes of governance associated with relevant measures at the national, regional and local levels. Through its chapters, it explores the implications for EPI of different modes of governance at different levels of governance – and vice-versa. The hope is to provide a comprehensive assessment of the progress which has been achieved in establishing and implementing EPI at these levels, describe relevant modes of governance and compare different experiences with a view to identifying modes of governance which tend to be more or less conducive to EPI.

In his opening chapter, Frank Convery takes an environmental economic perspective, defining a normative approach to EPI based on a standard economic assessment framework such as cost and benefit analysis, and discusses the behavioural impacts of 'suitable' price signals. According to the author, key to the achievement of EPI in the sense of ensuring appropriate consideration of the environment in decision-making, are: the availability of environmental information; public and private engagement; the existence of clear and appropriate price signals; and the right legal and institutional setup. The political effectiveness of the climate change and biodiversity debates is considered within this framework and the analysis seems to indicate that the growing importance of climate change in the political agenda worldwide can be at least partly attributed to the existence of the prerequisites needed to make EPI real.

The main strands in the literature on EPI at the national level are summarised by Alessandra Sgobbi in Chapter 2, with the ultimate aim to shed some light on the key component of a unifying framework for analysing EPI and its environmental effectiveness. At the national level, there are different interpretations of the axiom on environmental policy integration, as reflected in the literature discussing EPI. Four broad strands of literature are identified, focusing on: the strategic level; the national level in general; tools and strategies that governments at the central level may implement; and finally the assessment of EPI practices. Despite the large volume of literature on EPI at the national level, surprisingly few studies systematically compare processes, strategies and tools in individual countries in the pursuit of EPI. A clear assessment method must therefore be established to analyse progress, to use more effectively the wealth of experience with EPI and to establish how EPI may or may not work in different contexts. Progress will be slower in the absence of a clear benchmark against which to assess performance.

The challenge is even greater when focusing on environmental policy integration at the local and regional level, as shown in Chapter 3 by Michela Catenacci. Regions and local authorities have an important strategic role to play towards sustainable development, the protection of the environment and the development and implementation of policies, yet the vast majority of the literature dealing with environmental issues at these levels does not focus on EPI specifically, but rather addresses this topic within the broader context of sustainable development. Furthermore, the discussion of environmental matters at the regional and local level is dominated by a case study approach, with less emphasis devoted to the theoretical aspects of the environmental discourse.

An innovative and thought-provoking discussion on the strategic role of local entities in promoting EPI is presented by Bruno Dente. Throughout the centuries, the role of local entities has changed dramatically, from a strong welfare state in the post WWII period, with a tendency towards centralisation, to the anti-welfare backlash of the 1980s, that led to fiscal devolution, privatisation and an increasing role of local authorities. But the observed globalisation presents new challenges to local authorities, which have also strong implications for EPI at this level of governance. In particular, Dente's argument is not that everything can (and perhaps should) be integrated at the territorial level, with the choice depending on the level of participation and interaction required by the specific need for EPI. At the local level, EPI is better thought of as an outcome rather than a process, to bring about changes in the way actors interact at the local level, challenging existing power structures. In this context, the sphere of property rights is particularly complex, given the nature of public good as well as the existence of private vested interests in the protection of the environment. EPI effectiveness at the local level therefore depends on the inclusion of the property right dimension to bring about the necessary integration between state and non-state actors.

EPI must be considered as a policy outcome; however, EPI may also induce a process of policy learning by which policy makers, as well as other actors, become aware of sustainability issues and integrate them into their policy fields. This is the focus of Georgios Terizakis's chapter, where the concept of Governance for Sustainability is discussed: from an EPI perspective, then, the interactions and interdependencies between knowledge and sustainability become critical, with sustainability as a core crucial dimension of EPI. Knowledge and non-knowledge are crucial aspects of the environmental politics debate, which is framed by technical and scientific expertise shaping the discourse on sustainability. Yet, the gap between technical and scientific knowledge on the one hand, and local or everyday knowledge on the other, is increasingly clear. An exploration of the interaction between forms of knowledge and governance structure can shed light on the reasons for this gap and, with the help of two case studies, Terisakis shows how not only should research discuss EPI at different levels of governance, but also that different stages in the policy processes may exhibit different degrees of EPI.

Even if a specific governance structure may be appropriate to cross the boundaries between sectors, often seen as one of the major obstacles to EPI, this would not be sufficient to ensure EPI. This emerges from the work of Carolina Pacchi and Davide Zanoni, who assess the relevance of knowledge forms and governance modes for the approach to EPI adopted in the EPIGOV project. The concepts of knowledge forms and their interactions with local actors, and how power relations influence governance structures formally and informally, are discussed through a case study – the use of Strategic Environmental Assessment for the Provincial Master Plan of the province of Milan, Italy. The authors conclude that 'appropriate' modes of governance may be conducive to EPI, but that many other variables will influence their effectiveness, such as the patterns of the actors' interaction and the type of actors involved, the knowledge base extension, the inclusion of local knowledge, and inputs from external actors. Analyses of modes of governance for EPI should therefore be extended to additional variables, if a more accurate assessment is to be achieved.

Social system theory suggests that today the functional differentiation of social systems makes it more and more unlikely that environmental concerns are integrated in policy-making. However empirical research suggests that differentiated policy-networks in Europe may contribute to a greening of EU Regional Policy. Philipp Schepelmann explores this debate by assessing the degree to which EU regional funds have fostered EPI in the North Rhine-Westphalia region, using the concept of resonance. Resonance is defined as the active response of the social system to environmental problems, and is considered as a prerequisite for target-oriented EPI. By looking at selected indicators of the EU Lisbon process, the degree to which different policy networks react to environmental challenges indicates that there are areas of success, whose experience can be scaled up or transferred to other sectors. Furthermore, resonance analysis of policy systems with specific indicators is promising in helping to identify good and bad EPI practices on a case by case level, as it highlights that different governance patterns emerge depending on the indicator and the corresponding regional policy networks. Case-specific analysis will allow targeted interventions in order to close the gaps in policy-cycle promoting EPI.

The remaining chapters discuss country experiences, identifying success and failures of alternative modes of governance for EPI, with a focus on the UK, Central and Eastern European (CEE) Countries, and Spain. Moving to regional and country experiences on EPI, the success of country experiences such as the UK's one, traditionally acknowledged as an effective model for EPI, is challenged by Duncan Russel and Andrew Jordan. Light is shed on crucial variables such as the paucity of sustained political leadership, and the lack of external pressures from NGOs and other non-state actors, which have caused a breakdown of environmental coordination impairing the effectiveness of EPI. Overall, the UK has innovated, but the evidence presented in this chapter suggests that it has not been uniformly effective. Moreover, even though it has been in existence for fifteen years, the UK's EPI system appears to have not significantly improved the state of the UK's environment. Central leadership remains strong in the UK, though the UK appears to be embarking on a new phase of EPI with a dedicated focus on climate change. Aside from these developments, however, EPI in the UK has been achieved only partially, and the degree of success has not been consistent across departments. Russel and Jordan add to the body of literature depicting decision making in the UK as highly departmentalised. Where there has been successful cooperation, it has been driven by self-interest, and the portrayed success of the UK to achieve EPI is not as deeply rooted as it may seem at a first glance.

In parallel, the analysis of EPI in Central and Eastern European countries (CEE) provided by Keti Medarova-Bergström, Tamara Steger and Adam Paulsen suggests the need to carefully analyse regional specific characteristics in order to discuss alternative modes of governance and identify those favouring or inhibiting the EPI agenda. CEE countries provide an interesting ground for this exercise, being characterised by a rapid transition from a strong centralised regime to free market economies, with the emergence of multi-party regimes based on democratic principles, leading to new modes of governance for EPI. The emphasis on EPI dominant at the EU level is providing a strong leverage for CEE countries, coexisting with a strong bureaucratic administrative culture of national authorities. Successful examples of EPI exist, such as the introduction of the Environment and Strategic Impact Assessment, but a strong prevalence of top-down instruments remains. Furthermore, the introduction of instruments for EPI is severely hampered by a lack of ownerships and political will, while networks based on trust or political party affiliation remain an important mode of governance that should perhaps be exploited to further EPI. As such, the external drive for EPI provided by the EU can only be effective if adapted to the local context and characteristics, such as the positive legacies from the previous regimes.

Finally, barriers to effective EPI at the regional level in Spain are explored in the chapter by Kenneth Hanf. In Spain, the debate on sustainable development has dominated regional level decision-making processes, as opposed to a more specific focus on EPI. Institutional fragmentation and sectoral policy making remain a strong obstacle for effective EPI in the region, while efforts for more effective EPI should focus on building capacity and creating an enabling environment for deliberative decision-making at the regional level.

The diverse set of perspectives and experiences presented in this book contribute significantly to the debate on the means to achieve, and on the role of, environmental policy integration for sustainability. A recurrent theme in the book is the role of perspectives and context in determining whether a mode of governance will or will not be conducive to EPI – but also affecting the effectiveness of EPI efforts.

First of all, there is considerable variation with respect to the interpretation of EPI in different countries. The role of legal and administrative structures and culture, therefore, becomes crucial in influencing the extent to which EPI can be feasibly pursued, as well as the implementation strategies. This holds true for all levels of governance. An important contribution to understanding the role of administrative culture and practices in pursuing effective EPI is provided in the chapter on Eastern Europe, which fills a clear gap in the existing literature on EPI, focusing by and large on European countries. Greater emphasis should be placed on the potential positive role of history and past legacies as a potential avenue to effective EPI: it is indeed not always the case that more 'innovative' governance modes are better performing than top-down, regulatory instruments.

Perspectives to EPI also matter: so, for instance, environmental economics would entail a strong emphasis on the role of market and price signals in altering behaviour – thus calling for specific government interventions to change the relative prices of the environment *vis à vis* other sectors. On the other hand, social system theory calls for an analysis of the way societies respond to environmental problems, which can be measured by the concept of resonance, and monitored as well as fostered through appropriately designed target-based indicators. A focus on knowledge and non-knowledge provides interesting insights into the way governance modes and knowledge networks interact to shape the response of a social system to EPI pressures.

The stage of the policy cycle at which EPI is attempted also matters, and, to complicate matters further, the degree of integration plays a crucial role as well: in some circumstances partial integration may be more suitable than full integration, pursued through an additive multidisciplinary approach. Yet, these dimensions of EPI have often been neglected in the existing literature, and clearly warrant more attention.

Finally, as many of the chapters in this book show, EPI practices and their relation to governance modes do not neatly fall within set categories, but rather cross the boundaries of modes of governance and instruments, making it difficult to identify clear-cut relations between governance modes and successful EPI. Furthermore, universal criteria to assess successful EPI have not yet been identified, and strategies that may lead to EPI in theory have actually limited effect in safeguarding the environment in practice, as the UK and Spanish case studies indicate. A coordinated research effort based on comparative assessments of case studies would therefore help decision makers in learning from existing experiences, moving beyond an academic discussion of the merit and shortfalls of modes of governance for EPI.

The editors wish to thank the authors, all the partners of the EPIGOV project, the European Commission and FEEM's publication office for their precious support and contribution to the preparation of this volume.

NOTES

1. The conference was organised and hosted by Fondazione Eni Enrico Mattei (FEEM) and was held on 22–23 November 2007 in Milan, Italy. Additional contributions to the second conference and selected contributions to the other two conferences entitled 'Better Integration: Mainstreaming Environmental Concerns in European Governance' and 'Environmental Policy Integration at the Global Level and Multilevel Governance' and held, respectively, in Brussels (15–16 February 2007) and Stockholm (12–13 June 2008) are available in a separate volume by the same publisher.
2. The EPIGOV project was led by Ecologic, Berlin/Brussels/Vienna/Washington DC, and financially supported by the European Community's 6th Research Framework Programme (Contract no. 028661). For more information on the project, see http://www.ecologic.de/projekte/epigov/.

REFERENCES

European Environment Agency (EEA) (2005), 'Environmental policy integration in Europe: state of play and an evaluative framework', EEA Technical Report No 2/2005, Copenhagen, Denmark: EEA.
Homeyer, I. von (2006), 'EPIGOV common framework', EPIGOV Paper No. 1, Berlin, Germany: Ecologic – Institute for International and European Environmental Policy.

Homeyer, I. von (2007), 'Environmental policy integration and modes of governance – State-of-the-art report', EPIGOV Papers No. 2, Berlin, Germany: Ecologic – Institute for International and European Environmental Policy.

Jachtenfuchs, M. and B. Kohler-Koch (2004), *The Dynamics of European Integration: Why and When EU Institutions Matter*, Basingstoke, UK: Palgrave Macmillan.

Jänicke, M. (2006), 'Ecological modernisation: new perspectives', in M. Jänicke and K. Jacob (eds), *Environmental Governance in Global Perspective. New Approaches to Ecological Modernisation*, Berlin, Germany: Freie Universität Berlin, pp. 9–29.

Jordan, A. and A. Lenschow (2008), 'Environmental policy integration: an innovation in environmental policy?', in: A. Jordan and A. Lenschow (eds), *Innovation in Environmental Policy? Integrating the Environment for Sustainability*, Cheltenham, UK and Northampton, Ma, USA: Edward Elgar, pp. 313–42.

Pierre, J. (2000), 'Introduction: understanding governance', in: J. Pierre (ed.), *Debating Governance. Authority, Steering, and Democracy*, Oxford, UK and New York, USA: Oxford University Press, pp. 1–12.

Acknowledgments

The editors wish to thank the authors, all the partners of the EPIGOV project, the European Commission, and the staff of the FEEM publication office for their precious support and contribution to the realization of this volume.

1. Insights from Environmental Economics in the Integration of Environmental Policy into Decision-Making

Frank J. Convery

1.1 INTRODUCTION

There are two separate but related ways of addressing how integration of environment into the policy process can be addressed. The first is to focus on process – how environment and developmental policies are linked and coordinated, often with an emphasis on legal and regulatory frameworks and institutions, and the linking of sectoral development and environment. This strand is implicit in the OECD's sense of environmental policy integration, which defines it as:

> Early coordination between sector and environmental objectives in order to find synergy between the two or to set priorities for the environment where necessary.

The second is more explicitly normative and 'economic' in flavour, with an emphasis on costs, benefits and price signals, which I define as follows:

> Environmental policy integration is where the costs and benefits of environmental stewardship in the development process are recognised, and acted upon in the sense that the policy process ensures that 'environment' is given appropriate consideration in the articulation of choices, in the decisions made, and in their implementation, ideally with the use of a price signal that reflects the scarcity of the environmental endowment in question.

The World Bank attempted this sort of integration of environment and development in its lending and sectoral policies, described in Warford (1987) and Pearce and Warford (1993).

Sgobbi et al. (2007) make the point that with a process and institutional focus:

> It is very difficult to define criteria for assessing whether environmental policy

integration (EPI) has been achieved and to what extent. In fact, assessment exercises are still lacking [...] Furthermore, the efficiency of the EPI paradigm – that is the cost benefit ratio of following the EPI strategy – has never been quantified nor questioned. Yet the EPI does place additional burdens on sectoral actors, and whether EPI is the most cost effective strategy to follow to ensure environmental sustainability may be open to question. (p. 44)

In this chapter, I argue that environmental policy integration in the sense that I define it above (second definition) is achievable and appropriate where the following conditions are met:

- Widely accepted information on environmental performance is available that can be captured over time in a single variable;
- There is a conviction by business leaders that this is an issue of importance that does imply not only costs, but also opportunities; and
- A related understanding by the public of the importance of the issue in question;
- Direct market incentives via a price charge per unit of emissions can be mobilised;
- Relevant and appropriate legal, property rights and institutional arrangements are in place.

I will contrast the situation as regards climate change and biodiversity loss in terms of these prerequisites. I will then reflect on the traditional manner in which economists judge the effectiveness or otherwise of environmental policy integration, and the implications for the governance debate. The key is the use and usability of an appropriate price signal. If this is feasible technically, politically and administratively, then it is highly likely that 'environment' will be integrated in a manner where the benefits exceed the costs.

1.2   CLIMATE CHANGE AND BIODIVERSITY COMPARED

As regards information and performance measurement, the comparison between climate change and biodiversity is striking. In climate change, performance is measured mainly by emissions, expressed in tonnes of CO_2 equivalent.

The fact that we can combine emissions of CO_2, methane, nitrous oxide etc. in a single numeraire simplifies target setting and the evaluation of performance. The fact that the impact of a tonne of GHG is the same wherever it occurs also simplifies matters, since the particularities of the emission source or location have no bearing on impact. In contrast, biodiversity loss has many facets, with various estimates of species loss, fragmentation and loss of habitat, reported at different times and relating to different countries and regions.

In the world of business, mitigation of greenhouse gas emissions is towards the top of many agendas; many of the major energy-related global companies are focussed on business opportunities that arise in renewable development and deployment, in abatement of greenhouse gases, and increasingly in energy conservation. In regard to biodiversity, some business interests – notably Bodyshop in the UK – have made the business connection between species and habitat conservation and commerce, but at a much smaller scale than in the case of greenhouse gases. There is a growing body of work on how to ensure that local communities capture much of the benefits of conservation, on the basis that creating such an incentive to conserve is the only sustainable way to protect these assets, but overall the business engagement and profile is relatively low.

As regards public understanding, the plethora of climate change related articles and programmes in all of the media, and the linking of the issue to science in schools, and ethical behaviour in some churches, assures that, in many parts of the world, the public have a sense as to what is happening, and the need for intervention. There is also a parallel media and public interest in wildlife – typified in Europe by programmes by the late Jacques Cousteau and David Attenborough – that highlights the loss of habitat and species. A small terminological point. The use of the word 'biodversity' to characterise this field is probably a mistake. 'Nature' is much more meaningful to the public as a value to be protected.

In the case of greenhouse gas emissions, the market has been mobilised at European Union level by the European Union Emissions Trading Scheme (EU ETS) and by carbon taxes in a number of countries. In both cases, emitters face a price that signifies the scarcity of the capacity of the atmosphere to absorb such gases, that incentivises abatement, allows emitters to respond in the most cost-effective fashion, encourages innovation, and is fair in the sense that those who emit most pay most, and those who abate most gain most. Because there is no single 'emission' that can be priced in the case of biodiversity, there is no 'silver bullet' in the market place that can be mobilised to change behaviour. And because every situation and choice set is particular to a locality, it is difficult to generalise.

David Pearce et al. (1989) were perhaps the most successful proponents of integration at this level:

> Unfettered free markets will not solve environmental problems. They will make them worse. It is necessary to ensure that prices reflect the value of environmental

services used up in the production of goods and services. Sustainable development means changing the signals given to economic decision makers: from politician and civil servants to minister, from industrialist to consumer. Changing signals means changing prices and using the market. It does not mean leaving the environment to market forces.

In regard to the legal and institutional prerequisites, in the OECD countries generally, the frameworks for both climate change and biodiversity are largely in place, in the sense that information is available, government agencies of competence are designated to carry out policy, and the trajectory of performance is towards 'improvement'. I also argue that in terms of institutions and integration, the Minister for Finance or the Treasury is the key agent; without support from this quarter, integration is difficult to impossible.

This is because this Ministry has responsibility for overall macro-economic management, and decides on tax incentives and rates, and expenditure priorities. No policy area, and in particular environment, can be truly integrated into the development process without a degree of support at this level of government.

David Pearce made the wider point about processes and institutions, quoted in Convery (2007).

- If we must trade-off the various types of capital – if we cannot have environment and development – it is vitally important to value environmental assets correctly.
- The approach to project appraisal needs to be modified. Projects must be appraised in light of the fact that the environment clearly matters more than the weight placed on it in the past.
- The Treasury has the right to intervene in every economic decision that is made in this country and that is why every ministry has to answer to it. Why don't we say that every minister must answer to the Environment Secretary and say what my policies are doing to the environment?

As regards such relative engagement, support for biodiversity can take the form of subventions for acquisition of sites, and transfers to land owners to subsidise protection of nature. In regard to climate change, engagement is likely to be more central. Where a carbon tax or levy exists, there is necessary involvement, because this Ministry has to propose and implement such a tax, and in the use of the ensuing revenues. It will also have to approve tax and other subventions for renewable energy, and subsidy programmes for energy efficiency. The comparison can be schematically summarised as in Table 1.1.

Table 1.1   Comparison between Programmes

Indicator facilitating integration	Climate change*	Biodiversity*	Comments
Measuring performance	5	2	CO_2e provides unifying force for climate change
Business engagement	4	2	The 'big guns' from energy supply to retail outlets are taking climate change seriously. More niche concerns in the case of biodiversity.
Public understanding	4	4	High for both, but still progress needed.
Market mobilisation	4	1	Emissions trading and carbon taxes becoming mainstream
Institutional and legal prerequisites and Ministry of Finance engagement	4	2	Finance Ministries become mainstreamed in climate change; still peripheral in regard to biodiversity.

Note: * 5 = highest; 1 = lowest.

So there is plausibility to the view that in the case of climate change, the key elements that allow integration of this environmental strand into the policy are in place.

1.3   EVALUATING INSTRUMENTS FOR INTEGRATION

The following is the typical menu of mechanisms that can be mobilised to integrate environment and policy, illustrated in regard to climate change policy as it is evolving in Europe.

- Information on performance and options as discussed above. In Europe, the European Environment Agency (EEA) plays an important role in developing and disseminating performance data – especially emissions – at national and EU levels.

- Investment in hard and soft infrastructure that supports carbon reduction, including electricity grids and interconnections to support renewables, and road pricing.
- Regulation, for example legally binding efficiency standards in new housing, or carbon emission standards in new cars.
- Liability rules, for example obligation to repair any environmental damage.
- Research and development which creates new choices. The emergence of wind power as a viable alternative in electricity generation is a product in part of research and development.
- Subsidies, for example feed in tariffs above the market level for renewable, or subvention of carbon capture and storage.
- Voluntary agreements, for example where a sector agreed to meet certain emission targets.
- Market-based instruments (taxes and trading). The European Union Emissions Trading Scheme ran as a pilot from 2005 to 2007, is now in its second phase (2008–12), and a third phase will run from 2013 to 2020. It has been a learning-by-doing policy, with over – allocation in the pilot phase being corrected in phase 2, and auctioning to capture rents especially in the power sector likely to be characteristic in phase 3.[1] A number of countries have instituted carbon taxes or levies.

The policy instrument mix employed can be evaluated using the following criteria:

- Environmental effectiveness – are objectives achieved?
- Cost effectiveness – are objectives achieved at least cost?
- Dynamic efficiency – does integration stimulate innovation?
- Fairness – are the most vulnerable treated fairly?
- Feasibility – political and administrative?

The market-based instruments score highly on environmental effectiveness – especially in the case of emissions trading, which sets the quantity constraint – and in regards to cost effectiveness – abatement choices are left up to the emitters, so they have full scope to use the price signal to decide by how and how much to abate – and dynamic efficiency – there is an immediate financial dividend for technologies that can reduce emissions. As regards fairness, they are fair in the sense that those who emit most pay most, but – because poor households typically devote a higher share of expenditure to energy than rich people – a price that increases energy costs may bear heavily on such households unless other measures are taken. In regard to political and administrative feasibility, the situation is evolving in Europe, with trading in place, and with a more variegated situation pertaining to carbon taxes and levies.[2] In general, market-based instruments allow the others to be more effective, and in some cases to be complementary. For example, to stimulate innovation to the desired level will typically require both a price signal and subsidised research and development, and perhaps also subsidy for first users.

1.4   CONCLUSIONS

In considering the integration of environment into policy, it is important to remember that markets are the ultimate integrators, and if a price is 'manufactured' that reflects environmental scarcity, this mechanism on its own will integrate environment and development, and do so automatically, and 24 hours a day. Alan Bennett observed:

> The majority of people perform well in a crisis and when the spotlight is on them; it's on the Sunday afternoons of this life, when nobody is looking, that the spirit falters.

The market does not falter on Sunday or any other day. But of course integration is only a means to an end.

Institutions are also important, and effective integration requires that the most powerful institutions – which set priorities and have the resources and other levers of power to deliver – are committed. The Ministry of Finance or its equivalent is the first amongst equals in this regard.

In comparing climate change and biodiversity, it seems that the pre-requisites needed to make integration real are in place in regard to the former, but not yet so in the latter.

NOTES

1.   See Convery and Redmond (2007).
2.   See economicinstruments.com for more details.

REFERENCES

Convery, F. (2007), 'Making a difference. How environmental economists can influence the policy process: A case study of David W. Pearce', *Environmental and Resource Economics*, **37**(7), 7–32.

Convery, F. and L. Redmond (2007), 'European Union Emissions Trading Scheme (EU ETS): Market and price developments in the European Union emissions trading scheme', *Review of Environmental Economics and Policy*, **1**(1), 88–111.

Pearce, D.W. and J. Warford (1993), *World without End: Economics Environment and Sustainable Development*, summary version issued by World Bank, Oxford: Oxford University Press.

Pearce, D.W., A. Markandya and E.B. Barbier (1989), *Blueprint for a Green Economy*, London: Earthscan.

Sgobbi, A., A. Goria and M. Catenacci (2007), 'EPI at National Level – a literature review', paper presented at the conference Integrating the Environment into National Regional and Local Policies: Current Practises and Future Directions, Milan, 22–23 November.

Warford, J. (1987), 'Environment, growth and development', Paper Number 14, Washington DC, US: Development Committee, World Bank.

2. Environmental Policy Integration and the Nation State: What Can We Learn from Current Practices?

Alessandra Sgobbi

2.1 INTRODUCTION

Environmental policy integration (EPI) is recognised as one of the most important environmental policy axioms of the 1980s and 1990s, as well as a concept which has become central to sustainable development. This stems from the recognition that the achievement of sustainable development requires substantial institutional changes, and the integration of environmental concerns into other areas of public policies (WCED, 1987).

Several countries are incorporating the concept of EPI in their policy frameworks. For instance, EPI is one of the most ambitious basic principles of European environmental policy, and it has the same legal status as a constitutional provision (McCormick, 2001). In fact, the EU and European countries are leading in furthering the EPI concept – a bias which is reflected in the literature on EPI at the national level (Jordan and Lenschow, 2008a).

Together with the political buy-in of the principle, there is a growing attention in the research arena on EPI – both in terms of its definition and scope, and in relation to the tools and instruments available to foster it. This is also reflected in the wealth of research projects, conferences and policy briefs dedicated to this subject.

Yet, a precursory look at the literature highlights how different definitions of EPI persist, coupled with significant differences in the conceptual and analytical frameworks used to discuss EPI, its role and its implementation. These differences can hamper progress in the field. In particular, the issue of whether EPI is an effective route towards improved environmental management – which is indeed one of the least researched topics in the literature – may suffer from obstacles in transferring lessons, or drawing comparative research across EPI studies.

The objective of this chapter is therefore to summarise the main strands in the EPI literature, with the ultimate aim to shed some light on the key components of a unifying framework for analysing EPI and its environmental effectiveness.

As the body of work is vast, we will limit our attention to an analysis of EPI processes at the national level, considering therefore primarily private actors. Even though EPI takes place at different governance levels, the literature dealing with the strategic and national level is much more developed, and finding a unifying framework of analysis can be easier. Our objective is ambitious, and the critical review of the existing literate is but a first step in this direction. It does nonetheless highlight the current focus of research efforts, and areas that need to be further researched.

This chapter is organised as follows. Section 2.2 introduces the concept of environmental policy integration and the different perspectives to EPI found in the literature. Section 2.3 discusses EPI literature at the national level: first, the literature dealing with strategic policy documents is discussed (sub-section 2.3.1), then the implications of different administrative cultures are presented (sub-section 2.3.2). Sub-section 2.3.3 discusses papers dealing with country-specific studies, while sub-section 2.3.4 discusses cross-country comparisons and sub-section 2.3.5. Section 2.4 draws some initial lessons learned, while section 2.5 concludes this chapter.

2.2   CONCEPTUAL FOCUS

It is rather difficult to categorise the literature dealing with EPI at the national level. For one, often EPI is discussed within the context of National Sustainable Development Strategies and, even though the two concepts are related, EPI has a narrower focus than sustainable development in general. Secondly, there are significant overlaps in papers dealing with EPI, even though the focus may vary. So, for instance, some may deal with EPI at the national level, but instead of focusing on the strategic policy level, they also discuss sectoral examples of EPI.

While some authors discuss EPI within the existing institutional set-up and governance mode, others may focus on tools used to foster EPI, but including institutional set-up and organisation as a potential tool for EPI. Despite these overlaps and unclear boundaries, we have chosen to group the literature reviewed according to the main focus of the documents.

We thus identify four broad categories: literature dealing with EPI at the strategic level, thus focusing on political commitment and strategies; literature which discusses EPI at the national level in general; literature that focuses instead on the tools and strategies that governments at the central level may implement to foster EPI; and finally literature dealing with an assessment of EPI practices. Within the second category, we distinguish two further categories: there are first of all contributions with a country-specific focus, thus discussing several dimensions of EPI – strategic, sectoral, instruments – but for a specific country; and papers that attempt at comparing and contrasting experiences in different countries, with the objective of drawing some more generalised lessons as to what works and what does not work for EPI.

Before dwelling on the discussion of how the literature presents processes and tools to foster environmental policy integration at the national governance level, it is worth recalling what is meant by 'policy integration' in general, and environmental policy integration in particular. As will become apparent, the EPI literature is rich in definition of the concept, which does influence to varying degrees the perspective adopted by different authors on classifying, analysing and discussing EPI at all levels.

2.2.1   A Matter of Semantics?

Integration concerns the management of cross-cutting themes in policy making that transcend the boundaries of traditional policy fields. Importantly, integration requires overcoming the traditional allocation of policy responsibilities to individual organisations or departments within an organisation: as such, effective cooperation among institutions and actors is a *conditio sine qua non* for effective policy integration.

Environmental policy integration refers to the process of ensuring that environmental objectives are reflected in all policy areas. It is a strategy to change the way that people relate to their physical environment. The rationale is a move away from traditional *ad hoc* measures to counteract the negative consequences of economic activities on the environment ('end of pipe' or reactive measures), focusing rather on a more holistic, proactive approach, which avoids or minimises negative environmental impacts in the first place. EPI is thus seen as a key strategy towards sustainable development, as economic forces and changes in many of the economic sectors strongly influence environmental conditions and trends, thus enhancing or hampering the benefits of environmental policies.

As with most of these concepts and policy paradigms, definitions and perspectives abound. A full review of the definitions of EPI is beyond the scope of this chapter, although Box 2.1 summarises key definitions of EPI found in the literature.

Analytical perspectives to EPI

One of the aspects increasingly dealt with in the literature on EPI is its position with respect to national indicators such as governance structures, policy instruments, decision making and participatory processes, and so on. This EPI literature has a distinct focus on conceptual issues and the classification framework, in an attempt to bring some order to the vast body of literature which, on the other hand, has a case-specific focus – and which will be dealt with in subsequent section of this chapter. As pointed out by Schout and Jordan (2008), the choice of perspective can be strategic in that it depends on what we want to understand about EPI. A useful distinction is between normative and positive perspectives (Jordan and Lenschow, 2008): on the one hand, the normative approach focuses on what EPI ought to be, and how it should be enshrined in policy and legal frameworks, as well as institutions.

Box 2.1   Selected Definitions of EPI

Lenschow defines EPI as

the procedural principle and political aspiration [according to which] policy makers in non-environmental sectors recognise environmental repercussions of their decisions and adjust them when they undermine sustainable development'. (2002: 7)

Hertin and Berkout define EPI as

the inclusion of environmental concerns in processes and decisions of public policy making that are predominantly charged with issues other than the environment. (2003: 41)

Lafferty and Hovden define it as the

'incorporation of environmental objectives into all steps of policy making in non-environmental policy sectors, with a specific recognition of this goal as a guiding principle for the planning and execution of policies'. '[This] should be accompanied by: an attempt to aggregate presumed environmental consequences into an overall evaluation of policy, and a commitment to minimize contradictions between environmental and sectoral policies by giving priority to the former over the latter'. (2003: 12)

The OECD (1996) defines EPI as

'early coordination between sector and environmental objectives, in order to find synergy between the two or to set priorities for the environment, where necessary'.

EPI is therefore a process to ensure that environmental issues are fully taken into account in determining and/or implementing sectoral policies.

EPI is therefore seen as a policy principle which, however, still needs to be clearly defined for it to be implemented in practice. While, for instance, Lafferty and colleagues (2008) see EPI as calling for 'principled priority' to environmental matters in decision making, others (notably, Agenda 21, as discussed in Jordan and Lenschow, 2008) see environmental protection as one of three objectives which need to be balanced – the other two being economic and social development.

A positive approach, on the other hand, focuses much more on what EPI is in practice, and how it is put in place. Clearly, even in the absence of ambiguity over the normative understanding of EPI, the implementation of the concept in day-to-day governing decisions may differ, depending on political as well as economic driving forces. In the absence of an agreement over the normative definitions of EPI, the implementation practice becomes even more important. The focus of this work will be on the positive meaning of EPI and its implications for day-to-day policy making and governance structures.

In a recent work, Jordan and Lenschow (2008a) propose three perspectives which can be used to analyse EPI, at all levels of governance. At the highest level, EPI can be seen as a policy principle, which establishes the value of environmental protection vs. other policy objectives, within the broader sustainable development discourse.

EPI can also be seen as a governing process, of developing and applying different policy tools such as administrative changes or more specific policy instruments. Finally, the assessment of EPI processes can focus on their outcome, in terms of the impacts that EPI has on the environment.

EPI can be seen from a cognitive perspective, which understands EPI and its implementation in terms of the underlying factors leading to changes in the status quo, thus provoking changes in the way that people see the environment, for example Lenschow (2002: 17). The main focus of this literature is therefore on teasing out which factors favour or hamper cognitive learning and under which circumstances, for example Hertin and Berkout (2003) and Nilsson (2005).

Governance for EPI

There is generally agreement on the fact that the implementation of EPI, in any of its normative meaning, requires changes in institutions and decision-making processes. However, as in the case of the continuing divergences in analytical perspectives, we can identify several governance perspectives in the literature.

First of all, a subtle difference can be distinguished in the way that OECD countries and the EU see EPI. In the former case, EPI is seen as an instrument to gain mutual benefits from integration (Collier, 1994), whereas the EU stresses more the need that all sectors comply with the principle of mitigating the environmental impacts of their activities. There is therefore little consensus over how EPI is better achieved.

The European Environment Agency, for instance, distinguishes two main approaches to EPI at the national level (EEA, 2005a). Top-down approaches aim at embedding environmental concerns into high-level political spheres and within strategic, framework policy documents, and then provide the necessary incentives for all organisations to follow suite. Changes are thus achieved starting from the highest level, and expecting them to trickle down to the lowest level of implementation through a set of incentives or disincentives.

So, for instance, a department's budget may be conditional upon a satisfactory environmental performance. Intuitively, the stronger is the political commitment at the top, and the larger the number of (dis)incentives put in place, the more likely it is that EPI will realise. Bottom-up approaches, on the other hand, focus on encouraging and guiding departments in their efforts to integrate environmental issues, both in planning and implementation, and in their day-to-day operations. Bottom-up approaches are usually implemented through informal communication, training, exchanges of good practices, committees, task forces, guidelines and rules. The two approaches are not substitutes, but rather can complement each other, together contributing to progressive change in administrative culture.

The organisational perspective focuses on administrative practices and institutional set-up. It justifies EPI by the reported horizontal and vertical fragmentation of policy making, and concentrates on coordination processes and instruments. Authors adopting an organisational perspective are, among others, Peters (1998a), who uses incoherence, redundancy and gaps as indicators for effective integration; Metcalfe (1994), who further dissects the 'coordination problem' depending on the level of the required interactions – which can be, for instance, limited to data or information exchanges, or require joint planning between different institutions. Schout and Jordan (2008) lament the fact that the organisational dimension of EPI has received relatively little attention in the literature, and that there is still a lack of agreement with respect to the potential usefulness of organisational instruments to foster EPI.

The political perspective to EPI, on the other hand, focuses on the inherently competitive structures of public decision making, which constitutes one of the key obstacles to EPI – it focuses, therefore, on conflicting objectives.

The extent to which pressures from the top (high level politicians) or the bottom (public, activities, lobbies, and so on) are needed for achieving EPI will vary from country to country, depending on the level of competition among institutions. According to the classical theory, the support given to a specific issue will be dependent upon the position of institutions with respect to each other, but also on the position of individuals within an institution (Allison, 1971).

Finally, some controversies remain in the literature as to what extent traditional environmental policies remain valid, given efforts towards more effective and widespread EPI. For instance, Jordan and Lenschow (2008a) claim that 'if implemented, EPI would at a stroke remove the need for a stand alone approach to environmental policy'.

In contrast with this view, the European Environment Agency supports the view that EPI implies a change in the centrality of environmental issues with respect to decision making, yet 'Conventional environmental policies remain just as relevant, but need to be complemented by sectoral efforts to ensure their effectiveness' (EEA, 2005b: 12).

2.3   DISCUSSING EPI AT THE NATIONAL LEVEL

It is clear that the conceptual frameworks summarised in the previous section are not mutually exclusive, nor exhaustive; furthermore, the distinction is at times artificial, in that several elements of one perspective are found in different conceptualisations of EPI dimensions – so, for instance, the top-down approach proposed by the EEA has elements in common with both the organisational and political perspectives. These attempts represent nonetheless a useful starting point for further work on EPI at the national level.

Indeed, one of the main shortcomings in the literature is a lack of comparative country studies which assess in a rigorous manner the implications of different EPI strategies under different EPI perspectives. Most of the literature is based on case studies, either country-specific, or sector-specific: although useful in understanding progress in specific circumstances, the scope for drawing lessons and best practices is somewhat limited because of the lack of a common framework of reference and perspectives on EPI.

2.3.1   Political Commitment and Strategic Vision: 'Strategic' EPI

The importance of political commitment and leadership is one of the main themes underlying the literature on EPI (Lafferty, 2001; OECD, 2001; EEA, 2005a, 2005b).

Political will – in particular in the higher spheres of government – is seen as a key factor triggering institutional and behavioural change that can facilitate coordination and, therefore, EPI (Peters, 1998a).

According to Peters (1998a), the main obstacle to EPI is the failure to coordinate horizontally at the policy/strategic level, rather than at the managerial or implementation levels. Hence, effective EPI is a process to ensure that environmental concerns are taken into account in all policy phases, with steering from the top.

The first indicator of EPI at the strategic level is the existence of National Sustainable Development Strategies (NSDSs), supported by National Environment Action Plans (NEAPs) – even though the mere presence of these strategic documents is not an indicator of the successfulness with EPI.

The EEA, for instance, finds that the 'soft' nature of the NSDSs documents is one of the main shortcomings (EEA, 2005b), hampering their usefulness at the implementation level. Furthermore, these strategic documents tend to lack a clear prioritisation of objectives and the analysis of cost-effectiveness of the proposed strategies – as a consequence, given the lack of adequate funding, resources and costs associated with implementation are not addressed to a sufficient extent. Monitoring and assessment strategies are rarely present – or implemented: the EEA finds therefore little real evidence of progress with implementation of the NSDSs.

Swanson et al. (2004) examine 19 examples of National Strategies for Sustainable Development. Even though the focus is not on environmental policy integration, the NSSDs are seen as an overarching strategic framework within which EPI can take place. These authors also reach the conclusion that substantial progress has been made at improving planning at the strategic level, but there is still progress to be made with respect to implementation.

2.3.2   The Implications of Institutional Cultures and Administrative Practices

Several papers focus on the implications that different cultures and administrative practices have on EPI processes at the national level. This literature links the prevailing modes of governance at the national level to different levels of EPI – strategic commitment, processes and tools for integration.

The objective – stated or implicit – can be either to identify modes of governance which, at the national level, are more conducive to EPI; or to explore which strategic commitment, processes and tools for EPI are, in general, associated to which mode of governance.

A recent work by Steurer (2007) links policy integration as a means towards sustainable development to different institutional structures. By exploring the shortcomings of the current administrative structures, the author identifies the functioning of public administrations as one among other explanations for continued lack of integration. In this respect, Steurer highlights how strategic public management can be helpful, as a hybrid pattern of decision making, combining flexible strategy formulation with systematic planning.

The European Environment Agency includes 'administrative culture and practices' among its main categories for assessing progress with EPI (EEA, 2005b). In a subsequent technical report (EEA, 2005a), the European Environment Agency therefore concentrates on assessing the extent to which different national administrative practices can be conducive to effective and efficient EPI. The main finding of this report is that institutional structures in Europe can be categorised into five broad groups, which differ substantially in terms of horizontal and vertical EPI.

Table 2.1   European Institutional Structures According to the EEA

Southern European system	Legalistic and hierarchical, with a strong separation of political policy-making and administration/ implementation	May be counterproductive to EPI
German-speaking system	Power to judicial bodies, relatively little flexibility in implementing legal provision	If the law integrates EPI, may be conducive to it.
Anglo-Saxon system	Civil service tends to change structure depending on ruling government. Subordinate to political priorities.	If EPI a political priority, conducive to it.
Nordic countries	Strong administrative culture but growing specialisation with consequent fragmentation	The tendency to maintain the status quo may hamper EPI
Former communist countries	Political and strategic decisions are taken within the party structure, and not within the administrative structure	Lack of vertical and horizontal coordination may hamper EPI

A large body of literature sees EPI as a governing process of developing and applying different procedural measures (Jordan and Lenschow, 2008a). Furthermore, it is widely recognised that EPI has been difficult to achieve at the national level, despite its appeal, because of a widespread lack of institutional coordination (Hovden and Torjussen, 2002): despite recent progresses, further efforts towards improving coordination and collaboration among institutions are still needed (OECD, 2003). The importance of the implications of administrative practices on EPI cannot be over-emphasised, as it is administration and institutional decision-making processes that will, ultimately, determine whether EPI is successful (effective and efficient) or not. Yet, there is still a strong focus on policy rather than management, with the consequence that organisational implications and needs have not received systematic attention (Schout, 2001; Schout and Jordan, 2008). One of the main recurring themes of the EPI literature is that, despite the fact that institutional conditions are one important means to improve policy integration, the majority of institutional and decision-making structures are still ill-suited to foster integration of cross-cutting themes into sectoral policies. This problem is further compounded by the relatively scarce attention that the organisational perspective of EPI has received in the literature. For instance, Schout and Jordan (2008) highlight how there is still a lack of agreement over the potential role of administrative mechanisms to foster EPI – and, moreover, there is also a lack of agreement over what exactly the term includes, or what term should be used (for instance, administrative, bureaucratic, organisational, and so on, as shown in Table 2.2).

The literature agrees that the ultimate objective of institutional analysis should be to address the inefficiencies in the current systems, identify best practices, and foster policy coordination. As common with the EPI literature, those works that focus on what (Shout and Jordan, 2008) generally term 'administrative mechanisms' may look at the presence of absence of particular instruments (for example OECD environmental performance reviews); or at different combinations of administrative instruments in one state (Jordan, 2002), or in a small sample of states (Jacob and Volkery, 2008; Jordan et al., 2004). The new paper by Schout and Jordan attempts to look at the effectiveness of administrative mechanisms based on three broad conceptualisations of organisational science and public administration. Despite representing a step forward in our understanding of how different perspectives to administrative mechanisms change our view of EPI, the paper falls short of providing an assessment of the effectives of different arrangements and tools, but at least provides, under these three different views, different ways of thinking – and thus measuring – effectiveness.

One of the questions that still needs answering in the EPI literature is, therefore, what kinds of institutional arrangements and administrative tools perform better in terms of promoting the integration of environmental issues and concerns in other sectors and development strategies. The EEA (2005b) proposes six dimensions which could be used as reference for assessing progress with respect to the administrative dimension of EPI, summarised in Table 2.3.

Table 2.2   Different Types of Coordination Mechanisms

Author		Coordination mechanisms
Peters (1998)	Coordination devices	Core executive (centre of government) Ministerial organisations (vesting coordination task in one super-ministry) Inter-ministerial organisations Task forces and working groups Inter-department committees Informal coordination devices (local level delivery of services) Policy processes (budgeting, policy appraisal, evaluation) Coordination through interest groups and political parties
OECD (2002)	Institutional mechanisms	Budgeting Evaluation Reporting Institutional catalyst, where one institution takes the lead and other follow the example
OECD (2001)	Organisational approach	Coordination approaches to examine sustainability at strategic level (interministerial working groups, cabinet level committees, task forces,...) Structural approaches (i.e. altering structure of government, e.g. super-ministry) Strategic approaches (creating shared policy agenda by asking all ministries to develop their own integration strategies)

Source: modified from Schout and Jordan (2008).

In conclusion, there seem to be two opposing views over which form of institutional decision and policy making is more conducive to EPI: on the one hand, there are those who support the idea that strong and centralised bureaucracies and states are needed for the successful implementation of sustainable development strategies. The rationale is that these complex problems require a high level of coordination and cooperation among different institutional actors, which is better achieved when there is a strong central state (Khator, 1991). Some take this as far as saying that, in certain circumstances, even democracy can be sacrificed for ecological goals (Baker et al., 1997). On the other hand, there is a generalised tendency to associate a more effective promotion of EPI to 'new' governance models, based on integration participation, and devolution of powers. This view is often encountered in the more recent works on EPI and governance.

Table 2.3   Assessing Progress with Respect to the Administrative Dimension of EPI

Cross-governmental leadership and coordination
Restructuring ministries
Planning, budgeting and audit
Environmental Management Systems and green accounting
Coordination between administrative levels
Investing in capacity and resources for EPI

Source: EEA (2005b).

2.3.3   Country-Specific Studies

All 25 EU member states have taken steps towards EPI, which is a requirement of Art. 6 of the European Community Treaty ('environmental protection requirements must be integrated into the definition and implementation of the Community policies and activities … in particular with a view to promoting sustainable development'). Yet, as recently as 2003, the EEA confirmed that the EU still needed to invest additional efforts in formulating integrated policies, if its sustainable development ambitions are to be met (EEA, 2003). Even though existing assessment exercises of the effectiveness and efficiency of EPI at the regional or national level are not comprehensive, it is clear nonetheless that measures to address the environmental impacts of non-environmental sectors are still lagging behind what is envisioned in both EU and international commitments to integration.

The main studies looking at EPI from a national level perspective are: Nilsson and Eckerberg (2007) for Sweden; Hovden and Torjussen (2002) for Norway; Farmer (2002) and Farmer et al. (2004) for accession, candidate and Balkan countries; Jordan (2002) on the UK; Lewanski (2002) for Italy. Several new assessments for specific countries have been presented at the International Research Workshop on Innovation in Environmental Policy:

Integrating the Environment for Sustainability, Stockholm, 6–7 December 2006, and are forthcoming in a book: Jordan and Schout on the European Union; Wurzel on Germany; Lafferty, Larsen and Ruud on Norway; Nilsson and Persson on Sweden; Russel and Jordan on the UK; Hoornbeek on the US; and Dovers and Ross on Australia (the interventions are contained as chapters in Jordan and Lenschow, 2008b).

Not all studies adopt the same perspective on EPI, nor do they use the same terminology. To the extent that this is true, comparisons across studies and the identification of best practices are limited. Individual, country-specific studies do nonetheless offer precious insights with respect to lessons that can be learned to ensure a more efficient and effective application of the EPI axiom within a specific context. A notable exception is the collection of papers on EPI at the national level forthcoming in a book edited by Jordan and Lenschow (2008b): these papers first discuss the historical development of EPI in each country, and then present progress with EPI with respect to five broad categories of tools, namely: administrative mechanisms; green budgeting; strategies/strategy development processes; policy appraisal systems; Strategic Environmental Assessment; and mandatory requirements. Taken together, they represent a rich set of materials to undertake a thorough comparative assessment exercise to identify the conditions under which specific tools are effective in fostering EPI.

European countries
Several studies exist that look at EPI in Norway (for example Hovden and Torjussen, 2002; Lafferty et al., 2004). In the most recent works, Lafferty et al. (2007, 2008) present the progress with EPI in Norway. The authors are somewhat pessimistic as to the extent to which Norway has been able to translate the principle of environmental policy integration in practice, highlighting that the goal of achieving greater environmental policy integration has been sporadically pursued, in Norway – and this is despite the fact that Norway has been an 'early mover' in many cases. In Norway, attempts to institutionalise EPI have been by and large high-profiled. Yet, in contrast with the history in many other European countries, political support has declined since the 1990s. This, coupled with a reluctance of the institutions to undergo significant changes, have further weakened the efforts towards EPI, which has remained a political principle, with little empirical implications.

Nilsson and Persson (2008) and Nilsson and Eckerber (2007) examine the case of another Nordic country, Sweden, where a very different picture emerges. Sweden has been in the pursuit of EPI since the late 1980s, with a range of concrete measures that have been successfully implemented. The Swedish government has indeed being able to introduce a complex mix of mechanisms to foster EPI, even though the selection of tools has not followed a clear conceptualisation of EPI, but rather it has been dictated by ad hoc circumstances and experiences. Some institutional arrangement typical of Sweden, such as the committee of inquiry system and the management by objective approach, are highly conducive to policy coordination in general, and EPI has greatly benefited from them as well. EPI achievements at the sectoral level have been more modest, with some sectors lagging behind, where corporatism still prevails. An important step to bring all sectors up to speed with their efforts towards EPI is the 2000 management by objective strategy, which seeks to govern by objectives, leaving it to the discretion of sector and environmental agencies to reach the objectives. One of the obstacles to this approach is its reliance on political will and leadership which, in Sweden, is sometimes lacking for the environment at the level of sectoral agency heads and their counterpart ministries. The approach is also subject to changes in political orientations of the government – thus the call for a standardisation of public administration procedures (for example appraisal systems). Another important lesson can be learned from this chapter: sectoral responsibility is an important condition for any cross-sectoral EPI effort.

The German experience is described by Wurzel (2008). Despite being one of the main actors promoting domestic environmental policies in the early 1970s, interest for the environment in general – including EPI – had dwindled in Germany until the 1990s, when environmental issues were discussed in the domestic policy arena again. EPI has once again become part of the political discourse, mostly because of the new environmental challenge of climate change and legally binding EU commitments (for example the EU environmental directive on strategic environmental impact assessment). Crucially, however, integration has remained relatively low profile even within the environment sector, and several constitutional, structural and conceptual obstacles to EPI are identified by the author. These are coalition governments, the strong independence of different ministries and government agencies, the federal system, and a strong emphasis on BAT-driven environmental regulation. A notable exception is found in the German climate change policy, which adopted a mix of market-based instruments, voluntary agreement, fiscal reforms and subsidies to ensure that climate change issues are at the hear of sectoral actions. A more generalised discussion linking EPI to national sustainable development strategy is presented in Tils (2007) who concludes that the German sustainable development strategy still lacks high level political commitment partly because of its administrative executive policy orientation, designed, handled and coordinated as ordinary department business by chancellery and ministries of German government.

Lewanski (2002) discusses progress with EPI in Italy. His contribution focuses mainly on legislative developments – perhaps because the Italian governance system is characterised by a legal-formalistic policy style coupled with a lack of problem-solving capacity (La Spina and Sciortino, 1993). According to Lewanski's review, Italy is a latecomer in the field of EPI, and as such has been able to reap some of the benefits of learning from other countries' experiences. In addition to detailing progress with legislative initiatives and how the environmental dimension is addressed, the paper discusses the prevalent policy tools for fostering EPI. In Italy, one can see a strong preference for command and control instruments such as uniform standards of emissions, equipment, and so on. Starting from the early 1990s, however, one can see an attempt to supplement traditional tools with more innovative approaches based on the market, such as green taxes. Progress with EPI in several sectors is discussed in this chapter – namely transport, energy and production; the latter focusing on eco-industries. Lewanski arrives at the conclusion that progress with EPI in Italy has began late, and proceeded slowly, mostly because of the resistance of the Italian bureaucratic system to reform and concerted decision making. According to the author, progress is strongly related to the political party in power; furthermore, the effectiveness in implementing integrated policies and legislations has not yet been assessed.

Russel (2007) and Russel and Jordan (2008) assess the use of selected mechanisms for EPI in the UK. Contrary to the OECD finding, the authors argue that the UK does not have a very coordinated system of government, and that EPI has not been implemented nearly as effectively as portrayed in the existing literature (see also Jordan, 2002; Ross, 2005; Russel and Jordan, 2007). The UK was one of the first EU member states to develop a national EPI system (Schout and Jordan, 2005), and it has been a leader in developing mechanisms to improve policy coordination (for example environmental cabinet, policy appraisal procedures, and so on). Yet, the evidence presented in this chapter suggests that the various toolboxes have not been implemented effectively. One of the reasons why the EPI process has not been so effective in the UK is, according to Schout and Jordan (2005), the apparent lack of information flow on potential environmental spillovers from other sectors. This is also why attempts to integrate sustainable development in the Comprehensive Spending Review have not been very effective, thus conditioning sectoral budget on their environmental impacts/performances. Of course (lack of) information flow is not the only obstacle to EPI in the UK. For instance, like in the case of Sweden, there is a lack of political commitment at the high level in line ministries and government agencies, including DEFRA, which is mandated with supervising the EPI system. The authors thus conclude that the UK EPI system is not as effective as one may think, but rather it is quite sectorised and not well coordinated, unless it is in the interest of individual departments to coordinate, or there are strong controls (similar findings in Jordan, 2002; Richards and Smith, 2002).

Non-European countries

Hornbeek (2008) discusses the use of policy instruments for EPI in the US Importantly, the author points out that EPI in the US has not developed as an overarching policy principle – which is the case in Europe, for instance – but rather 'EPI activities' are the result of practices that have accumulated over time.

Six broad categories of EPI instruments are discussed in the paper (administrative mechanisms; green budgeting; strategies/strategy development processes; policy appraisal systems; Strategic Environmental Assessment; and mandatory requirements), and progress with respect to each of them is discussed at the federal, national and local levels. A more detailed analysis of EPI efforts in specific sectors is presented – namely agriculture, energy and transport. Some interesting conclusions can be drawn in the paper: so, for instance, administrative tools have been mostly implemented in a top-down fashion, and as such have been subject to the vagaries of politics – notably, the change from the Clinton to the Bush administrations. Furthermore, the US relies quite heavily on subsidies to provide incentives for EPI at the sectoral level – for instance, through green budgeting programmes in the agriculture, energy and transport sectors. Furthermore, very few of the efforts have been motivated explicitly by the pursuit of EPI – so, for instance, despite being a front runner in Regulatory Impact Assessment, in the US very little systematic environmental policy appraisal is conducted. Mandatory regulations are seen as playing a key role in fostering EPI. Despite the considerable progress with EPI in the US at the practical level, the author concludes that America's fragmented policy structures and processes have proved an obstacle to a holistic approach to EPI. In particular, the widely recognised fragmentation in American policymaking structures is seen as a key obstacle to effective EPI: America's system of separated powers at the national level and divided powers between national and state governments is not conducive to building nationwide consensus.

Dovers and Ross (2008) discuss the EPI experience in Australia. The same categories of instruments as in Hoornbeek (2008) are analysed, as both papers originate in the same context and are part of the same book. Nonetheless, some differences in the perspectives adopted by the two authors remain. Specific examples discussed include climate change and natural resources management. Contrary to the US approach, Australia has been experimenting with market-based instruments and voluntary agreements between government and private actors, as opposed to a hierarchical and centralised approach (Papadakis and Grant, 2003). The authors find that, even though Australia has not been at the forefront of EPI, it has adopted some distinctive institutional and instrumental approaches to EPI in specific sectors – such as natural resource management and climate change. Other sectors, however, do not explicitly address sustainability objectives – notably industry, transport and health. Dovers and Ross discuss in quite some length the success factors, barriers and gaps affecting EPI in Australia, which the authors categorise in: strategic, leadership, structural, procedural and capacity building. Interestingly, the authors highlight how changes implemented in Australia in the pursuit of EPI may have produced some improvements in terms of policy coordination, but they have resulted in additional costs for the government – which may in some cases outweigh the benefits of making the change. Furthermore, the experience in Australia indicates that structures and strategies are not sufficient for EPI, but leadership, political and administrative culture and capacity have an important role to play. There is no ideal set of structures, strategies and processes for EPI, which will be more difficult in sectors were economic and individual interests are strong.

2.3.4 Cross-Country Studies

EPI is a concept that all EU25 countries are committed to, as it is enshrined in the provisions of the EU treaties. The transition economies of eastern and central Europe subscribed to the principle too (at the 1991 Environment for Europe Conference in Dobris), recognising the importance of integrating environmental concerns earlier on in the process of transition from centrally planned to democratic political system and market based economies.

A comprehensive review of progress with EPI at the national level in EU member states was carried out by the European Environment Agency in 2005 (EEA, 2005a, 2005b).

Jacob and Volkery (2008) survey 20 OECD countries, examining the extent of EPI under several respects. The survey is then extended to 30 countries in their 2006 paper (Jacob and Volkery, 2008). In their comparative framework, they distinguish between centralised and decentralised EPI strategies – a classification that somehow overlaps with the EEA top-down vs. bottom-up distinction. Within these two categories, however, they do not distinguish among strategic level support and policies (for example NSDSs and NEAPs), decision-making organisations and processes (for example parliamentary committees, green cabinets, and so on) and specific tools for EPI (for example Strategic Environmental Assessment, green budgeting, and so on).

Reviewing different strategies and tools within their centralised and decentralised framework, Jacob and Volkery (2008) conclude that OECD countries adopt a mix of the two. Perhaps surprisingly, they find that there has not been a move away from centralised towards decentralised approaches and, as such, EPI is still seen, in the majority of the cases, as a task for environment departments. According to the authors, the continued dominance of a centralised approach is caused by the prevailing administrative culture, which is still based on specialisation and compartmentalisation. Moreover, governments tend to avoid processes and tools that could alter the power structure or influence resource allocation. Jacob and Volkery therefore conclude that 'the environment is far from being effectively mainstreamed within the institutional context of government'.

Despite the extensive coverage, the review does not address what, in the terminology of Jordan and Lenschow (2008a), would be the outcome of EPI. In fact, there are virtually no studies comparing progress with EPI across countries, in terms of the effectiveness of EPI strategies in improving the environment.

2.3.5 Focus on Tools for EPI

The EPI literature is relatively well developed in this field, but the focus is mostly on commonly used mechanisms, such as green cabinets, mission statements and environmental ministries.

The literature tends to be rather descriptive, without a detailed analysis of the pros and cons of the different instruments, and the situations under which they may or may not be effective. Horizontal mechanisms such as rules, procedures and teams are less used in practice – and this is reflected in the relatively limited literature discussing them.

It is important to point out that the distinction between categories (vertical vs. horizontal integration, but also market- vs. non-market-based mechanisms) is sometimes artificial. Depending on the objectives the tool is expected to achieve, circumstance and the implementation programme, an instrument may belong to more categories. So, for instance, teams composed of civil servants from different ministries are an example of horizontal integration, whereas teams of civil servants at different level of governance (Prime Minister's office, line ministries, regional authorities, and so on) are an example of vertical integration.

The difficulty in categorising the tools, however, may also be due to differences in the terminology adopted by the various authors. By and large, EPI literature is not providing the assessment needed to know either the current patterns of use provide an effective or sufficient response to the challenges of EPI (EEA, 2005b).

Mechanisms to promote horizontal and vertical integration currently in place in several countries include: interdepartmental committees, commissions, working groups and steering committees, which bring together representatives from different departments or institutions.

Tools to detect policy conflict – and thus favour integration – are limited to strategic environmental assessment of policy and programmes (for example Finland, Germany, Lithuania, and so on). Joint ministerial conference can also help with this respect – in Belgium, for instance, a joint ministerial conference is held on transport and the environment.

There are therefore a multitude of different instruments, which are not mutually exclusive, but rather may complement each other, as well as interact with non-EPI-related factors such as technological change, characteristics of the democratic system in place, legislative framework, public opinion, and so on. Two of the classifications proposed in the literature is summarised in Table 2.4.

An important strategy to promote integration is the use of market-based instruments (MBI) to create a more sustainable operating market. Jordan et al. (2003, 2005) provide an extensive review of MBIs such as eco-taxes, as well as a review of other tools such as voluntary agreements and environmental management systems. Public participation and consultation are increasingly applied to develop or fine tune policies and strategies, but the framework for public participation remains weak, in particular in developing countries. Access to environmental data has also improved recently. League tables and the 'exercise of shaming' (Knill and Lenschow, 2005) can also be quite successful in promoting EPI at the national level.

In fact, an interesting suggestion can be put forward: according to Drezner (2001: 57), 'states alter institutions and regulations because a set of beliefs has developed sufficient normative power that leaders fear looking like laggards if they do not adopt similar policies or models'. We could therefore postulate that if a sufficient number of states adopt EPI as a prevailing mode of policymaking at the national level, other countries will follow suit. The EU is likely to be a leading actor in this respect.

2.4   LEARNING FROM THE LITERATURE

Highlighting best practice examples and key obstacles recurrently reported in the literature, we discuss in some detail the main factors that emerge as key constraints to EPI.

It will become clear that, despite the differences in national context and socio-economic development level, the key obstacles to EPI are common to several countries, and relate to a difficulty in coordinating the activities of different departments or ministries; and the difficulties in championing EPI by high level politicians. Despite the difficulties in considering within a unified framework all the contributions to the EPI literature, therefore, some guiding principles can be identified, which could form the basis for developing an analytical framework for future EPI studies.

Table 2.4   Tools for EPI

a) Centralised vs. decentralised tools (Jacob and Volkery, 2008)

Centralised	Decentralised
National environmental plans,	Sectoral strategies
Sustainable development strategies	Special environment units/ environmental correspondents
Constitutional provisions	
Independent institutions for EPI for evaluation and monitoring (for example parliamentary committees, national court of auditors, and so on)	Strategic environmental assessments/impact assessments
Extension of competencies of the department of the environment (for example consultation rights, veto rights, and so on)	Green budgeting
	Obligations to report
Amalgamation of departments	
Interdepartmental coordination for EPI (for example green cabinets, interdepartmental working groups, and so on)	
Strategic Environmental Assessment	
Green budgeting and conditionalities	
Obligations to report	

b) Implementation type

Policy instruments	National funding programmes, government of public investment, constitutional provisions, and so on
Economic instruments	Environmental taxation, tax differentiation, subsidies, emission trading schemes, eco-labelling, public participation and consultations
Spatial planning	National and sectoral plans, river basin planning, Regulatory Impact Assessment (RIA) and Strategic Environmental Assessment (SEA)
Certification	Environmental management systems (EMAS)
Other instruments	Voluntary agreements, league tables and exercise of shaming

2.4.1   National Level EPI and Modes of Governance

Looking at the experience with EPI from the perspective of individual countries is instructive in terms of determining which mode of governance is more conducive to EPI.

The conclusions drawn are subject to all the necessary caveats, given the still small and not systematic body of literature analysing EPI processes at the country level. Some general remarks can nonetheless be made.

First of all, even though most of the innovation with innovative tools for environmental management is seen at the national level (Jordan et al., 2003), market-type[1] modes of governance are seldom employed to further EPI practices (Jordan and Lenschow, 2008a). Networks[2] are sometimes useful for EPI at the national level, as they can help to bridge differences of opinions and objectives. Yet, network types of governance are expected to be conducive to EPI only when there is a very strong political commitment at the top.

Finally, hierarchical forms of coordination are steered from the top, where actors or institutions at the high level compel lower level actors or institutions to coordinate or integrate cross-sectoral aspects.

Even though there is, at the moment, a strong tendency to equate 'good governance' with coordination based on decentralisation and stakeholder-oriented mutual learning – thus dismissing hierarchical forms of coordination – hierarchical modes of governance, and the tools available, are still the most commonly used and, in the short term, likely to be the most efficient and effective option to bring EPI forward at the national level.

This finding seems supported by a recent review of strategies and approaches adopted in 30 OECD countries to foster EPI (Jacob and Volkery, 2008), described in more detail in the following subsections. In fact, the emphasis is on soft approaches rather than on tools that have the potential to alter the existing power of actors or the allocation of resources (Jacob and Volkery, 2008).

2.4.2   Obstacles to EPI at the National Level

There is now a wide consensus over the fact that EPI will require structural institutional changes rather than marginal and incremental changes, coupled with more commitment and enforcement power of the ministries responsible for the environment.

EPI requires advocacy in other ministries, information dissemination and awareness raising, but it also requires a stronger role and power of the environment ministries. The risk is that integration results in loss of enforcing capacity and financial resources, if it is not coupled with adequate enforcement ability ('rubberstamping' in policy documents without real implementation). Key strategies to overcome obstacles to EPI are summarised in Table 2.5.

There are several different institutional set-ups designed for integrating environmental and economic decision making. Given the cross-sectoral nature of sustainable development goals and variation among countries in terms of size, political structure, geographical condition and so on, there is no 'model' structure which suits all the countries.

The institutional framework itself may be appropriately setup but other external factors (such as lack of resources, financial and human) may deter the efficient functioning of the framework. Furthermore, different institutional frameworks are not mutually exclusive and there are models that make use of several frameworks in combination. Thus more than one framework may exist in one country. Within governments, the level of political, high level commitment to environmental issues remains scanty. The processes through which administration and public bodies work are still ill-suited for integration. Other external factors will affect the success of EPI efforts, such as the nature of the economic or sectoral activities, the extent to which it affects the environment, the perception of society and of key actors, as well as the wider political and economic contexts.

Furthermore, government institutions are a constraint in the extent to which they can adapt and re-organise. The key administrative challenge of EPI is to move away from a culture of fragmentation and policy/sectoral specialisation, and make departments more receptive to environmental issues. The overall aim is to ensure that all departments and institutions contribute to environmental protection and the achievement of sustainable development. In addition to the potential lack of political will and the related struggle for power and influence, the problems which are often encountered by governmental institutions in the strive for EPI can be summarised into three categories:

- Lack of information exchange.
- Insufficient capacity to handle environmental information.
- High transaction and coordination costs.

Institutional restructuring may not be sufficient to guarantee EPI. For instance, there is a strong need to mandate 'police' and enforcement powers to environmental ministries, as currently EPI tasks are devolved to ministries without a special responsibility for the institutions explicitly dealing with the environment – 'voluntary compliance' with the paradigm of EPI is therefore assumed. According to some authors, there is a tendency to distribute responsibility without building administrative capacity, in the hope that coordination with take place through competition for influence through self-organising processes (Schout, 2001).

Several factors related to the institutional set-up and countries' administrative history will prevent or hamper progress with EPI. Of course, these will depend, to some extent, on government styles and personalities – so, for instance, one could expect both vertical and horizontal coordination to be easier in smaller counties.

There are also key external factors that affect progress with EPI, related to the external, socio-economic context in which the public administration is operating. Key external factors include:

- The nature of the sector and the impacts of EPI requirements: so, for instance, EPI demands which are not neutral, but rather imply some limitation on production or consumption, are likely to encounter strong opposition.
- The views of society and interest groups: the political power of different stakeholders may be significant, thus influencing the political class. Increasing transparency and public participation may limit the power of lobby groups.
- A country's commitment to international treaties will necessarily affect EPI at the national level. So, for instance, the WTO discussion relating to subsidies are important drivers of change at the national and EU level.

Effective EPI requires commitment, strategic vision and a clear division of responsibilities among institutions. Effective and transparent communication channels are also needed, to enable cooperation among institutions and flow of information and knowledge. Above all, appropriate budgeting is needed, as EPI activities are likely to impose an additional burden on sectoral and institutional activities.

2.4.3 Transferring the Lessons Learned

The concepts and practices of policy integration are very wide, and it is neither feasible nor advisable to prescribe a fixed institutional set-up or decision-making process that is expected to promote EPI. Rather, several institutional conditions may help in fostering EPI, and their feasibility and effectiveness will depend on country-specific conditions – such as the prevailing culture, the interest of the general public, and so on and so forth.

The exchange of experience about practical aspects of policymaking is often advocated in fields at the frontier of public policy, particularly for cross-cutting issues such as gender mainstreaming and the environment. Yet 'policy learning' requires a thorough understanding of the prevailing cultures and modes of governance in both the 'sending' and 'receiving' countries – processes and tools that work perfectly well in some settings are bound to fail when necessary conditions for their successful implementation are lacking. So, for instance, the establishment of water users' associations – so much thrust forward by the World Bank – has proved very successful in countries where governance was more participatory and inclusive anyway, but has proved almost detrimental in countries where water users are not accustomed to taking decisions for the community, or taking responsibility for operation and maintenance of water delivery infrastructures (for instance, in Bulgaria).

Similarly, although the analysis of practices conducive to successful EPI at the national level may be instructive, care must be taken in transferring them *tout court* in a different context.

Several conditions may favour the positive uptake of best practices. First, the harvesting of policy solutions builds on both positive and negative experiences – hence both should be highlighted. Second, whenever non-governmental actors are involved, the focus shifts from position- to results-oriented decision making, and transferring lessons learned is more successful and less problematic. The socio-economic environment of the 'sending' and 'receiving' countries must be similar; at the same time, environmental and socio-economic pressures and priorities must be aligned to avoid a mismatch between the introduction of new policy paradigms and actual needs of the receiving countries. The legal system must be similar as well, in order to ensure smooth implementation or a smooth transition to a new institutional setting. In fact, this is also shown in the rate of convergence of policies among EU member states, which are faced with the task of implementing essentially the same legislation in very diverse socio-economic, environmental and legal settings.

In Turkey, the restructuring of the institutional set-up led to the merging of the forestry and environment sectors. Yet, rather than facilitating EPI, the merge is expected to lead to a further weakening of an already weak Ministry of Environment. Whether restructuring efforts can be effective or not depends on the degree to which existing ministries and departments are willing to move away from sectoral objectives, adopting a more issues-oriented approach to planning and implementation. 'The lesson is that ministerial structures alone are not a sufficient determinant for integration, but assessment must be coupled with an analysis of inter-ministerial relations'.

Overall, there is little understanding of what resources are required for EPI, and assessing the resources already available may be quite difficult as well.

2.5   CONCLUSION: TOWARDS A COMMON FRAMEWORK. ASSESSING PROGRESS WITH EPI

A review of the literature on EPI at the national level reveals that there are surprisingly few studies systematically comparing processes, strategies and tools in individual countries in the pursuit of EPI, thus limiting the scope of learning from existing experiences. A few general remarks can nonetheless be made.

First, there is considerable variation at the national level, with respect to interpretation of the EPI axiom in different counties. The difference is mostly attributable to differences in legal and administrative structures that necessarily influence the extent to which EPI can be feasibly pursued, as well as the implementation strategies. So, for instance, the Netherlands recognise the need for a deep change in societal attitudes for the effective implementation of EPI, whereas the UK government sees EPI as a tool to further the efforts of improving government coordination (Jordan and Lenschow, 2000; Lenschow, 2002). Sweden, on the other hand, sees EPI as an integral part of the country's sustainable development strategy (Nilsson and Persson, 2008).

The intrinsic diversity of political decision-making processes, as well as societal attitudes, also means that the obstacles faced by individual countries in their efforts to EPI vary considerably. So, for instance, the main obstacle faced by the German government is the need to change the institutional structure of the public administration, whereas Italy is confronted with the need for deep changes in its legal and administrative culture, rather than structure, as well as dwindling political will (Jordan, 2002; Lewanski, 2002; Müller, 2002).

Vertical integration concerns the extent to which sectoral policies address environmental concerns in their strategies and implementation activities. On the other hand, horizontal integration refers to the extent to which there exist cross-sectoral strategies and mechanisms to coordinate and foster cooperation among institutions.[3] Of course these two dimensions are strongly affected by the existing external factors such as the prevailing administrative culture, institutional set-up, the opinion of the general public and of interest groups, and so on. In some cases, however, vertical integration may not suffice: that is, when multisectoral issues are present, both vertical integration and horizontal coordination are necessary – not only among the environment sector and the sector for which the policy is developed, but also between the latter and other sectors that may influence it. So, for instance, energy policy clearly needs to integrate environmental concerns (vertical integration), but it will also affect to a significant extent agricultural practices (through, for example, its stand on biofuels): coordination between the energy and agriculture sector is needed as well.

Clear assessment methods must be established to analyse progress and use more effectively the wealth of experience with EPI – processes and tools – and how they may or may not work in different contexts. Without a clear benchmark against which to assess performance progress will be slower.

Assessing progress with EPI is rather difficult, given the ambiguities inherent in the definition of the concept – which is indeed the outcome of a political process. In fact, according to Richardson, EPI 'is sufficiently vague to allow conflicting parties, factions and interests to adhere to it without losing credibility' (Baker et al., 1997: 107).

Table 2.5   Some Strategies to Overcome Challenges to EPI

Problem	Possible solution
High-level and clear political commitment to EPI: often, support to EPI from high-level political class is lacking, either because of the (short term) socio-economic implications of EPI, or because of the political implications. Similarly, environmental issues are rarely at the top of the political agenda.	Political commitment could be secured through information on the consequence of (in)action, or through political pressure. Strategic statements or commitments could also be used. League tables and exercise of shaming.
Compartmentalised government: there is a tendency of government departments and institutions to maintain the 'traditional' decision-making processes, with a strong sectoral focus, despite the increasing recognition of the interdependent nature of SD. Furthermore, departments may be unwilling to take on new responsibilities (Wandèn, 2003).	One way to deal with excessive fragmentation is to create clear and shared internal visions and mission statements, and through restructuring the current institutional set up. Resources and capacity of government officials can be enhanced, also by getting people to work in several departments. Information dissemination, public consultation, decision support tools, are all instruments that could help ensure information flows, and that decisions reflect environmental considerations.
Environmental authorities may lack sufficient authority (Lafferty, 2004).	The responsibility for EPI could be given to an ad hoc authority, together with the power to enforce it. Alternatively, assign responsibility for EPI to a more influential Ministry (e.g. Finance?) or the Prime Minister's office. This second option may be better in fostering EPI: not only would the new institution need to establish its mandate and authority, but also it would require significantly more additional financial and human resources than assigning the same role to an existing institution.

Table 2.5   Some Strategies to Overcome Challenges to EPI (Continued)

Problem	Possible solution
Integration between levels of governance: vertical integration can be a challenge, but is increasingly important in the face of growing devolution of decision making and planning authorities.	Multi-level structures, committees and communication channels can promote vertical integration during the decision making process.
Multitude of institutions involved: the cross-sectoral nature of EPI inevitably requires the involvement of numerous institutions and actors.	

Furthermore, EPI strategies as they have been implemented in the majority of the countries fall short of providing a tool to make trade-offs among often competing objectives. Yet, there are many cases in which real conflicts of interest exist over environmental issues, which are likely to increase as EPI is strengthened (Lafferty and Hovden, 2002). The emphasis on mutual benefits of EPI may thus be misleading, underplaying many of the challenges which are inherent to the objective of integration (p. 14).

A number of international organisations are attempting to monitor and assess progress with EPI. The OECD and UNECE environmental performance reviews (EPRs) are, to date, the more systematic attempt, even though they approach EPI from an economic perspective. The OECD's work on indicators to measure the link between environmental impacts and sectoral activities is also an important source of information. Finally, the EEA (2005b) presents a framework for evaluating sectoral and cross-sectoral EPI.

Assessing EPI can be done at eight fundamental levels:

- *Strategic level*: commitment of policy makers to EPI, and how the commitment feeds to strategic planning;
- *Governance level*: changes in administration structures or decision-making processes that facilitate EPI;
- *Resource and capacity building*: level of human resources – ability as well as power – that administrations have available to push forward EPI;
- *Policy instruments and implementation tools*: ability and power to implement tools and processes that facilitate EPI at different governance levels;

- *Monitoring, reporting and information*: strategies and channels (formal and informal) to report on steps undertaken and progress, to improve transparency and accountability;
- *Changes in drivers and pressures*: indicators to monitor and assess outcomes of EPI strategies.

It is very difficult to define criteria for assessing whether EPI has been achieved, and to what extent. In fact, assessment exercises are still by far lacking.

There may, for instance, be cases in which environmental objectives are legitimately overridden by socio-economic priorities – in themselves consistent with the principles of sustainable development. In such cases, agreement on whether EPI was successful or not is difficult to attain. In fact, the effectiveness of EPI can only be assessed in terms of the outcomes of the processes that assist integration – quite difficult to quantify. Furthermore, the efficiency of the EPI paradigm – that is, the cost–benefit ratio of following the EPI strategy – has never been quantified, nor questioned. Yet, EPI does place additional burdens on sectoral actors, and whether EPI is the most cost-effective strategy to follow to ensure environmental sustainability may be open to questions.

Despite the importance of the administrative structure and capacity, relatively little attention has been devoted to the requirements for effective and efficient EPI (Jordan et al., 2004). Assessing the suitability of institutional set up to deal with EPI requirements requires answering the following questions (EEA, 2005a):

- Do regular planning, budgetary and audit exercises reflect EPI priorities?
- Are environmental responsibilities reflected in the internal management regime?
- Is there a strategic department/unit/committee in charge of coordinating and guiding EPI?
- Are there mechanisms to ensure environment/sector coordination and communication?

Thus, the successful EPI requires that environmental protection is a key objective of policy appraisal, design and implementation, together with consideration of the socio-economic needs of development. Yet, the EPI discourse has not extensively addressed the means and instruments to trade-offs among the objectives, or ways to establish the relative weights of the different objectives.

There are some efforts in this respect, for instance Lafferty and Knudsen (2007) take a somewhat radical position, calling for EPI to be given priority over other dimensions of sustainable development, and claiming that the definition of 'sustainable development' provided by Our Common Future itself implies a principled authority to the environmental dimension of the concept. This claim is likely to raise a lively debate, in particular in any attempt to implement it, as the interests of other interested parties and lobbies, traditionally stronger than the environmental lobby, are likely to oppose it. Further efforts are therefore needed to find ways for implementing EPI and aiding decision makers in trading off several, conflicting policy objectives. Furthermore, it is not clear what institutional architecture and what tools would be needed to make such a principle operational.

Finally, one should bear in mind that EPI cannot be a panacea to solve environmental problems, and more than that, it may not be warranted under all circumstances. EPI will be needed whenever there are clear failures deriving from the inability of sectoral policies to coordinate with environmental issues. In some circumstances, on the other hand, other types of approaches, more traditional, perhaps, based on environmental policies to mitigate negative impacts, may be more cost-efficient – as EPI may place an excessive burden on non-environmental sectors. Furthermore, integration is a matter of degrees, and in some circumstances partial integration may be more suitable than full integration: that is, an additive multi-disciplinary approach may suffice, rather than an inter-disciplinary approach to policy making (Dovers, 2005).

ACKNOWLEDGMENTS

This study was supported by funding under the Sixth Research Framework of the European Union within the project 'Environmental Policy Integration and Multi-Level Governance'.

The author gratefully acknowledges the substantial contributions of Michela Catenacci and Alessandra Goria, as well useful comments on previous versions of this chapter by all EPIGOV partners.

NOTES

1. Market-type coordination mechanisms imply the existence of an exchange relationship between the administrative parties concerned.
2. Networks comprise of a range of actors who are part of the same community because of a (real or perceived) need to collaborate.
3. Lafferty and Hovden (2002) adopt different definitions of vertical and horizontal integration: in their view, the former refers to the extent to which a government sector has taken on board and implemented environmental objectives, whereas the latter refers to the extent to which a central authority has developed a comprehensive cross-sectoral strategy for EPI. In the authors' definition, therefore, efforts at vertical integration are not only more common, but also more effective than horizontal integration – perhaps because vertical integration involves departmental conflict and less change in the overall allocation of sectoral winners and losers.

REFERENCES

Allison, G. (1971), *Essence of Decisions: Explaining the Cuban Missile Crisis*, Boston, MA: Little, Brown.
Baker, S., M. Kousis, D. Richardson and S. Young (1997), *The Politics of Sustainable Development: Theory, Policy and Practice within the European Union*, London: Routledge.
Collier, U. (1994), *Energy and Environment in the European Union*, Aldershot: Ashgate.
Dovers, S. (2005), 'Clarifying the imperative of integration research for sustainable environmental management', *Journal of Research Practice*, **1**(3), M1.
Dovers, S. and A. Ross (2008), 'Australia', in A. Jordan and A. Lenschow (eds), *Innovation in Environmental Policy? Integrating the Environment for Sustainability*, Cheltenham, UK and Northampton, MA, USA: Edward Elgar.
Drezner, D.W. (2001), 'Globalization and policy convergence', *The International Studies Review Globalization and Policy Convergence*, **3**(1), 53–78.
EEA (2003), *Europe's Environment: The Third Assessment*, Copenhagen: European Environment Agency.
EEA (2005a), *Environmental Policy Integration in Europe. Administrative Culture and Practices*, Copenhagen: European Environment Agency.
EEA (2005b), *Environmental Policy Integration in Europe: State of Play and an Evaluative Framework*, Copenhagen: European Environment Agency.
Farmer, A. (2002), *Environmental Policy Integration and Sustainable Development in the Accession, Candidate, and Balkan Countries*, Background Paper, Copenhagen: European Environment Agency.
Farmer, A., H. Bennett, C. Bowyer and P. Keles (2004), *Environmental Policy Integration and Sustainable Development in Accession, Candidate, and Balkan Countries*, Background Paper. Copenhagen: European Environment Agency.
Hertin, J. and F. Berkout (2003), 'Analysing institutional strategies for environmental policy integration: The case of EU enterprise policy', *Journal of Environmental Policy and Planning* **5**(1), 39–56.
Hoornbeek, J. (2008), 'The USA', in A. Jordan and A. Lenschow (eds), *Innovation in Environmental Policy? Integrating the Environment for Sustainability*, Cheltenham, UK and Northampton, MA, USA: Edward Elgar.

Hovden, E. and S. Torjussen (2002), 'Environmental policy integration in Norway', in W.M. Lafferty, M. Norskag and H.A. Aakre (eds), *Realizing Rio in Norway: Evaluative Studies of Sustainable Development*, Oslo: ProSus, pp. 21–42.

Jacob, K. and A. Volkery (2008), 'A comparison of environmental policy integration instruments in 30 OECD countries', in A. Jordan and A. Lenschow (eds), *Innovation in Environmental Policy? Integrating the Environment for Sustainability*, Cheltenham, UK and Northampton, MA, USA: Edward Elgar.

Jordan, A. and A. Lenschow (2000), 'Greening the European Union: what can be learned from the "leaders" of EU environmental policy?', *European Environment* **10**(3), 109–20.

Jordan, A. (2002), 'Efficient hardware and light green software: environmental policy integration in the UK', in A. Lenschow (ed.), *Environmental Policy Integration. Greening Sectoral Policies in Europe*, London: Earthscan, pp. 35–56.

Jordan, A. and A. Lenschow (2008a), 'Integrating the environment for sustainable development: an introduction', in A. Jordan and A. Lenschow (eds), *Innovation in Environmental Policy? Integrating the Environment for Sustainability*, Cheltenham, UK and Northampton, MA, USA: Edward Elgar.

Jordan, A. and A. Lenschow (2008b), *Innovation in Environmental Policy? Integrating the Environment for Sustainability*, Cheltenham, UK and Northampton, MA, USA: Edward Elgar.

Jordan, A., A. Schout and A. Zito (2004), *Coordinating European Union Environmental Policy: Shifting from Passive to Active Coordination*, CSERGE Working Paper. University of East Anglia, UK, Centre for Social and Economic Research on the Global Environment.

Jordan, A., R. Wurzel and A. Zito (2003), *New Instruments of Environmental Governance? National Experiences and Prospects*, London: Frank Cass.

Jordan, A., R. Wurzel and A. Zito (2005), 'The rise of "new" policy instruments in comparative perspectives; has governance eclipsed government?', *Political Studies*, **53**(3), 477–496.

Khator, R. (1991), *Environment, Development and Politics in India*, Lanham: University Press of America.

Knill, C. and A. Lenschow (2005), 'Compliance, communication and competition: patterns of EU environmental policy making and their impact on policy convergence', *European Environment*, **15**, 114–28.

La Spina, A. and G. Sciortino (1993), 'Common agenda, southern rules: European integration and environmental change in the Mediterranean states', in D. Liefferink, P. Lowe and J. Mole (eds), *European Integration and Environmental Policy*, London: Belhaven, pp. 217–36.

Lafferty, W.M. (2001), 'Adapting Governance Practice to the Goals of Sustainable Development', OECD PUMA seminar, 22–23 November.

Lafferty, W.M. (2004), 'From environmental protection to sustainable development. The challenge of decoupling through sectoral integration', in W.M. Lafferty (ed.), *Governance for Sustainable Development: The Challenge of Adapting Form to Function*, Cheltenham, UK and Northampton, MA, USA: Edward Elgar, pp. 191–220.

Lafferty, W.M. and E. Hovden (2002), *Environmental Policy Integration: Towards an Analytical Framework?* Oslo: ProSus.

Lafferty, W.M. and E. Hovden (2003), 'Environmental policy integration: towards and analytical framework', *Environmental Politics*, **12**(3), 1–22.

Lafferty, W.M. and J. Knudsen (2007), 'The issue of "balance" and trade-offs in environmental policy integration: How will we know EPI when we see it?', First EPIGOV Conference, Brussels, 15–16 February 2007.

Lafferty, W.M., J. Knudsen and O. Mosvold Larsen (2007), 'Pursuing sustainable development in Norway: living up to Brundtland at home', *European Environment*, **17**, 180–88.

Lafferty, W.M., O. Mosvold Larsen and A. Ruud (2008), 'Norway', in A. Jordan and A. Lenschow (eds), *Innovation in Environmental Policy? Integrating the Environment for Sustainability*, Cheltenham, UK and Nothampton, MA, USA: Edward Elgar.

Lafferty, W.M., A. Ruud and O. Mosvold Larsen (2004), *Environmental Policy Integration: How Will We Recognize It When We See It? The Case of Green Innovation Policy in Norway*, Oslo: ProSus.

Lenschow, A. (2002), *Environmental Policy Integration*, London: Earthscan.

Lewanski, R. (2002), 'Environmental policy integration in Italy: Is a green government enough?', in A. Lenschow (ed.), *Environmental Policy Integration: Greening Sectoral Policies in Europe*, London: Earthscan, pp. 78–100.

McCormick, J. (2001), *Environmental Policy in the European Union*, Houndmills: Palgrave.

Metcalfe, Les (1994), 'International policy coordination and public management reform', *International Review of Administration Sciences*, **60**, 271–90.

Müller, E. (2002), 'Environmental policy integration as a political principle? The German case and the implications of European policies', in A. Lenschow (ed.), *Environmental Policy Integration. Greening Sectoral Policies in Europe*, London: Earthscan, pp. 57–77.

Nilsson, M. (2005), *Connecting Reason to Power. Assessment, Learning, and Environmental Policy Integration in Swedish Energy Policy*, Stockholm: Stockholm Environment Institute.

Nilsson, M. and K. Eckerberg (2007), *Environment Policy Integration in Practice*, London: Earthscan.

Nilsson, M. and Å. Persson (2008), 'Sweden', in A. Jordan and A. Lenschow (eds), *Innovation in Environmental Policy? Integrating the Environment for Sustainability*, Cheltenham, UK and Northampton, MA, USA: Edward Elgar.

OECD (1996), *Building Policy Coherence: Tools and Tensions*, OECD Public Management Occasional Paper, Paris: Organisation for Economic Co-operation and Development.

OECD (2001), *Environmental Performance Reviews: Achievements in OECD Countries*, Paris: Organisation for Economic Co-operation and Development.

OECD (2002), *Improving Coherence and Integration of SD: a Checklist*, Paris: Organisation for Economic Co-operation and Development.

OECD (2003), *Environmental Performance Reviews – Poland*, Paris: Organization for Economic Co-operation and Development.

Papadakis, E. and R. Grant (2003), 'The politics of "light-handed regulation": "new" environmental policy instruments in Australia', *Environmental Politics*, **12**(1), 27–50.

Peters, G.B. (1998a), 'Managing horizontal government', *Public Administration*, **76**, 295–311.

Peters, G.B. (1998b), *Managing Horizontal Governance: The Politics of Coordination*, Research Paper, Ottawa: Canadian Centre for Management Development.

Richards, D. and M.J. Smith (2002), *Governance and Public Policy in the UK*, Oxford: Oxford University Press.

Ross, A. (2005), 'The UK approach to delivering sustainable development in government: A case study in joined-up working', *Journal of Environmental Law*, **17**(1), 27–49.

Russel, D. (2007), 'The United Kingdom's sustainable development strategies: leading the way or flattering deceive?', *European Environment*, **17**, 189–200.

Russel, D. and A. Jordan (2007), 'Gearing up government for sustainable development: Environmental policy appraisal in central government', *Journal of Environmental Planning and Management*, **50**(1), 1–21.

Russel, D. and A. Jordan (2008), 'The United Kingdom', in A. Jordan and A. Lenschow (eds), *Innovation in Environmental Policy? Integrating the Environment for Sustainability*, Cheltenham, UK and Northampton, MA, USA: Edward Elgar.

Schout, A. (2001), 'Managing environmental policy integration at the national level: From event to issue coordination', Seventh ECSA Biennial Conference, Madison, 31 May–2 June 2001.

Schout, A. and A. Jordan (2005), 'Coordinated European governance: self-organizing or centrally steered?', *Public Administration*, **83**(1), 201–20.

Schout, A. and A. Jordan (2008), 'Administrative mechanisms', in A. Jordan and A. Lenschow (eds), *Innovation in Environmental Policy? Integrating the Environment for Sustainability*, Cheltenham, UK and Northampton, MA, USA: Edward Elgar.

Steurer, R. (2007), 'From government strategies to strategic public management: An exploratory outlook on the pursuit of cross-sectoral policy integration', *European Environment*, **17**, 201–14.

Swanson, D., L. Pintér, F. Bregha, A. Volkery and K. Jacob (2004), *National Strategies for Sustainable Development: Challenges, Approaches and Innovations in Strategic and Co-Ordinated Action*, Winnipeg, Manitoba, Canada and Eschborn, Germany: International Institute for Sustainable Development (IISD) and Deutsche Gesellschaft für Zusammenarbeit (GTZ).

Tils, R. (2007), 'The German sustainable development strategy: facing policy, management and political strategy assessment', *European Environment*, **17**, 164–76.

Wandèn, S. (2003), *Society, Systems and Environmental Objectives – a Discussion of Synergies, Conflicts and Ecological Sustainability*, Naturvårdsverket Report, Stockholm: Swedish Environmental Protection Agency.

WCED (1987), Our Common Future, Oxford: Oxford University Press.

Wurzel, R.K.W. (2008), 'Germany', in A. Jordan and A. Lenschow (eds), *Innovation in Environmental Policy? Integrating the Environment for Sustainability*, Cheltenham UK and Northampton, MA, USA: Edward Elgar.

3. Environmental Policy Integration at the Regional and Local Levels: Setting the Problem into Context

Michela Catenacci

3.1 INTRODUCTION

A great deal of the implementation and integration of environmental policies, often aimed at addressing global problems, takes place among sub-national actors at the local and regional level.

According to the Network of Regional Governments for Sustainable Development, regions have a wide strategic role to play towards sustainable development and the protection of the environment. The sub-national or regional sphere of government is growing in importance worldwide and from the point of view of proximity, efficiency and spatial dimension, regions are considered to be strategically located as a necessary and crucial sphere of government for the development of policy and for implementation of sustainable development.

Regions are perceived as an important level for policy implementation, which includes efforts for policy integration. Due to their proximity to the citizens and other important stakeholders, regions are able to tailor their action to people's needs, and to strategically link different areas of policy. Regional governments are therefore best placed to make sustainable development a practical reality.

The role local authorities fulfil within environmental policy, as the front line of the environmental concern, is an important aspect of integration. Local authorities can be approached as autonomous, decentralised authorities, but also as the executors of central environmental policy.

The aim of the present chapter is to capture the main literature dealing with EPI at the regional and local level, including scientific articles, policy studies and sectoral case studies, carried out at the international, national and sub-national level.

Since EPI is addressed in several heterogeneous contexts, the chapter tries to focus on the main currents of both theoretical and policy-oriented literature. The scientific debate on regional and local EPI is not limited to academic studies and literature, but is broadly addressed within several research projects, which analyse the effectiveness and results of specific policy procedures or tools to improve EPI in sectoral strategies. Opportunities to obtain benefits from EPI, on both the environmental and the economic fronts, are searched across a wide variety of sectors. The chapter will therefore include a few case studies to concretely assess the application of the theoretical principles exposed in the academic literature.

The analysis will address three related research questions, namely:

- Which are the main contributions to the scientific and academic debate on regional and local EPI?
- What instances of regional and local EPI do they look at?
- What are the most important points of agreement and disagreement among them?

This chapter is therefore organised as follows. Section 3.2 defines the meaning of region and of local level, and clarifies the crucial concepts of sustainable development, vertical and horizontal integration, and multi-level integration.

Section 3.3 introduces the theoretical debate which assesses the peculiar features, potential and limits of the implementation of EPI at the regional and local level. Sub-section 3.3.3 discusses the characteristics of the Local Agenda 21 process, while sub-section 3.3.3.1 focuses on the strategic role of the integration of environmental and natural resource issues in poverty reduction strategies at the local level. Section 3.4 considers the debate on regional and local EPI arising from the implementation of research projects, at the global and EU level.

Section 3.5 discusses two categories of instruments that promote the diffusion of EPI and are broadly analysed in the literature: the EU Structural and Cohesion Funds, and the Strategic and Regional Environmental Assessment processes. Section 3.6 evaluates the potential of the networks of regions to share good practice and encourage actions for integrating the environment into regional development programmes. Finally Section 3.7 provides four examples of regional EPI carried out by single countries at the sub-national level. Section 3.8 concludes this chapter.

3.2   KEY CONCEPTS

This section introduces and clarifies some important concepts which are central to the debate on regional and local EPI.

As Persson (2004) suggests, a number of assumptions should be specified when analysing the EPI concept. It is important to identify if the ultimate objective of EPI is environmental protection, environmental sustainability or broadly sustainable development, whose aim is to ensure economic growth while protecting the environment. The nature of EPI has to be defined, distinguishing between horizontal and vertical integration. At the same time the role and characteristics of each different level of governance should be specified, in order to study their influence on the achievement of EPI.

3.2.1 Definition of Region and of the Local Level Concept

It is almost impossible to identify a generally accepted definition of 'region' in the literature, due to the ongoing theoretical debate on the issue.

The present chapter will therefore refer to a spatial entity which fulfils certain criteria (spatial, political/administrative, functional). The term 'region' is understood in a broad sense as a territory where a system of governance exists, which is the largest and first level of political subdivision within an individual country represented at the United Nations, and which is above the municipal level (Tauras, 1997).

Because of possible confusion in terminology, a distinction has to be made between 'world-regions' and 'regions' at the sub-national level. A 'region' in the UN context is the supranational geographical area comprising the different regions of Africa, Asia, Europe, Latin America and the Caribbean, Northern America and Oceania, whereas the chapter will mainly focus on sub-national regions.

There are many different types and names for regional governments in different parts of the word. Berger and Pohoryles (2006) offer three different definitions of regions:

1. Homogeneous regions: The first definition refers to regions as homogenous spatial entities, which comprise, for example common historical roots, language, culture, and so on.
2. Functional or polar regions: In the second case regions are defined with regard to the function which is carried out on their spatial areas, for example economic regions, labour market regions or cultural regions. Environmentally defined regions, like water regions or bioregions, can also be comprised in this definition. Some suggestions have been made in favour of 'bioregions' (that is, spatial units which are defined by environmental characteristics) which should be governed on an environmental and sustainable use basis (McGinnis, 1998). Others argue that regions are somehow distinct geographical areas which have an identity that does not correspond with existing administrative or political boundaries (Lafferty and Hovden, 2003).

3. Administrative and programming regions: The third definition refers to regions as political-administrative entities, and therefore includes entities at the first sub-national level below the nation state which have political and/or administrative competences. Regions as sub-national political-administrative entities show distinct competences in the different countries, depending on whether they are federal states or more centralised states.

David (1998), in his contribution to the 6th Conference of EEAC, sums up the concept of 'local level' as the elected level of government which is closest to the people, and broadly refers to every directly elected level of government below that of central level. Among the directly elected authorities he considers municipalities, provinces, and the like, while among the indirectly elected authorities, which are created on the orders of the directly elected ones, he enumerates the inter-communal associations, municipal or provincial regions, non-profit associations, local platforms an so on. He therefore suggests considering, when assessing the integration of environmental policy at the local level, the division into diverse hierarchical sub-levels, and the specific forms of management authorities in the different countries.

3.2.2   Economic Development and Environment

Within the context of economic development, integrating environmental policy has commonly been perceived as a negative and constraining factor. Academic analyses and institutional developments have encouraged a more positive view, and have produced explanatory theories in the form of 'ecological modernisation'.

The 'zero-growth' option, asking for a reduction or even a complete halt in economic development, has been substituted by the sustainable development concept. Ecological considerations are therefore viewed as providing a framework for development and constituting a necessary precondition for growth.

The concept of sustainable development challenges the traditional division of competences among the different levels of government, due to the multi-level character and the shared responsibility system which is at the core of such a commitment. According to this idea, regions should play a strategic role in promoting sustainable development, through their intermediate position in the local/global axis (Morata, 2002).

3.2.3   Vertical and Horizontal Integration

Basically all theoretical studies and policy conclusions agree on the importance of establishing a strong interaction among the different authorities and government.

The cooperation among the authorities is generally considered from two perspectives (David, 1998):

- The vertical line, that goes from the global to the local level which is closer to the local population, and is defined on territorial basis. Vertical integration means achieving benefits for the environment through effective and efficient co-ordination between different levels of government (local, regional, national, European or global).
- The horizontal line, that means the integration of environmental concerns into other areas of policy, such as zoning and spatial policy, economy, traffic and transport, agriculture, education and so on. Therefore horizontal integration is the integration of environmental considerations within sector and across sectors. It can also be between different actors requiring co-ordination between all relevant authorities and agencies of the same policy level (for example financial and health authorities, as well as environmental authorities).

At the regional and local level, all forms of integration of environmental policy can be applied.

3.2.4   Multi-Level Governance

Multi-level governance can be seen as a consequence of the dispersion of political authority among different territorial levels of governance. The implementation of EPI may be considered in a multi-level governance perspective, analysing the contributions of each specific level of governance to EPI in a particular sector or policy.

The institutions and processes that promote the integration of the environmental concept into policies and sectors can be seen as an integral part of a single system. Cooperation between different tiers of government, from the local to the global level, proves to be essential from the analysis of the literature and of the applied projects.

Moreover, the 'crisis of legitimacy' (Morata, 2002) impacting the traditional notion of governance, no longer admit centralised policy approaches and single responses to face complex and integrated problems regarding, for example, environmental decision-making processes.

Institutional transformation is therefore required, which transfers some policy functions to sub-state levels, and decentralises the authority to carry out the governance patterns. The transfer of some areas of competence to regional and local levels is already taking place in several countries. In the

European Union this process is contributing to the redefinition of traditional functions of subnational governments. Moreover, in several countries the most functionally relevant unit which has emerged is not the regional or the provincial level, but the metropolitan or city region.

3.3   THEORETICAL DEBATE

3.3.1   Regional EPI

During the past two decades sustainable development concerns have emerged as important elements in the design and operation of a range of EU and member state spatial and sectoral policies associated with regional planning and development. In part this recognition and incorporation of sustainable development concerns reflects a new realisation that the consequences of unthinking and irresponsible economic growth are more serious than originally envisaged, but it also represents the rediscovery of the merits of what in previous eras was called a 'balanced' approach to regional planning and development (Roberts, 1994).

Morata (2002) provides a detailed research on the strategic role played by regions in promoting environmental integration and sustainable development. Their particular function should be the translation of sustainability principles and concepts into concrete actions, through the implementation of policies and agreements defined at the national and international level, and the management of specific programmes related to sustainability. Regions are in charge of promoting public debate and stakeholders' participation in defining the tasks and sharing responsibilities to cope with it. Morata focuses his analysis on the EU regions, which are increasingly experiencing a transferring of competencies from the national and European authorities. Despite appreciating the enhanced awareness about environment and sustainable development at the different levels of governments, he also notes that there is insufficient concern about 'the institutional changes and capacities needed to cope with such a commitment' (p. 51), and therefore underlines the need to create an appropriate set of institutions at the sub-national level and improve political and social skills of officials and citizens, in a 'joint multi-level collective action'.

Morata specifies that the effort towards sustainable development should come jointly from public and private actors, since the former cannot hierarchically impose the behavioural changes on which sustainability depends, while the latter are not able to deal with problems that overcome their abilities to internalize the issues and to mobilize the resources needed to face them. The quality of the relationships between different actors and levels of governance is a crucial issue. Therefore, the essential contribution to EPI is not confined to institutions and governmental authorities, but is widely dependent on citizens and local actors, who increase the awareness, understanding and acceptance in the development of integrated policies and approaches.

A number of scientific articles assessing the integration of the environment into regional development in the European Union are collected in a Special Edition of the *European Environment* journal.

The first two papers of that issue consider in broad terms how the role of the environment has developed within EU regional policy. In the article 'Incorporating the environment into structural funds regional programmes: evolution, current developments and future prospects', Roberts (2001) examines the concept of ecological modernization that underpins the belief that environmental gain can be a significant part of regional development. Clement (2001) illustrates in his paper 'Strategic environmental awakening: European progress in regional environmental integration' how the European Commission has steadily adopted many of the tenets of ecological modernization, both in the development of its strategy, and also in the provision of new tools for its implementation, before observing that the next stage in integrating the environment into regional planning must focus on the strategic aspects of sustainability.

The subsequent two papers look at current progress in this respect. Glasson and Gosling (2001) consider, in the article 'SEA and regional planning – overcoming the institutional constraints: some lessons from the EU', the institutional obstacles that may impede progress towards strategic environmental assessment of regional policies, plans and programmes both within the Commission and at the level of the individual member state. Given that a new directive in this area was expected in time for the next round of funding for the Structural Funds, they examine how strategic environmental aspects are currently accommodated in the regional planning systems of England, the Netherlands and Spain, and the guidance that can be drawn from this for future developments.

Karl and Ranné (2001) examine the German situation, where transfers of resources through regional policy form a central element of government development strategy. They find that, although one may identify individual examples where environmental gain appears to drive some aspects of German regional policy, there is no concerted strategic element to environmental policy at a regional level at present, despite the existence of a strong green movement and federal structure.

In the final paper, 'Sustainable development and environmental partnership at the regional scale: the case of Sustainability North West', Shaw and Kidd (2001) consider these issues at regional level within a member state, assessing progress towards sustainability within the North West of England. Their paper suggests that the concurrent emergence of English regional governance and the growing emphasis in regional policy on sustainable development and public–private–community partnerships, epitomized by Sustainability North West, provide pointers to the way in which environmental strategy can be accommodated in UK regional development practice, and may also perhaps serve as an example which can be adopted more widely in the EU. As all the papers in this issue clearly demonstrate, there is a growing pool of best practice available to policy makers within the EU seeking to integrate the environment into regional development.

The recent *Environmental Integration Handbook* (European Commission, 2006a), provides an operational framework for integrating the environment into EC development cooperation modalities. It illustrates the main tools and procedures to be applied at the national and regional levels, and dedicates a particular focus to the importance of integrating the environmental component in country and regional analyses, response strategies and multi-annual programming. Coherent with the traditional policy position of the EU, the document proposes a precautionary approach to enhance the efficiency of development activities and projects, which considers environmental issues from the very start of the cycle of operations. That implies a duty to take action in the face of unfavourable trends, and to integrate environmental considerations at an early stage of decision making. The optimum approach would be therefore to integrate environmental considerations upstream at the policy making and programming stage, and in the first phases of the cycle of operations. Integration of the environment early in the decision-making process has however certain limitations: in particular the uncertainty of the real impacts of decisions taken. Follow-up monitoring is therefore necessary.

In order to adequately inform regional co-operation strategies, the key tools proposed by the EU Commission are the Regional Environmental Profiles (REP). The REP focus on environmental issues common to a group of neighbouring countries (including transboundary issues) such as those linked to the shared management of ecosystems, which can be more effectively addressed at the regional level. The REP represent the regional version of the Country Environmental Profiles (CEP), which contain a description and broad assessment of a country's environmental situation, policy and regulatory framework, institutional capacities and environmental co-operation.

In order to design integrated development programmes at the regional level, with the specific inclusion of the environment, Clement (1997) underlines the potential of multi-disciplinary teams. Experts from different disciplines or departments (or authorities) should work together on a specific issue. As Clement points out, regional economic strategies are increasingly incorporating a range of multi-disciplinary and sectoral perspectives. Therefore programme preparation has moved from 'being the territory solely occupied by economists', to an integrated approach including different professionals.

Clement brings examples from regional economic programmes in European countries, which highlight how multidisciplinary teams approach environmental integration. They generally tend to treat environment as a horizontal issue, that should be included across all other sectors without the need for an independent priority. To avoid the risk of losing environmental perspectives during programme implementation, the role of the environmental specialist and the formation of ad hoc environmental sub-groups are increasing in significance.

3.3.2   Local EPI

David's article on 'Environmental policy integration at a local level' (David, 1998) explains that in the EU, according to the principle of subsidiarity, every decision must be taken at the most appropriate level and the various authorities must be open and prepared to cooperate.

The nature and the scale of the environmental problem is decisive for the choice of which is the most appropriate forum: local, central, European or global. The local policy level should cooperate with the higher hierarchical levels and benefit for its own environmental objectives. In the environmental management framework, the interaction between the governmental strata is referred to as 'partnership'.

Morata (2002) specifies that the modern concept of subsidiarity can be seen as a multi-level approach that goes beyond the simple territorial distribution of competencies to include relationships between authorities at different levels, allowing local actors and citizens to take a proactive approach and give their own contribution to the overall policy process.

David (1998) explains that the active role of local authorities in the development and implementation of the environmental policy of central government is an example of vertical integration.

The horizontal line is related to the causally-orientated approach to environmental problems. This can be applied to all levels of management, dealing with how environmental issues can be integrated into the environmental apparatus itself (internal integration) and into other areas of policy (external integration).

Whenever local authorities have special tasks and powers for local circumstances such as public health, safety and so on, this offers an opportunity for horizontal internal integration. We speak of horizontal external integration when local authorities have major executive responsibilities such as, for example, the laying and maintenance of sewers, the maintenance of non-navigable watercourses, management of road verges and management of its own patrimony (for example forests and nature reserves, parks). This enables them to integrate environmental policy into other policy sectors.

The development of a more coherent policy on both the vertical and horizontal lines and the harmonisation of both lines represent the aim of the integration of environmental policy at the local level.

David's article presents a number of aims to achieve a coherent integration, such as mutual strengthening the government action, reducing overlapping environmental problems to a minimum, promote a movement towards sustainable development at all levels of society.

Moreover, the general conclusions of the 6th annual conference of EEAC (1998) enumerate four general principles of integration and subsequent implementation that are equally valid at European, national, regional and local level:

1. The development of sector-specific integration strategies and action plans including: defining co-operative mechanisms, raising awareness and understanding, developing economic and fiscal initiatives. The development of appropriate financial incentives and the strengthening of instruments to encourage integration and implementation are important. Appropriate mixes of financial incentives must be designed to reward good environmental practice (and penalise bad practice) and instruments strengthened to promote communication, establish clear methods and goals for achieving sustainability and cross-compliance, for example, requiring compliance with environmental criteria as a precondition for the receipt of grants or subsidies.
2. Examination of institutional decision making arrangements to ensure effective delivery of integration.
3. The establishment of environmental audit systems within sector, identifying (and rewarding) best practice.
4. For each sector the clear definition of indicators and targets which are linked to sustainable development. Medium-term targets should be set as realistic milestones that take us towards achieving integration and environmental sustainability.

According to the conclusions, it is essential that the process of environmental integration is established at the earliest possible point within the development of policies, plans and programmes.

In this process it is important to clearly establish the responsibilities of all government departments and ministries; this forms the basis and commitment to design and implement integrated policies. Strong cooperation is necessary between Ministries (for example Finance, Agriculture, Health, Employment and Environment) and so, for example, in agriculture between consumers, farmers, environmentalists and Advisory Councils. It is important, however, to avoid an exclusively sectoral approach. A dual approach should be taken; one of integration within sectors and an overarching approach between sectors.

David's article (1998) explains that the integration of environmental policy at the local level can lead to a number of contentious issues, mainly due to the fact that:

- planning of local environmental policy is still in its early stages;
- the level of integration at the central level is often low itself;
- people, resources, organisation and expertise are still inadequate to cope with the new tasks;
- integration is still too often considered an irrelevant cost element;
- perceptions of the environmental problems at the various levels still differ greatly;
- the horizontal integration of local environmental policy is limited by the fact that it is inadequately harmonised with the central level;
- environmental information is inadequately managed;
- the priorities for the integration of environmental policy with other policy sectors will vary depending on the degree of importance given to typically local problems.

David identifies different support policies for the integration of environmental concerns at the local level. First of all, he suggests that central government should enhance the integration of environmental concerns at the local level by developing a stimulus programme covering key aspects, such as communication planning, development of abilities, financing and consultation structures. The central and local authorities can commit to environmental or cooperative agreements, to promote the extension of 'front-line environmental care'.

The planned development of the local environmental policy should be stimulated and gradually harmonised with environmental planning at the central level. Therefore central government, in consultation with local authorities, should formulate a number of conditions regarding substance, form and methods, considering for example:

- how the integration principle can be adapted by local authorities;
- a correct and complete inventory of the existing situation in terms of a given area of policy;

- an inventory of contentious issues;
- strategic aims;
- the instruments and means to achieve these aims;
- programming and organisation of its implementation.

Concrete and measurable criteria to assess the level of integration should be finally established. The whole policy is seen as a common learning process, that leads to a common approach towards the subdivision of environmental issues, the assessment of environmental problems and the organisation and planning of environmental policy, through mutual consultation, guidance and awareness rising.

Local planning can form the basis for a local Agenda 21 which will help bring about the global concept for sustainable development at the local level (see sub-section 3.3.3). Central government must provide stimulus for the establishment of a local Agenda 21. In order to stimulate the introduction of this concept into local policy, David's article proposes that the model projects for the implementation of local Agendas 21 might be brought together to form a 'scenario for sustainable development'. The advantage of introducing the issue of integration at the local level via a project and/or issue approach, rather than a top-down approach, is tested. Finally, David considers that, in addition to measures which provide stimulus, the central government could impose integration of environmental policy through appropriate regulations. The inclusion of environmental aims in the general objectives of a local authority is one such possibility.

3.3.3   Local Agenda 21

Agenda 21 is the global plan of action towards Sustainable Development adopted at the UN World Summit on Sustainable Development held in Rio de Janeiro, Brazil, in June 1992.

The onus of implementing the key objective of Agenda 21 has been placed clearly on local governments and its constituent communities. The real roots of Agenda 21's success therefore lie at the micro, local level.

Chapter 28 of the Agenda 21, titled 'Local Authorities' Initiatives in Support of Agenda 21' highlights the vital role that local authorities have to play in educating, mobilising and responding to the public to promote sustainable development, pointing out that 'Local authorities construct, operate and maintain economic, social and environmental infrastructure, oversee planning processes, establish local environmental policies and regulations, and assist in implementing national and sub national environmental policies. As the level of governance closest to the people, they play a vital role in educating, mobilizing and responding to the public to promote sustainable development …'.

Chapter 8, 'Integrating Environment and Development in Decision-Making' contains the following programme areas:

- integrating environment and development at the policy, planning and management levels;
- providing an effective legal and regulatory framework;
- making effective use of economic instruments and market and other incentives;
- establishing systems for integrated environmental and economic accounting.

They comprise an adjustment or even a fundamental reshaping of decision-making, in the light of country-specific conditions, in order to put environment and development at the centre of economic and political decision-making, achieving a full integration of these factors.

In recent years, some governments have also begun to make significant changes in the institutional structures of government in order to enable more systematic consideration of the environment when decisions are made on economic, social, fiscal, energy, agricultural, transportation, trade and other policies, as well as the implications of policies in these areas for the environment. New forms of dialogue are also being developed for achieving better integration among national and local government, industry, science, environmental groups and the public in the process of developing effective approaches to environment and development.

According to Article 8 of Agenda 21, the responsibility for bringing about changes lies with governments in partnership with the private sector and local authorities, and in collaboration with national, regional and international organisations, including in particular UNEP, UNDP and the World Bank.

To support a more integrated approach to decision-making, the Article requires, among the other things, to adopt integrated approaches to sustainable development at the regional level, including transboundary areas; delegate planning and management responsibilities to the lowest level of public authority consistent with effective action; establish procedures for involving local communities in contingency planning for environmental and industrial accidents, and maintaining an open exchange of information on local hazards.

Local Agenda 21 (LA21) is a local-government-led, community-wide, and participatory effort to establish a comprehensive action strategy for integrating the environmental protection with economic development and community well-being in the local jurisdiction or area. This requires the integration of planning and action across economic, social and environmental spheres. Key elements are full community participation, assessment of current conditions, target setting for achieving specific goals, monitoring and reporting. The 'Localising Agenda 21' section is an effort to outline a four-step process by which a LA21 plan can be developed or improved:

1. Data collection: it gathers pertinent baseline information, on which future actions are based and evaluated. This information is used to develop a comprehensive environmental profile.
2. Planning and development: it is the formulative stage where the information gathered is used to develop an environmental vision, state the goals and objectives, and output an environmental strategy.
3. Plan management: in this phase a large range of activities that involve various stakeholders and the community at large are initiated.
4. Monitoring and evaluation: it takes a critical view of the actions being taken and evaluates them against a set of indicators, and monitors the implementation of the LA21 plan.

Braun (2006b) affirms that carrying out long-term actions put forward by the Agenda 21 at the local level represents one of the main challenges as municipal government in general do not have the capacity to effectively implement the process.

Paredis et al. (2002) point out that, especially in the industrialised countries, parallel ideas have developed concerning what a Local Agenda 21 process should now contain. These ideas have grown strongly on the basis of practice, including under the influence of major campaigns. These campaigns are a second important source of discourse on LA21. This is the case, for example, of the worldwide campaign on LA21 organised by ICLEI (International Council for Local Environmental Initiatives, an international association of cities and urban organizations), and the European Sustainable Cities and Towns Campaign (launched in 1994 with support from the European Commission among the others, and known because of the Aalborg Charter which was signed by the participating cities).

All of these campaigns give raise to a number of key concepts (see Lafferty, 1999; ICLEI, 2001): integrated approach to policy making, participation and consultation of stakeholders, long-term perspective and translation of global concerns to the local level. This implies extra efforts to establish the link between local actors, decision and rules on the one hand, and their global impact, both in the environmental area as well as relating to equity and justice at the global level.

In 1996 ICLEI published a Local Agenda 21 Planning Guide, which is used as a source of inspiration in many campaigns.

ICLEI (2001) produced also one of the few comparative surveys of LA21 projects at global level. A more quantitative description is provided by the

SUSCOM (SUStainable COMmunities in Europe) project, which ran from 1999 to 2001, bringing together studies relating to LA21 in 12 European countries (Norway, Sweden, Finland, Great Britain, Ireland, Germany, Austria, Italy, Spain, Denmark and France) and analysing them. The results show that the LA21 label is used in very different cases and realities.

3.3.3.1 Poverty reduction and environmental management

Within the broad concept of sustainable development, one of the pillars of the Agenda 21 programme is the interest towards the poverty issue. Poverty can be described as the condition when basic human needs are unsatisfied because of the lack of capital and the inequitable distribution of wealth. Livelihoods are therefore closely dependent on the productivity of natural resources and of labour. This makes the poor vulnerable to any decline in the productivity of natural resources and to any unhealthy conditions that affect their capacity to work. Thus degraded environmental conditions have a direct and important relationship with poverty. The poor are also the most vulnerable to natural disasters such as floods, droughts, crop pests and environmentally-related conflicts.

There is a growing coverage of environmental and natural resource issues in poverty reduction strategies documents. The present section acknowledges the importance of the environmental component for economic development and growth policies carried out at the local level, and underlines the close links between poverty, vulnerability and the environment.

Especially for developing countries, environmental and natural resources provide foundations for the growth sectors: notably agriculture, forestry, fisheries and tourism. Poor people are dependent on land, water, wood fuel and clean air. The state of natural environment needs to be protected and harnessed to its full potential in order to promote pro-poor growth.

In a joint document of the Department For International Development, the European Commission, the United Nations Development Programme and the World Bank (DFID, EC, UNDP and WB, 2002) the strong link between environmental protection and poverty reduction is demonstrated, with the aim of forging a more integrated and effective global response to both issues.

Sound and equitable management of the environment is considered integral to achieving the Millennium Development Goals, in particular 'to eradicating extreme poverty and hunger, reducing child mortality, combating major diseases, and ensuring environmental sustainability'.

The document identifies many different opportunities to reduce poverty by improving the environment. A crucial point is the importance of decentralisation for environmental management by integrating poverty–environment issues into sub-national policy and planning processes and sectoral investment programmes. Civil society needs to be empowered, expanding public access to environmental information, decision-making and justice.

Environmental management needs to reflect the multidimensional and dynamic nature of poverty–environment linkages. Many countries, such as for example Malawi, Tanzania, Egypt and Sri Lanka, have introduced district-level environmental planning. Decentralisation in rural areas has given local government control over many key natural resources. However, it is important that decentralised environmental planning is integrated into the mainstream local planning process. Moreover, efforts to empower communities to manage natural resources locally should be taken, to safeguard against corruption and unsustainable behaviour, and to build local capacity for participatory management.

Finally, devolution of power to the local level can increase pressure on natural resources in view of the income, employment and revenue needs of local government. Financial transfer from the outside, for example through national subsidies or international funds, such as the Global Environmental Facility (GEF), can make a make a big difference as to how these issues are resolved. The Global Environmental Facility grants can cover the incremental costs associated with transforming a project with local and national benefits that may have global environmental costs to one with both internal and global benefits.

3.4   RESEARCH PROJECTS ON REGIONAL AND LOCAL EPI

A significant part of the study on the EPI issue comes from the analysis of research projects carried out at the regional and local level. Due to the increasing concern with the environmental component, and the important role of legislation, the formulation of several projects takes into account environmental conditions such as efficiency and sustainability.

The problem analysis and the strategy analysis in the logical framework approach take into account the linkages between the social and economic conditions and the environment. Many projects are designed in such a way that they will use available opportunities to enhance the positive impacts and ensure that they will not result in significant negative impacts on the environment when implemented. Monitoring and subsequent evaluation of the projects also address linkages with the environment as part of the assessment criteria.

3.4.1   At the Global Level

The UNESCAP (1999), in order to fill the gap in the existing knowledge about the integration of environmental and sustainable development issues into the economic decision-making process of almost all the countries of the Asia-Pacific area, executed a project entitled 'Integrating environmental considerations into economic policy-making processes'. The purpose of the project was to assist member countries in building their capacity to devise effective institutional frameworks for policy formulation and implementation for integrating environmental consideration into economic policy-making processes. The project aimed at enhancing the capacity of the government at all levels, focussing in particular on the provincial and local levels, promoting interaction and coordination between various departments and agencies in the formulation of environmentally sound and sustainable development policies and programmes.

The first set of studies focuses on the existing institutional arrangements for incorporating environmental considerations into economic policy-making process. This topic has been further divided into studies at the national, provincial/local and sectoral levels. Each study includes: a review of the institutional modalities for making policy decisions and undertaking coordination between ministries/agencies and the analysis of their strengths and weaknesses; a critical analysis of the types of measures being used to integrate environmental considerations as well as the monitoring and enforcement mechanisms in terms of perceived effectiveness in achieving stated policy objectives; a review of training and information needs of government officials; a set of recommendations for making improvements in all the above areas.

The second set of studies analyses the effectiveness of various methods used for assessing environmental problems such as land use, soil erosion and hazard management, and the way in which those assessments are fed into policy decision-making processes. Each study focuses on a major area of concern for the selected country and analyses the use of different methodologies for assessing the problem, the capacity of the various agencies in the assessment of trade-offs between environmental concerns and economic development objectives.

Volume II of the country studies assess the 'Institutional arrangements and mechanisms at local/provincial level', and carries out country studies on Shenyang in China, Suva in Fiji, Kuala Lumpur in Malaysia and North West Frontier Province in Pakistan.

3.4.2   EU Projects

Regions act as the interface between the local level and the EU and global levels. The EU Commission is opening the way for sub-national decentralisation as a response to socioeconomic and territorial transformations. At the same time the Commission has taken advantage of the process by building coalitions with regional authorities to overcome central governments' resistance (Morata, 2002). Through Community initiatives and projects, such as, for example, REGIONET, ALTENER and SAVE, the Commission has improved cooperation among subcentral actors and communication between different levels of governance.

According to Morata (2002), a complementary action at the EU level is necessary in three areas, to build a coherent partnership across the levels of governance.

First of all the Commission should ensure that peculiar conditions at the regional and local level are taken into account when developing policy proposals. That emphasises the importance of greater flexibility in the implementation of legislation and programmes, and the need for coherent and balanced policies when dealing with complex and integrated issues. In order to do that, the Commission is expected to improve the communication with regions and cities within the Member States.

REGIONET project

The Treaty of Amsterdam gave the Union the task of ensuring sustainable development, with priority attached to maintaining a high level of environmental protection. Article 6 of the Treaty establishes that environmental protection requirements must be integrated into the definition and implementation of Community policies.

Such integration is a reality for regional development and the environment which, far from being contradictory, are necessarily complementary. Certain regions must bear higher environmental protection costs than others. The quality of life also contributes to the attractiveness of a region.

The European Commission consequently ensures that projects developed under regional policy are respectful of the environment: an assessment of their environmental impact must be conducted by the Member States concerned.

As Jeffery (2002) states, 'regions were envisaged both as an institutional building block for EU constitutional debates, and as mechanisms for reconnecting the citizens with Europe'. European regions were considered as one important level of EU policymaking.

REGIONET, an EU thematic network project funded by DG Research under the 5th Framework Programme, was running between 2002 and 2004. The overall objective of the project was to investigate the efforts in the European regions to implement sustainable development. It was also an aim to bring together the various stakeholders who have experiences in the study and/or implementation of regional sustainable development in order to discuss the experiences made so far as well as the new needs and challenges being faced.

The work and the findings of REGIONET were based on two main approaches. On the one hand, four international workshops were organised by the project team. These workshops included academic and policy-related papers as well as workshop and plenary discussions, with participants coming from more than 25 European countries, Canada and Australia. The workshops allowed having a comprehensive state-of-the-art of regional sustainable development in Europe and elsewhere. The workshops covered the following topics:

1. regional sustainable development and the role of Structural Funds;
2. strategies for effective multi-level governance;
3. evaluation methods and tools for regional sustainable development;
4. cross-fertilisation and integration of results of the project.

On the other hand, national reports on regional sustainable development were prepared to give an extensive overview of how this topic is perceived and what practical policy implications it has in the different European countries. The project team developed a template for the national reports which served as the basis for each of the seventeen reports.

The following main sections are covered within each national report:

- National background on regional development: this includes not only the history of regional development of each country, but also the political and administrative system and hierarchies as these are of major importance in giving a framework for policymaking. This section also includes a reflection about national initiatives for sustainable development.
- Regional sustainable development: here the national reports reflect upon national and regional initiatives for regional sustainable development. The role of Structural Funds in fostering sustainable development at the regional level is underlined.
- Multi-level governance: this section focuses on the involvement of the different political/administrative levels in policymaking – from the EU, to the national and regional level – as well as on the multi-level interaction between the different stakeholders. Additionally, it analyses how cross-sectoral policy integration in regional sustainable development is carried out by the different levels.
- Evaluation methods and tools for regional sustainable development: the current evaluation methods, tools and indicators are described in this section, that studies the different types of measurements for regional sustainable development, and the potential harmonisation of the different tools.

- Analysis of regional sustainable development: the last section summarises the practical experiences with regional sustainable development across Europe. It also evaluates the general trade-offs, top-down and bottom-up relations characterising European regional policy. The post-2006 period, when new Structural Funds regulations will be implemented, is finally considered.

Berger and Pohoryles' article (2006) uses the findings of the REGIONET project and assesses the potential of regions to contribute to the practical application of SD and, in this context, it investigates two main aspects:

- the integration of policies across various policy sectors;
- the concept of capacity building, which refers to the means and resources of regional institutions and stakeholders in their attempts to formulate and/or implement sustainability policies.

The article focuses on the experiences with the above two issues in the following fields:

- multi-level governance and its implications for the regions;
- the Structural Funds regime and how it promotes sustainable development;
- evaluation methods and tools for sustainability in the regions.

Berger and Pohoryles study the meaning of EPI and underlines the lack of concrete implementation efforts at the EU level. The problems identified, mainly due to the insufficient consistency of the Cardiff process, are the lack of political commitment, the unclear priorities, the missing strategic approaches, and finally the lack of delivery, implementation and review mechanisms.

Among the most severe shortcomings there are the sectoral strategies as a result of the Cardiff Process (difficult cross-sectoral integration) and the lack of implementation of EPI on the ground.

Jordan et al. (2004), quoted also by Berger and Pohoryles (2006), underline the importance of embedding EPI in MICRO policy processes. Until now, the bottom-up formulation and implementation of EU policies and integration processes on the various government levels has not been fully realised.

The authors argue that 'if EPI is to mean anything, it has to bite at the level of daily policy-making, otherwise grand political and legal commitments to principles such as integration and sustainability will not be translated into daily practice'.

From these results, Berger and Pohoryles conclude that policy integration cannot be delivered by the Commission alone, but must involve all different levels of government as well as the various stakeholders. Therefore, they evidence the necessity to examine whether different capacities and resources exist at the micro level (that is regional and local level) which can facilitate EPI processes.

They also examines the capacities of regions for the implementation of sustainable development policies. They focus on the concept of 'capacity building' (p. 5) and explain that for SD to have any practical implications and meaning on the ground, in terms of institution-building, policy formulation and implementation as well as development management, it is important to have skills, knowledge and resources at the individual and institutional level.

The overall objective of capacity building (UN Rio Declaration) is 'to develop and improve national and related sub-national and regional capacities and capabilities for sustainable development, with the involvement of non-governmental actors'.

ALTENER and SAVE projects

Local and regional actors, decision processes and initiatives are of prime importance for implementing measures in the area of energy efficiency, renewable energy and clean urban transport. Energy efficiency measures and renewable energies are decentralised technologies, and there are many players to be mobilised. Activities on the local or regional level therefore constitute a type of bottom-up approach, which is more oriented to market needs than national or global solutions. The development and implementation of renewable energies and energy efficient measures is not only a matter of technological innovation and profitability, but also of motivation and social influence.

The SAVE Programme addressed studies on non-technological aspects of energy efficiency, while ALTENER is the Community programme for the promotion of renewable energies.

To achieve the objectives of stimulating measures, encouraging investments and creating favourable framework conditions for energy efficiency, one of the explicit schemes of SAVE were studies on 'specific measures to improve energy management at urban and regional levels with a view to achieving greater cohesion between Member States and regions in the field of energy efficiency'.

This target was tackled mainly by setting up SAVE agencies regionally, on islands and in cities in order to disseminate information and good practice examples, and by creating networks between local and regional authorities. Renewable energy is by definition local energy, so that the local aspect is generally included in projects in this field. In addition, the ALTENER II Programme made explicit reference to the local aspect of renewable energy.

Local action with respect to energy efficiency and the use of renewable energy resources is indispensable to achieving the EU's energy target. The EU has further emphasised the promotion of activities on a local level within the 6th Framework Programme, of which CONCERTO is a major part. This is an EU initiative to support local communities in developing sustainable and highly energy-efficient initiatives. It aims at motivating communities to work towards a completely integrated energy policy, harmonising a substantial use of renewable energy sources with innovative technologies and systems to minimise energy consumption and improve citizens' quality of life.

All the projects funded by the ALTENER and the SAVE programmes contribute to local sustainable development. They analyse barriers to and potentials for energy efficiency and the use of renewable energies and use an integrated approach in most cases.

The awareness and behaviour of citizens are highlighted as essential factors with regard to sustainability, as is the involvement of local players and the partnerships between them. Some of the projects also include social aspects such as communication patterns, support for less favoured social groups, improving the quality of life, social cohesion and, above all, the insight that local sustainability policy is a social process. Exchanging experience between communities through networking, the identification and dissemination of good-practice examples, and providing appliance-oriented tools to a large group of users are considered important measures for success on the local level.

3.5   TOOLS FOR EPI AT REGIONAL LEVEL

Morata (2002) specifies that institutional and financial instruments are necessary, but often not sufficient to enhance the role of regional government in the development and integration of the environment into policies and sectors. This would also require other ingredients such as strategic projects, problem-solving capacities, cooperative arrangements, social cohesion and an adequate economic environment (Keating, 2002).

Two significant examples of instruments that promote the diffusion of EPI, and are broadly analysed in the literature, are the EU Structural and Cohesion funds, and the Environmental Impact Assessment (EIA) procedures. The present section will consider two forms of EIA, specifically targeted for regional and local management.

3.5.1   EU Structural and Cohesion Funds

Article 6 of the 1997 Treaty of Amsterdam stipulates that environmental protection requirements must be 'integrated into the definition and implementation of Community policies and activities, in particular with a view to promoting sustainable development'. Financial instruments, including Structural Funds, are required by this article 'to work, simultaneously and in the long term interest, towards economic growth, social cohesion and the protection of the environment; in other words sustainable development'.

Structural Funds comprise a series of programmes designed to assist problematic regions, that range across the different EU Member States. Designated on the basis of an index of disparities, these regions generally face economic problems including outmigration, declining industrial strength, rural depopulation and peripherality (Clement, 1997).

Over the last ten years, a number of factors have impacted on the Structural Funds to raise the importance of the environment. In particular, the EU Environmental Action Programmes introduced the concept of environmental integration into economic development (Johnson and Corcelle, 1995); the Single European Act made environmental protection a component of the Community's other policies; and the White Paper on Growth, Competitiveness and Employment proposed a new development model that reversed the current negative relationship between economic growth and environmental pollution (Commission of the European Communities, 1993).

EU General Regulation 1083/2006 on Structural Funds makes environmental sustainability a key feature of regional funding. Article 3 states that socio-economic objectives will be strengthened 'by protecting and improving the quality of the environment'. Article 17 makes clear that 'the objective of the Funds shall be pursued in the framework of sustainable development and the Community promotion of the goal of protecting and improving the environment'.

Clement (2001), in his research article on European progress in regional environmental integration, reviews progress in regional environmental integration within the EU Structural Funds, specifically in the economic development programmes for disadvantaged regions. He explains that in Europe the challenge of integrating environment and regional economic development is progressively being met through the EU Structural Funds. Although the beginning was characterised by conflict between these two themes, considerable progress has been made in successive rounds of programmes, accompanied by a gradual raising of awareness and the development of new mechanisms for integration.

Clement underlines the crucial support of environmental guidance offered by the European Commission to achieve this progress, with handbooks designed to raise new ideas and suggest innovative ways of approaching the task.

Current programmes incorporate extensive environmental profiles to support programme development, and new methods of combining both horizontal and vertical integration show considerable promise for the realisation of environmental objectives in programme implementation. To facilitate further integration, Clement identifies the main priorities for research, including the role for environmental strategies, the production of an index of environmental integration, the identification of measurable environmental indicators and confirmation that sustainable development is acting as a catalyst for environmental gain.

The establishment of the Cohesion Fund has added further impetus to the environmental dimension of the Community's Cohesion Policy. This fund constitutes for the Member States concerned the most important instrument to address their needs, particularly in the field of protection and management of water resources, as well as the collection, treatment and recycling of waste.

The importance of the Cohesion and of the Structural Funds marks the increasing awareness that the environment and regional development are of complementary character.

Already in 1995, in a thematic Communication on *Cohesion Policy and the Environment*, the European Commission presented what it considered as the main options for achieving greater synergy between the Community's cohesion policy and its policy on the environment, focussing on improving the monitoring and assessment of the environmental impact of regional programmes, and on the tightening up of the criteria on which projects are selected to ensure that they have a marked impact in economic, social and environmental terms. The Commission supported establishing a dialogue between all the parties involved, including the non-governmental organisations.

3.5.2   Strategic Environmental Assessment

Strategic Environmental Assessment (SEA) is a systematic process for evaluating the environmental effects of proposed plans, programmes and policies. In the EU, SEA is required for regional development plans and programmes if they meet the criteria specified in the Directive 2001/42/EC on the assessment of the effects of certain plans and programmes on the environment.

The GRDP 'Toolkit for integrating the environment into regional development' shows how regional development planning and SEA are mutually reinforcing tools within a robust planning system which deliver a more sustainable approach to development.

According to the Toolkit, SEA is an important tool for helping programme development authorities address environmental considerations at the earliest stage of decision making, alongside economic and social factors. It supports plan and programme developers in achieving both environmental and development benefits and advance innovation and sustainable development.

Braun (2006a) demonstrates the effectiveness of regional environmental assessment (REA) in supporting local sustainable development processes. From the analysis of a case study in the Brigida sub-region (Brazil), Braun proves that REA is a useful tool not only to understand the causes of cumulative impacts and analyse regional unsustainable developments and local environmental problems, but also to formulate local sustainable development actions and to support the implementation of strategies for the Agenda 21 environmental plans.

3.6   NETWORKS OF REGIONS

Networks of regions are aimed at sharing information and experience and co-ordinating actions for environmental and regional development programmes. In the context of greening development programme, networks bring together those working on economic development and environmental issues to strengthen the synergy between the environment and economic growth. Well-organised and focused networks are key tools for integrating environmental issues with economic and social objectives in regional development programmes.

According to Morata (2002), interregional and transregional networks provide more opportunities for defining common strategies and fostering mutual learning, increasing regional influence on central governments. However, the different characteristics of each region, and also the lack of correspondence between environmental territorial problems and administrative boundaries, could undermine this coalition. A solution could be to refer to the concept of 'ecologically defined regions', which are based on basic challenges (that is, tourism).

The present section comments on some of the main outputs of regional networks, which contribute to the debate on EPI.

The Network of Regional Governments for Sustainable Development (nrg4SD) was formed in 2002 during the World Summit on Sustainable Development, which took place in Johannesburg. The nrg4SD Network aims to be a voice for, and to represent regional governments at the global level, promoting sustainable development and partnerships at the regional level around the world.

The nrg4SD Network is an excellent platform and basis for sharing information and experience about sustainable development in the regional sphere and promoting collaboration. Individual regional governments have a great deal to learn from one another about the practice and implementation of sustainable development. Within the nrg4SD Network, regional governments have the opportunity to collaborate and establish partnerships, both with near neighbours and with others in more distant parts of the world. Bilateral cooperation projects and partnerships that contribute to this shared learning process have been agreed and signed among member regions in the framework of nrg4SD, in addition to partnerships between nrg4SD and other international organizations.

The regions belong to several nations, such as Australia, Spain (Basque and Catalan councils), Argentina, Belgium, Brazil, South Africa, Germany, USA, France and the United Kingdom.

The network's website provides reports on its activities and a series of strategies which have been implemented by the nrg4SD members at regional and local government levels. They consist of simple actions, which can easily be carried out.

The Greening Regional Development Programmes (GRDP) project is a network of partners and associated organisations from nine EU Member States, funded by the INTERREG IIIC programme.

INTERREG IIIC is a European Community Initiative designed to strengthen economic and social cohesion in the European Union. Operations funded under INTERREG IIIC should multiply the effects of other regional development policies, such as programmes supported by the European Regional Development Fund (ERDF), through large-scale exchange of information and know-how, and sharing of experience. The overall objective is to improve the effectiveness of regional development policies and instruments. The main target groups of INTERREG IIIC are regions and municipalities.

GRDP partners share good practice and develop advice on integrating the environment into regional development programmes. The aim is to encourage organisations across Europe to demonstrate commitment to balancing economic prosperity with environmental benefits by signing up to the GRDP charter. GRDP affirms that identifying the environment as a driver for regional development can also give regions a more competitive edge, save resources and money, create a positive public image, manage risks and facilitate compliance with policies and funding requirements.

The GRDP partnership launched its 'Toolkit for integrating the environment into regional development' with a particular focus on new Member States (European Commission, 2006b).

This set of fact sheets and reports help public sector bodies throughout Europe give full weight to environmental issues alongside more traditional economic and social objectives in the 2007–2013 round of development programmes supported by the EU. The toolkit explains the aims of developing the environment as a driver of a region's economy, which mainly regards the increased economic competitiveness by reducing business costs through more efficient use of resources, and the increased productivity by developing sectors of the economy that achieve integrated economic and environmental benefits.

The toolkit reports some case studies, such as the Güssing Region in Austria, where the regional authority took advantage of Objective 1 funding to turn the area into Europe's leading centre for renewable energy. Güssing has boosted its economy by becoming an energy self-sufficient region through investing in a network of generation plants (for example biomass and biogas and photovoltaic systems). The city of Güssing is also enjoying the development of 'ecoenergy tourism', which gave a boost to the tourism development in the region. And now the city is aiming at becoming the first Austrian Centre for further education in the field of renewable energy.

Another case study regards the Piedmont region, in Italy, where the 'Environment Park', a Science and Technology Park (STP), combines environment and business and is part of a project involving four other STPs in the region. The project is a cluster in which small and medium-sized enterprises, research bodies and start-up companies can share services, join in new initiatives and develop new projects. The project has been made possible through close cooperation between all the local authorities and business associations. Environment Park's facilities were planned according to the principles of 'green architecture' and made intensive use of innovative technologies, particularly in energy and water management. Environment Park is an innovation among European STPs thanks to its ability to combine technological innovation and eco-efficiency, hosting several companies and research institutes operating in both environmental protection and information and communication technology.

The GRDP paper suggests actions that regional development programme managers can take to foster the development and implementation of greener programmes and projects, and provides examples of the results achieved around Europe.

The toolkit also provides a section on the development of sustainable communities at the local level. It explains that the overall aim of the renewed EU Sustainable Development Strategy is to identify and develop actions to enable the EU to achieve continuous improvement in the quality of life for present and future generations.

This requires the creation of sustainable communities able to manage and use resources efficiently and tap the economy's potential for ecological and social innovation, ensuring prosperity, environmental protection and social cohesion. The new regulatory framework for cohesion policy reinforces the importance of sustainable communities, and directs that support in towns and cities should focus on the development of participatory and integrated strategies capable of tackling the high concentration of economic, environmental and social problems that affect urban areas.

GRDP also produced a paper to summarise good practice in managing current EU Structural Funds assistance through partnership, focusing on the involvement of environmental partners in the programmes. The report studies the use of partnership in programming, in implementation, in monitoring and evaluation. It underlines the advantages in terms of a more integrated approach, with the reduction of conflicts and of resources waste. The involvement of stakeholders can ensure a greater understanding of the actions that a programme plans to support.

3.7   SECTORAL CASE STUDIES

This section presents four boxes containing representative case studies, which report significant experiences of regional EPI carried out by single countries at the sub-national level.

The great availability of case studies dealing with regional and local EPI issue makes it difficult to report all the single experiences. The United Nations Economic and Social Commission for Asia and Pacific, for example, in its section dedicated to 'Integrating environmental considerations into the economic decision-making process' (UNESCAP, 1999), collects several cases of integration at the local/provincial level, carried out in South Asia (for example Pakistan), Pacific Islands (for example Fiji), East and Southeast Asia (Malaysia, China), together with some specific sectoral studies.

Since environment plays a key role in human well-being and activities, several sectors are particularly and directly dependent on the environment. These include, for example, health, as many diseases are caused by pollution or other degraded environmental conditions, and areas directly involved in the use of natural resources, such as fisheries, agriculture and forestry. However, because sectors are interdependent, all are influenced in some way by the environment.

Some sectors are more vulnerable to environmental changes, others produce higher impacts, and all sectors have the potential for environmental integration.

3.8   CONCLUSIONS

The aim of the present chapter is to clarify how the main contributors to the scientific and policy debate on regional and local EPI assess the issue.

The crucial role of regions and of local authorities in integrating the environmental factor into policymaking processes has emerged throughout the literature, mainly linked to the proximity to citizens and stakeholders and to the potential for direct implementation of policies.

The academic literature mainly addresses the crucial issue of achieving the economic growth while ensuring environmental protection. The focus is therefore less centred on the environmental component, and more concentrated on the broader issue of sustainable development, sometimes defined as 'ecological modernisation'.

The literature basically agrees on the need for applying a more decentralised approach involving all different levels of government as well as the various stakeholders, throughout the policy chain, therefore embedding EPI in micro policy processes.

The development and integration of environmental policies into economic sectors and decision-making processes is not only a matter of technological innovation and economic profitability, but also of motivation and social influence. It comprises, as important elements, communication, co-operation and the participation of as many players as possible.

Box 3.1   Sustainable Development in Flanders

Humbeeck et al. (2004) produced a policy summary to contribute to the discussions at OECD level on horizontal innovation policy, but also to the discussion in Flanders on governance for sustainable development and in particular on the implementation of the Innovation Platform on Environmental Technology that was created by the Flemish Government in May 2004. The framework of the analysis was the issue of public governance for policy coherence, as a starting point for building a sustainable development policy in Flanders.

The authors affirmed that the Federal level had proceeded with an explicit sustainable development strategy and formal governance bodies, but with little political commitment and results. The Flemish government had not yet elaborated an explicit strategy, but had initiated several policy processes to implement sustainable development, without formal coordination.

Several initiatives were expected to be taken to better integrate economic, environmental and social goals within the mandate of each policy sector, not to comply with international agreements but to improve the policy performance of the government. In order to achieve that, it was necessary to use specific measures to build and strengthen a sound policy cycle in every individual policy sector (vertical coherence), measures to improve the coordination of sectoral policies (horizontal coherence) and measures to allow for the modulation of short-term and long-term objectives (temporal coherence).

Box 3.2   Water Management and Spatial Planning in the Netherlands

Van der Brugge and de Graaf (2006) analyse the integrating development between water management and spatial planning in the Netherlands, on three levels: national, regional and local. The objective is to evaluate the 'transformative capacity' of the water management system, which is the system's capability to adapt to changing circumstances. The Rotterdam area is taken as a case study to understand the tipping point between transformative capacity and resilience. The paper represent an interesting study on integration at the macro level (national), meso level (regional) and micro level (local).

Box 3.3   Sustainable Development in Galicia

The Centre for Sustainable Development of the Galician Ministry of the Environment provides a very useful example of horizontal integration at the regional level (Urquijo Zamora, 2003). The paper exposes the structure and the implementation of the Galician Strategy of Sustainable Development. The strategy focuses its attention on the integration of the environmental component into all the sectoral policies dependent on the Galician Government, to serve as an example and to demonstrate the decisive will of its policies to foster a new model, more appropriate to the new paradigm of development. The paper underlines the lack of coordination across the various ministries of the government, and therefore the need of contemplating the environment as one more item at the moment of taking decisions, planning strategies and so on. It emerges that an integrated policymaking is missing that takes into account the environmental aspects throughout the policy spectrum. The first phase of the strategy is therefore based on a series of steps, including:

1. Elaboration (analysis of programmes and plans of the different sectoral policies; meetings with general Directorate of various Ministries; personal interviews with experts)
2. Implementation (approval of the draft document)
3. Monitoring (appropriate follow-up through annual report; approval of a specific decree; system of indicators to measure the degree of efficiency of the proposed measures and their actual application)

The experience evidences the necessity of a pragmatic approach to tackle an integrated policy making. The emphasis is very practical and the procedure is structured to foster environmental policy integration.

Box 3.4   Industrial Clusters and Eco-Districts

Porter (1998) defines clusters as 'geographically proximate groups of interconnected companies and associated institutions in a particular field, linked by commonalities and complementarities'.

Clusters are important, because they allow companies to be more productive and innovative than they could be in isolation.

The Italian industrial background is, for example, characterised by the presence of small and medium-sized enterprises (Ambiente Italia, 2003). Industrial clusters are therefore required not only to share the costs of energy and infrastructures, but also to internalise the concept of 'environmental responsibility' within the different productive areas, to save energy and resources, to obtain environmental certifications, to comply with environmental legislation requirements.

Box 3.5   EIA in the Walloon Region

The CEDD carried out an extensive multi-sector field study of the EIA system in the Walloon Region of Belgium (Frendo and Zaccai, 2004), with the aim of evaluating the performance of the procedure. The study includes the analysis of the inputs and interactions of all the actors involved: the project developer, the author of EIA, environmental and other administrations, advisory bodies, and the public.

Results show the importance of:

- capacity building among the actors;
- development of accessible data;
- juridical institutionalisation;
- differences among sector types;
- EIA as a basis of dialogue among various actors;
- specific means to be devoted to these tasks.

Although some progress in taking environmental aspects into account among project developers can be perceived from the results of the study, some aspects of the system have been criticised for their 'lengths', posing the question of a balance between environmental efficiency and means to be devoted to this objective compared to other requirements.

Communication and interaction need to be enhanced both 'vertically' and 'horizontally', involving all the different levels of governance and allowing the interaction between public and private actors.

This implies that EPI strategies are moving away from the state-centric and sectorised perspective. Cooperation among different groups and levels of governance are crucial for the implementation of EPI, and policies need to be defined with an integrated approach, which avoid too sector-specific logics. Policy documents increasingly propose an approach centred on citizens' and stakeholders' participation, and an acknowledgement of territorial and local knowledge and characteristics.

At the same time, the integration of the environmental component in regional and local policies needs governmental action, administrative organisation, and public resources to enforce and monitor the effectiveness of the process. Therefore, an institutional ability to manage the processes towards decentralisation of competencies, an integrative approach to problems and collective learning, need to be enhanced and coordinated at all levels of action. The theoretical suggestions of the academic literature are applied and commented on in several policy documents, which provide interesting evaluations of the implementation of different combinations of policy processes and instruments.

Local Agenda 21 emerges as a structured effort which establishes a comprehensive action strategy for integrating environmental protection with economic development and community well-being. In the same way, the design of several projects, at the global and EU level, increasingly reflects the intention to use available opportunities to enhance the positive impacts and ensure that they will not result in damages on the environment when implemented.

The need to ensure appropriate instruments to promote the diffusion of EPI, and enhance the role of regional and local authorities, is addressed in several policy documents which acknowledge the potential of EU Structural and Cohesion Funds. On the other hand, the implementation of Strategic Environmental Assessment and Regional Environmental Assessment processes answers the request to integrate environmental considerations upstream in the policymaking and programming stage, in the first phases of operations.

Networks of regions are considered in the analysis, and emerge as well organised and focused approaches to share information and experience, and develop advice on integrating the environment into regional development programmes.

The case studies finally show a growing concern on bringing the level of governance closer to the people, recognising the role of local and regional institutions to effectively deal with both local environmental problems and global environmental challenges. As a result, appropriate policies at the regional and local level can bring major benefits on both the environmental and the economic fronts, and opportunities are searched across a wide variety of sectors.

REFERENCES

Ambiente Italia (2003), *Ecodistretti 2003: Politiche Ambientali Innovative nei Sistemi Produttivi Locali Italiani*, Research promoted by Club dei Distretti Industriali, Legambiente and Padova Fiere.

Berger, G. and R. Pohoryles (2006), 'Policy integration and capacity-building in regional sustainable development: Analysis of experiences in Europe', in J. Martin and K. Jacob (eds), *Greening of Policies – Interlinkages and Policy Integration*, Proceedings from the 2004 Berlin Conference on the Human Dimensions of Global Environmental Change, FFU-Report, ICCR Vienna.

Braun, R. (2006a), 'Regional environmental assessment (REA) and local Agenda 21 implementation', *Environment Development and Sustainability*, **10**(1), 19–39.

Braun, R. (2006b), 'Sustainability at the local level: Management tools and municipal tax inventive model', *Environment Development and Sustainability*, **9**(4), 387–411.

Clement, K. (1997), 'Multi-disciplinary teams and environmental integration: European programmes', *Team Performance Management*, **3**(4), MBC University Press.

Clement, K. (2001), 'Strategic environmental awakening: European process in regional environmental integration', *European Environment*, **11**(2), 75–88.

David, H. (1998), 'Environmental policy integration at a local level', 6th Annual Conference on Policy Integration and Implementation, 17–19 September 1998, Tuusula, Finland.

DFID, EC, UNDP and WB (2002), *Linking Poverty Reduction and Environmental Management, Policy Challenges and Opportunities*, Washington DC.

European Environmental Advisory Council (EEAC) (1998), 6th Annual Conference on Policy Integration and Implementation, 17–19 September 1998, Tuusula, Finland.

European Commission (1995), *Cohesion Policy and the Environment*, Communication from the Commission to the Council, the European Parliament and Social Committee and the Committee of the Regions, COM/1995/509.

European Commission (2006a), *Environmental Integration Handbook, for EC Development Co-operation*, Europe-AID Co-operation office.

European Commission (2006b), *Beyond Compliance: How Regions Can Help Build a Sustainable Europe. A Toolkit for Integrating the Environment into Regional Development*, Project part-financed by the EU, Interreg IIIC and GRDP.

Frendo, L. and E. Zaccai (2004), *Integration at Local Level: Lessons Learned from the Environmental Impact Assessment (EIA) System in the Walloon Region (Belgium)*, Berlin Conference on the Human Dimensions of Global Environmental Change, Berlin, 3–4 December 2004.

Glassoon, J. and J. Gosling (2001), 'Strategic environment assessment and regional planning', *European Environment*, **2**, 89–102.

Humbeeck, P., J. Larosse and I. Dries (2004), *Governance for Linking Innovation Policy and Sustainable Development in Flanders (Belgium)*, Berlin Conference on the Human Dimension of Global Environmental Change, Berlin, 3–4 December 2004.

ICLEI (2001), *Local Authorities Self Assessment of Local Agenda 21 (LASALA)*, Accelerating Local Sustainability – Evaluating European Local Agenda 21

Processes – Volume I, II, Reports of the LASALA project team.

Jeffery, C. (2002), 'The "Europe of the Regions" from Maastricht to Nice', *Queen's Papers on Europeanisation*, Issue No. 7.

Johnson S. and G. Corcelle (1995), *The Environmental Policy of the European Communities Second Edition*, The Hague: Kluwer Law International.

Jordan, A., A. Schout and A. Zito (2004), *Coordinating European Union Environmental Policy: Shifting from Passive to Active Coordination*, Working Paper (EDM 04–05), CSERGE, University of East Anglia.

Karl, H. and O. Ranné (2001), 'Regional policy and the environment – The case of Germany', *European Environment*, **11**(2), 103–11.

Keating, M. (2002), 'Territorial politics and the new regionalism', in P. Heywood, E. Jones and M. Rhodes (eds), *Developments in West European Politics*, New York: Palgrave, pp. 201–20.

Lafferty, W.M. (ed.), (1999), *Implementing Agenda 21 in Europe, new initiatives for sustainable communities*, Oslo: ProSus.

Lafferty, W.M. and E. Hovden (2003), 'Environmental policy integration: Towards an analytical framework', *Environmental Politics*, **12** (3), 1–22.

McGinnis, M.V. (ed.) (1998), *Bioregionalism*, London: Routledge.

Morata, F. (2002), *The Role of Regions in the Local/Global GSD Axis*, Final report of the workshop on 'Governance for sustainable development', CADS and IIG.

Paredis, E., P. De Baere and B. Mazjin, (2002), 'Towards an analysis framework for Local Agenda 21', paper for the VLIR Policy Preparation Research Project, Sustainable Urban Development, Local Agenda 21 in Development Perspectives.

Persson, A. (2004), *Environmental Policy Integration: An Introduction*, Stockholm: Environmental Institute, PINTS project.

Porter, E.M., (1998), 'Clusters and the new economics of competition', *Harvard Business Review*, **76**(6), 77–90.

Roberts, P. (1994), 'Sustainable regional planning', *The Journal of the Regional Studies Association*, **28**(8), 781–7.

Roberts, P. (2001), 'Incorporating the environment into structural funds regional programmes: Evolution, current developments and future prospects', *European Environment*, **11**(2), 64–74.

Shaw, D. and S. Kidd (2001), 'Sustainable development and environmental partnership at the regional scale: The case of sustainability North West', *European Environment*, **11**(2), 112–23.

Tauras, O. (1997), *Der Ausschuss der Regionan: Institutionalisierte Mitwirkung der Regionen in der EU*, Agenda, Münster.

United Nation Economic and Social Commission for Asia and Pacific (UNESCAP) (1999), *Integrating Environmental Considerations into the Economic Decision-Making Process*, Volume II: Local and Provincial Level.

Urquijo Zamora, S. (2003), *Monitoring Environmental Policy Integration: The Strategy of Galicia*, Prepared for the REGIONET workshop III: Evaluation methods and tools for sustainable development, Manchester (UK), 11–13 June 2003.

Van der Brugge, R. and R. De Graaf (2006), *Transformation and Resilience of Water Management Regimes, Integration of Water and Spatial Planning in Rotterdam*, Conference on the Human Dimensions of Global Environmental Change Berlin, 17–18 November 2006.

4. The Transformations of Regional and Local Governments: Implications for Environmental Policy Integration

Bruno Dente

4.1 THE EVOLUTION OF LOCAL GOVERNMENTS IN WESTERN COUNTRIES

The aim of this chapter is to present a possible scenario for the evolution of local government systems in developed countries and draw some consequences about the possibility of Environmental Policy Integration (EPI).

The underlying assumption is that linking the two terms of the equation is really essential in order to avoid major mistakes. Local government systems – as all political institutions – have been evolving over a long period of time, and are the result of the superimposition of different principles and values. Furthermore they are quite different from one another for different reasons.

First of all they have different starting points (Hesse and Sharpe, 1991):

- In most Napoleonic states (by and large the bulk of continental Europe) they were a substantially weak part of the machinery of government, entrusted with regulatory policies (for example land use) and the provision of public services with low externalities (street lighting, refuse collection, and so on) as well as with a substantial amount of activities in which they acted as representatives of central government. The result was a low level of local government autonomy, partly compensated by their political relevance according to the structure of political parties.
- In Anglo-Saxon countries the tradition of self-government made the importance of local governments in service provision much bigger, and the level of autonomy much higher, even if, mostly in the United Kingdom, their political relevance was limited by the principle of parliamentary sovereignty.

These different traditions were of paramount importance when, in the industrialised countries the welfare state started to expand in the aftermath of World War II. Anglo-Saxon countries were certainly best equipped to manage the transition, but also in most north-European countries the adaptation was fairly rapid. Basically during this period local governments become the primary providers and producers of many if not most public services and welfare policies. This implied a big increase in the scope of activities performed at the local level, a huge increase in local finance and in many cases (but not in southern Europe) an increase in the size of local governments through the so called territorial reform (Kjellberg, 1985). But this implied also a relevant trend towards centralisation, basically because of the need of redistributive policies implicit in the welfare state expansion. The instruments of centralisation were on the one hand the huge increase of financial transfers (in the form of conditional grants) severely limiting the freedom of local governments to decide where to invest their monies, and on the other hand the strong reliance on (mostly sectoral) planning and programming defining the targets to be met by the different components of the machinery of government, in an effort for co-ordination that actually never worked satisfactorily.

It was during the anti-welfare backlash of the 1980s that the different traditions made a lot of difference. The lower relevance of local political systems left the British – and to a lesser extent American – local governments at the mercy of the neo-liberal trends dominant at the national level, and therefore the attack on public expenditure meant an attack on local government. Under the *mot d'ordre* of fiscal responsibility, not only were the central transfers substantially cut, but a whole array of policies were imposed in the direction of privatisation of public services and/or contracting out of many activities. In continental Europe the trend was certainly less marked, as local governments were able to defend themselves in the national political arena, but equally active. Paradoxically the outcome was in many cases an increase in decentralisation, through a push towards federalism and the growing importance of direct local taxation.

This exceedingly schematic account of a secular evolution – from the liberal, to the welfare and post-welfare state – leaves a lot to be desired, and however is important as a background of the present situation.

4.2   LOCAL GOVERNMENT IN THE GLOBALISED WORLD

With the collapse of the Soviet Union and the rise of globalisation a new scenario is opening up for the political institutions and for local government as well.

The ICT revolution, coupled with the establishment of global financial markets and the general evolution of the economy, creates a situation in which a lot of old values and principles have lost their meaning. Two aspects are particularly important as far as our field of analysis is concerned.

In the first place the political systems at all levels are transformed by the demise of old partisan allegiances as the ideologies that characterised the twentieth century become increasingly obsolete and tend to lose their meaning. This poses a problem in the legitimacy of political systems because party allegiance is not any more an important factor of collective identity.

The second aspect regards public policies. The growing interdependencies between different spheres of society and different regions of our planet determine the emergence of new, seemingly intractable, problems. From global security to sustainable development, from social exclusion to the resurgence of fanatism, those 'wicked problems' have in common the lack of clear-cut solutions, basically a level of uncertainty unknown by the optimistic ideologies of the previous centuries (Rittel and Webber, 1973).

These 'mega trends' have direct consequences on local government.

For one thing, they (re)establish the locality as the root of the political process. The need to provide the necessary collective identity in a very globalised and fragmented society reinforces the role of territorial politics, as shown by, for instance, the trends towards federalisation and devolution, the direct election of mayors in many countries, and so on. The Tocquevillian spirit seems to be back, and with a vengeance. The American saying 'All Politics Is Local' never felt so true (Pratchett, 1994) .

In the second place, in the economic sphere there is an increased focus on the local dimension. The 'New Economic Geography' school, of which Paul Krugman (1991) is the best known member, emphasizes the need to look at the resources available in a given territory in order to understand the process of economic growth. This does not mean necessarily that 'All Economic Development is Local', but certainly poses a challenge to local institutions, as we will see.

Finally the emergence of intractable problems gives rise to new governance theories. The idea that the business of governments is 'steering not rowing', one of the tenets of the 'New Public Management' proposed by Osborne and Gaebler (1992) and popularised by the National Performance Review led by Al Gore in the Clinton years, is variously articulated in the different countries, but certainly asks for new ways of coping with collective problems.

These transformations bring about direct consequences on the way in which local government is structured and acts. We have already mentioned the reinforcement of local (representative) democracy through the direct election of mayors, but we could also mention other points like the rise of territorial political parties. More important, however, are other aspects.

The first is that, perhaps for the very first time, socio-economic development becomes a local government mission. It certainly was not so neither in the liberal nor in the welfare phase, and during the neo-liberal period local governments certainly were too busy in trying to readjust to the new situation to be able to take major policy initiatives. This is a major shift in priorities as in the previous period the local services in which were mainly in the sphere of consumption rather than production, with only an indirect bearing on economic development, considered a national preserve. The forms in which this transformation manifested itself are various: think of strategic planning as a way to boost the potential of a city in the international competition for investment and jobs or the experiments in integrated planning in order to consider simultaneously urban revitalisation, the fight against social exclusion, socio-economic development and indeed environmental protection. This trend has therefore a direct bearing on the role of localities in environmental policy: if in the previous period the emphasis was mostly on remedial activities and/or in changing patterns of household consumption, now the attention is shifted on the issue of sustainable development, with all the ambiguities that this term implies.

But also the nature of the relationship with the other levels of governments changes substantially. The so-called crisis of the nation-state, the rise of international policy making (Kyoto, WTO and of course European policies) and the growing importance of the regional dimension (in Spain, Italy, Belgium but also in unlikely places like the United Kingdom) all together change the institutional landscape. If in the past one could talk of 'intergovernmental relations', trying to understand their basic principles (separation, domination, coordination, and so on), now the scholars are forced to describe the situation in terms of 'multilevel governance' basically meaning that in each and every policy field the outcomes are determined by the simultaneous involvement of a plurality of institutions (some of them democratically elected and some based on different forms of political legitimacy) at different territorial levels, that become interdependent in a non totally predictable way.

A third important trend takes place in the relationship between the population and local institutions. The loss of relevance of traditional political ideologies creates a situation in which popular participation acquires a structurally different importance. The multiplication of conflicts at the local level, a side effect of the demise of hierarchical principles in the inter-institutional dimension, creates a situation in which consensus building becomes a permanent feature of local political systems. This creates a new interest in all forms of direct democracy, up to the point that deliberative democracy becomes an important dimension of conflict resolution (Andrew and Goldsmith, 1998).

All these trends are by now very apparent, and therefore the keywords with which we can characterise the present phase are certainly complexity and globalisation but also terms like integration, interdependence, empowerment, and the like. All of them have in common the idea that political power has to be shared between different institutional and non-institutional actors, but one should be careful to avoid the idea that this is 'simply' a value change towards a more mature democratic system. In fact it is necessary to remember that one of the major forces behind change is also the emergence of the already mentioned intractable or 'wicked' problems. Looking from this point of view, the new somewhat confused system of governance that most countries seem to possess can also been interpreted as the way in which the blame for the inevitable policy failures can be shifted or at least shared between different actors.

Be that as it may, this is more or less the picture of the present status of regional and local authorities in most western countries: a complex maze of bodies with high level of interdependence across government levels and jointly in charge of collective problems apparently defying the available 'solutions'.

It is against this background that the introduction of Environmental Policy Integration at the regional and local level should take place.

Before trying to draw some conclusion, or at least giving some indication, however, three qualifications, or cautions, should be made.

The first and most obvious is that the picture presented above is indeed schematic and largely incomplete. Trying to distil the basic features that have in common largely different political and institutional systems is a very difficult exercise possible only at a very high level of abstraction. The reader is advised to take the previous indications much more as an ideal-typical model than as the actual description of the reality.

The second caution – reinforcing the first – is that, as we have seen at the beginning of this chapter, institutional systems very rarely substitute each other. This basically means that at each and every time different, and often conflictual, principles are simultaneously at work. In other words some typical features of the welfare state, as well as of the liberal state and of the anti-welfare movement, are still very much at work even because the present situation is not defined by some overarching general principle commonly shared.

The third, and probably the most relevant, qualification is that the system is far from stable, and that one should expect the evolution to be sudden and probably fast. In which direction the system will move is hard to say with certainty. But all in all the available cues tend to point out that the pendulum between centralism and decentralisation is quite ready to swing back. The emergence of issues as security, immigration and energy policies as defining the present political climate (for instance the American presidential race) means that the likelihood of 'bringing the Nation-state back' (Evans, Rueschemeyer and Skocpol, 1985) at the centre of the political scene is certainly not negligible. This will probably entail a series of consequences, among which one should emphasize the following:

- policy making will become increasingly multinational and international,
- political leadership will become increasingly based on charisma, and
- policies will become increasingly symbolic, that is based on communication.

Some of these trends are not particularly reassuring, as they are typical of critical periods of history in which 'terrible simplifiers' – as Jacob Burkhardt warned us – tend to emerge with dire consequences. The combination of these factors will probably decrease the level of democracy as we know it in developed countries. However one should remember that the interdependence between political actors will certainly not decrease and therefore the complexity of public deliberation is likely to stay at a high level, securing against the worst forms of despotism.

4.3   IMPLICATION FOR ENVIRONMENTAL POLICY INTEGRATION

The consequences of the present state of things (and of the possible trends for the future) against the background of a secular evolution, for EPI at the territorial level are, as the whole of this chapter, obviously tentative.

For clarity's sake we will divide them into three distinct, albeit interdependent, aspects. The first concern what can really be integrated at the regional and local level, the second how EPI can be brought about and the third who are likely to be the main actors of the process.

The first point is maybe the most important. The use of the territorial dimension in order to integrate different sectoral policies makes sense mostly because it reduces the level of complexity, limiting the number of actors involved as well of the issues to tackle. It is not by chance that 'integrated territorial planning' has become one of the main instruments of socio-economic development both in urban and in rural areas. And, as we have seen, socio-economic development, nowadays sustainable development, has become one of the main missions of modern local governments. To link EPI with local development will certainly increase the possibilities of success.

However, if what we have said about globalisation and the possible future trends make sense, not everything can be integrated at the territorial level. As we will see, integration implies the active participation of interested actors. It seems highly unlikely that in some issues there will be real interest at the local level and therefore the main strategy should be the segmentation of the problem. A possible division of labour could therefore be the following:

1. Special issues like greenhouse gases reduction, minimal standards, and so on should be dealt with mostly at the international and to a lesser extent at the national level, through representative democracy or intergovernmental decision making and treated at the territorial level as external constraints in the form of targets to be met in a given period of time.
2. Most active policies (for example energy saving and biodiversity protection, not to mention all local services like refuse reduction, water protection, and so on) should be the main object of EPI at the regional and local level. This implies strong interaction, multilevel governance and consensus building.

What I am proposing here is actually to depart from the tradition of the Local Agendas 21, in so far I would not advise to use EPI as a way of raising environmental awareness, but rather as an instrument to create positive sum games in which the idea of sustainable development is shown to be working also in the interest of the present generation and not only of the future ones.

The second point is probably the most obvious, but it is always useful to remind some well known, even if sometimes forgotten, truths. The basic point can be stated in this way: EPI should be conceptualised as an outcome and not as a process. The risk to be avoided is to equate EPI with the need of policy co-ordination, with the aim of taking into account all the possible inter-dependencies. This entails the idea of comprehensive planning and rational decision making as a 'superior' form of governance. As we have mentioned in passing when we were referring to the welfare state era, the problem is that all the forms of meta-decision making, including obviously rational comprehensive planning, do not work. There are theoretical reasons – shown by Charles Lindblom (Lindblom and Woodhouse, 1993) and Fritz Scharpf (1986) many years ago – why this cannot be the case, and in any case the empirical evidence seems to be overwhelming.

On the contrary conceptualising EPI as an outcome means shifting the focus on the many possible ways through which an interaction between self-interested actors can be used in order to create positive sum games for all or most of the participants. This implies the ability of managing simultaneously the form and the content of the interaction and therefore the presence of some actors able to understand the process and to adapt it to the contingent needs of the given situation. In other words one has to conceptualise EPI as the goal of one or several actors, who, in order to reach it, are prepared to engage in negotiations and to spend their resources.

Integrating policies, one has to remember, usually means to overcome the resistance of well entrenched policy communities, formed by technical bureaucracies, special interest groups and, more often than not, elected politicians, who are likely to oppose any alteration of the status quo, but at the same time are prepared to bargain in order to get short-term gains.

The latter observation brings us to the third and final suggestion, concerning the actors of the integration policy game. What we have learned from the rise of the governance theories at the end of last century is that governments are far from all-powerful, and that they have to take into consideration the existence of pre-existing rights and interests. In complex societies the state and the political actors – including the political parties and the citizenry – do not have the monopoly of 'power', but they must come to terms with the fact that there are individual rights that cannot be – except in special circumstances – ignored or nullified.

This is particularly important in the case of environment protection because many of the goods to be preserved – soil and water for instance – are often the private property of individual or firms, and cannot be disposed of without the consent of the owner. Hence the need to include these actors in the policy game in order to reach some sort of agreement with them, having in mind that sometimes these actors are even more interested in protecting the integrity of their patrimony than to maximise the economic value of it.

From this point of view I find more useful to speak of 'integrated regimes for environmental protection' rather than EPI, because this includes the simultaneous consideration of public policies and property rights. But this is obviously less important than to understand the need of including the property right dimension in bringing about the necessary integration (Gerber et al., 2009).

REFERENCES

Andrew, C. and M. Goldsmith (1998), 'From local government to local governance – and beyond?', *International Political Science Review*, **19** (2), 101–17.
Evans, P., D. Rueschemeyer and T. Skocpol (1985), *Bringing the State Back In*, New York: Cambridge University Press.
Gerber, J.D., P. Knoepfel, S. Nahrath and F. Varone (2009), 'Institutional resource regimes: Towards sustainability through the combination of property-rights theory and policy analysis', *Ecological Economics*, **68**(3), 798–809.
Hesse, J.J. and L.J. Sharpe (1991), 'Local government in international perspective: some comparative observations', in J.J. Hesse (ed.), *Local Government and Urban Affairs in International Perspective*, Baden Baden, Germany: Nomos Verlagsgesellschaft, pp. 603–21.
Kjellberg, F. (1985), 'Local government reorganization and the development of the welfare state', *Journal of Public Policy*, **5**(2), 215–39.

Krugman, P. (1991), *Geography and Trade*, Cambridge, MA: MIT Press.
Lindblom, C. and E.J. Woodhouse (1993), *The Policy-Making Process*, 3rd ed., Englewood Cliffs, NJ: Prentice Hall.
Osborne, D. and T. Gaebler (1992), *Reinventing Government: How the Entrepreneurial Spirit is Transforming the Public Sector*, Reading, MA: Addison-Wesley Publishing.
Pratchett, L. (1994), 'Local autonomy, local democracy and the "new localism", *Political Studies*, **52**(2), 358–75.
Rittel, Horst, and M. Webber (1973), 'Dilemmas in a general theory of planning', *Policy Sciences*, **4**, 155–69.
Scharpf, F.W. (1986), 'Policy failure and institutional reform: Why should form follow function?', *International Social Science Journal*, **38** (2), 179–89.

5. Sustainability and Environmental Policy Integration: Local Level Sustainability through Knowledge Involvement and New Governance Arrangements

Georgios Terizakis

5.1 INTRODUCTION: FROM EPI TO GOVERNANCE SUSTAINABILITY

Environmental policy in general and Environmental Policy Integration (EPI) in particular has become a relevant theme for the policy makers and academic community of Europe over the last 20 years and remains so.[1] This upswing is related to various phenomena. For one thing we observe an increasingly undisputed diagnosis of environmental damage as anthropogenic, that is in the case of climate change. The 'natural causes' scientific diagnosis was long part of the controversial debate and instrumentalised by sceptics to reject any kind of nature protection policies. These attitudes are changing due to increasing expert and scientific knowledge on climate change. For another, we come to the insight that we can manage this kind of problem only if we give environmental policy an adequate weight in daily politics. Symbolic solutions seem to have been marginalised and more substantial reforms have joined the agenda. One part of this new agenda is EPI. But EPI is not a given concept or daily experience, and therefore multiple interpretations and implementations of this concept have arisen over recent years. Nevertheless there are only few systematic studies that compare EPI experience at different levels and in different countries (see Lafferty and Hovden, 2003; Sgobbi, 2007).

Another important debate in this context is the sustainability issue. The rise of this concept is a real success story despite its being vague and contested. But this semantic openness can also be an advantage: it increases the freedom of action and of choice of the discourse arenas and the involved actors by which a commonly agreed paradigm for joint action is achievable

(Heinelt, 2000: 59–64). This sort of process could be a basis for collective learning and reflexivity (see Heinelt et al., 2007). The same applies to EPI, viewed as a concept of policy learning by which policy makers become aware of sustainability issues and integrate it in their policy fields. And by the same token, all policies should integrate the environment into their daily work. But there is a difference: sustainability refers to more than the environment. It refers also to social and economic dimensions which have to be integrated just as strongly into sustainability policy.

This chapter will show the value of a sustainability concept for EPI called Governance for Sustainability (GFORS). This sustainability concept interacts with two other relevant concepts, knowledge and governance. Sustainability in this sense is not a quantitative approach in search of the right criteria for measuring sustainability. In fact sustainability is a qualitative and context-sensitive approach that exemplifies itself in the tripartite relation between governance, knowledge and sustainability in a specific context.

5.2   THE CONCEPT OF GOVERNANCE FOR SUSTAINABILITY: WISHFUL THINKING OR A SOLID BASIS FOR ANALYSIS?

EPI is about policy integration and more specifically about integrating environmental objectives into other (potentially all) policy fields.[2] This tremendous generality of the concept allows different strategies in dealing with EPI; in any case it should promote sustainable development at its core (see Lafferty and Hovden, 2003).[3] Therefore it seems helpful to reflect on the sustainability side of EPI.

The basis for the following argumentation is developed by the European project consortium 'Governance for Sustainability' (GFORS). GFORS is an FP6-funded project involving 12 partners from 10 European countries. In order to broaden the basis for analyses and to make the outcomes of the empirical research more adequate the team contains partners from western, eastern, southern and northern Europe. Each national team has carried out at least two in-depth local case studies, making a minimum of 18 case studies. All the case studies employed a common theoretical and methodological framework, which I will present in this chapter.

The aims and task of the project are to develop an innovative analytical model for the study of governance for sustainability, focusing on the synergy between new governance modes and different forms of knowledge. For this purpose, we identified a range of different forms of knowledge and analysed how these different forms of knowledge may interact in the context of particular governance arrangements. The design of an innovative analytical model to study governance for sustainability was a major milestone for the project because it integrated governance and knowledge concepts in one new design. The project seeks analytical tools to evaluate the effectiveness of governance arrangements to make environmental policy integration more sustainable.

The point of reference from which the research began is what might be referred to as an 'epistemological deficit' or 'the problem of ignorance', which becomes most obvious in situations in which decisions are taken against a background of 'risk' in the 'knowledge society' (see Willke, 1992).[4] These issues are particularly important for policies addressing the environment and sustainability, where uncertainty and disagreement about how to formulate and implement policy is rife (Beck, 1986). Often, judgements are made not on the basis of empirical (hard) facts but using foresight studies, scenarios and models. These forms of knowledge are always insecure, incomplete and provisional.

Despite the fact that the growing relevance of various types of knowledge and non-knowledge in contemporary societies is applicable to all policy fields, its significance is particularly high in the field of environmental politics and its integration into other policy fields. Environmental politics is framed within by an extensive knowledge infrastructure that produces a huge body of technical and scientific expertise, shapes discourses on sustainability, and influences political decisions. Furthermore the environmental policy arena provides fertile ground for the investigation of new governance arrangements (Heinelt et al., 2001) and emerging architectures of knowledge. What has often been observed in environmental decision making is the marked gap between technical-scientific knowledge on the one side and local or everyday knowledge on the other. It has been suggested that this gap may be closed by developing decentralised and participatory procedures associated with particular modes of governance (for example network modes and civil society involvement). For instance Fischer (2000: 222) has argued: 'Today, deliberative participation is not only seen as a normative requirement for a democratic society but serves increasingly as a counter to the uncertainties of science.' Thus the sustainability issue provides an ideal testing ground for examining the construction of and the interrelationships and interactions between governance arrangements and different knowledge forms.

Starting from this position, GFORS sought to investigate the interaction of governance arrangements and knowledge forms systematically and to analyse the problem-solving capacities of specific arrangements/arenas with reference to sustainability. The basic objective of the project was therefore to determine how the concrete institutionalisation and practical enactment of certain governance modes impact upon the effectiveness and legitimacy of policies aimed at sustainability objectives by using and developing different types of knowledge. Most approaches that seek to measure sustainability are based on quantitative criteria using a fixed catalogue of indicators (for example, the Brundtland Report, WCED, 1987 or WWF, 2007). The GFORS perspective raises doubts about this approach on two counts:

1. Catalogues of indicators tend to neglect contextual effects and issues. In our view sustainability is not an absolute but a relative concept that cannot be fully analysed outside a particular governance context or dissociated from its political, social, economic and planning context. We hold that sustainability is highly dependent on local knowledge, because the local level is the level at which schemes operate and are confronted with the life world of the citizens.
2. Indicator-based approaches to sustainable development are unable to fully measure and take into account interdependency, thus they fail to provide strategic guidance for policy integration. This is why we draw on the notion of reflective knowledge. It represents the creative interaction of, and awareness of the interdependency between, these knowledge forms within a certain context.

In a general and widely accepted understanding, sustainability has to do with environmental, economic and social concerns. Sustainability is an issue of environmental policy integration (but not exclusively). Moreover it implies a concern for long-term dynamics or a long-term vision. Therefore, we conceived sustainability as a form of inter-sectoral coordination and inter-temporal integration – as a qualitative approach that focuses on the dynamic and learning capacities of stakeholders. A dilemma for research still remains: how to compare different cases from this 'relative' point of view? One answer is that every case deals with the same directive as a common basis (see next chapter).[5]

However, while there is a considerable quantity of empirical work on changing governance arrangements and institutional capacity building for sustainable development, the knowledge dimension is largely absent from the debate on sustainability (see, for an exception, Rydin, 2007). Our case studies as well the theoretical frame are therefore situated in the triangle of knowledge, governance and sustainability. We do not assume clear, unidirectional causalities. None of our three categories can be considered stable.

The contested interpretation of what may be termed sustainable or unsustainable at the local level is embedded in societal and national political systems – from a local level to the meta-governance level. The substance of the concept of sustainability, as well as societal rules, is subject to forms of knowledge and practices of knowing. Concrete actions as well as normative evaluations of measures are based on knowledge. The identification of a certain sustainability problem such as climate change or PM_{10} is connected to an idea of the appropriate governance arrangement needed to (re)solve it.

On the background of this discussion, the research began from two interrelated sets of questions

- Forms of governance: Which forms of governance and their arrangements facilitate exchanges and flows of knowledge? Which forms of governance encourage mutual learning between individuals as well as within and between organizations? Which forms of governance seem, in this respect, to be most appropriate for policy learning that supports sustainable development?
- Forms of knowledge: Which forms of knowledge are essential to governance for sustainability? Which forms of knowledge are dominant and which forms are missing within successful (or unsuccessful) governance arrangements for sustainability? What different forms of knowledge need to be combined for the development of successful governance and institutional arrangements, and what is the relative influence of each? Can a certain form of reflexivity (reflective knowledge) be identified as influential?

The operationalisation of the governance discussed is located in a governance arena model. In this governance arena we can find three types of governance arrangements: hierarchy, network and market. These governance modes are 'pure' or 'ideal' types which hardly will be found as such empirically. Nevertheless these types tend to favour different types of rules and actors. For example, the 'market' modus produces contracts and properties and prefers profit maximisers with egoistic orientations as actors.

Generally speaking, the GFORS concepts focus on new modes of governance rather than on traditional government:

- Non-hierarchical networks of autonomous, interdependent public and private actors reaching a binding coordination of interactions through bargaining.
- Non-hierarchical networks relying on argument to influence societal binding decision making.
- Besides these political modes of governance characterised by their deliberate attempts to coordinate societal interactions by influencing binding decision making, societies are also governed (unconsciously) by the 'hidden hand' of the market, that is by constraints and abilities to (inter-)act imposed by price variations driven by the law of supply and demand (and a respective allocation of resources) (Heinelt et al., 2007).[6]

Nevertheless hierarchy or hierarchical interventions will play a crucial role for analysis. A democratic political system is predominantly based on majority decisions and hierarchical intervention through the state apparatus. Moreover, we will find hierarchical organisation in companies or in administration.

With regard to the forms of knowledge that interact in these governance arrangements we identified nine, based on the knowledge concept proposed by Matthiesen (2005), who distinguishes:

1.   Knowledge of everyday life.
2.   Expert/professional/scientific knowledge.
3.   Product knowledge.
4.   Steering/management/leadership knowledge.
5.   Institutional knowledge.
6.   Economic and market knowledge.
7.   Local knowledge.
8.   Milieu knowledge.
9.   Reflective knowledge.

These knowledge forms interact in a 'flower of knowledge forms' (see Figure 5.1). Matthiesen (2005) starts from the assumption that modern knowledge societies depend heavily on different knowledge forms. Traditional dualistic knowledge approaches like Polanyi's lack the sensitivity to detect and distinguish the variety of different knowledge formations. The proposed flower of knowledge integrates different mouldings and logics of the modern society. Moreover, it is open toward the life world because it recognises everyday life as the basis for all knowledge forms. Everyday knowledge has drawn the attention of environmental policy concepts in recent years (Fischer, 2000). Besides, Matthiesen places special emphasis on reflective knowledge as an outcome of cooperation (and the process of communicative interpretation and discursive practice) which is crucial for sustainable processes. This social constructivist understanding of knowledge makes the knowledge concept interesting for new modes of governance; they can be related.

We conceived of different knowledge forms as having, to varying degrees, institutional bases that led to them being more or less clearly defined and in some cases accredited by the state and/or professional bodies. As such these forms of knowledge could be drawn upon and articulated by actors in specific situations to achieve certain ends in relation to particular issues/problems. In this process the knowledge enters the action arena of a governance arrangement and builds up a certain KnowledgeScape. This filtering process is realised in three kinds of choices: choice of knowledge, choices of interpretation and choices of action (Nullmeier, 1993, see Heinelt et al., 2007).

Figure 5.1   Knowledge Forms According to Matthiesen (2005)

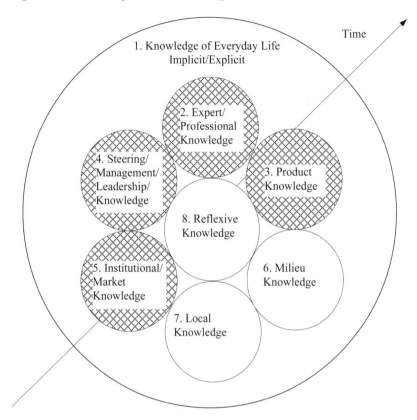

On the other hand we conceive of everyday life knowledge as having a transversal and mediating role. Knowledge of everyday life is present in all forms of knowledge serving as a general reference and a starting point for knowledge differentiation. Reflective knowledge is a product of learning and evaluating, of knowledge-in-action coupling and re-coupling the whole process of knowledge utilisation involving other knowledge forms. As a kind of meta-knowledge, reflective knowledge enables the development of forms of self-description of the various knowledge forms and governance arrangements. Therefore reflective knowledge is, for us, a key aspect for sustainability. Of course these different forms (or ideal types) of knowledge do not exist in 'pure form'; empirically they exist only in particular combinations or what we label 'bundles of knowledge'.

Utilising these concepts we have described and analysed the different empirical manifestations and associated combinations of forms of knowledge that materialise from these interactions. We use the term KnowledgeScapes to describe the particular socio-spatial and institutional topographies that develop from these interactions. It is important to emphasise that combinations of KnowledgeScapes and governance arrangements only exist within particular contexts and have to be constructed, they are always hybrid forms. The interaction of governance arrangements and KnowledgeScapes, along with more general societal structuring processes, create an action arena that in turn structures and facilitates the creation of action situations within which organisations and individual actors operate to produce actions/outputs, one of which may be the creation of 'reflective knowledge'.

We recognised that if we were to achieve this aim GFORS needed to develop a new, integrated and innovative theoretical and methodological framework (see Figure 5.2). We sought to assess the degree to which the mix of different knowledge forms and governance arrangements contributed to a more integrated, effective and legitimate understanding of sustainability. One of the most innovative aspects of this research is that it brought together two bodies of academic knowledge that had hitherto existed largely in isolation from one another – political science research on governance and sociology of knowledge. Political science and governance research is particularly represented by Ostrom's institutional analysis and development framework (1999) and Kooiman's governing order model (2002). In modern network modes of governance, actors are placed in an action situation 'with participants in positions who must decide among diverse actions in light of the information about how the actions are linked to potential outcomes and the cost and benefits assigned to actions and outcomes' (Ostrom et al., 1994: 29). Therefore knowledge is a crucial source of modern politics. The integration of sociological research – or, more precisely, social constructivist and pragmatist approaches – brings the knowledge side into the GFORS concept (Matthiesen, 2005). Integrating these two approaches and developing an associated methodological framework provided the basis for the subsequent empirical research (for an in-depth explication of the model see Heinelt et al., 2007).

From this perspective, EPI approaches seem closer to traditional policy- and decision-making models. Traditional models are vertical and hierarchical, and based strongly on sectoral specialisation and the division of work. Environmental policies are like every other policy field. The Brundtlandt report heralds a turning point in this kind of thinking. Integration of different approaches and substantial institutional change are seen as fundamental to promoting sustainable development.

The integration of environmental policy in other areas became a conditio sine qua non (WCED, 1987).

Figure 5.2   The GFORS Concept

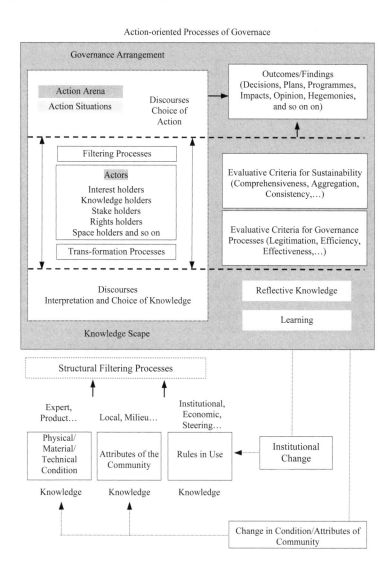

Source: Heinelt et al. (2007).

The European Union's environmental policy is the most striking example. Nevertheless EPI has occurred since the 1990s at all levels of policy making – local, national and European.

5.3   SOME EMPIRICAL INSIGHTS: SUSTAINABILITY[7]

Local politics are crucial for promoting sustainability. This is true for two reasons. Firstly, the local and regional level is the level where national and European schemes are implemented. Secondly, the local level is the level of life world of the citizens and is therefore the testing ground of the effectiveness of sustainability measures. We therefore selected three empirical fields in nine countries as case studies for the GFORS project:

1. Air Quality (and particularly PM_{10} and $PM_{2.5}$): This field was originally a mixture of health and environmental policies. It is important to mention that the driving force behind the air quality schemes was the realisation that fine dust was shortening the lives of European citizens by about ten months. 'Air Quality' also addresses the general quality of life and therefore tends to integrate with other policy areas. We expected this field to be shaped by the network mode of governance and a differentiated knowledge arena.
2. Emissions Trading Policy: Here, we find a mixture of economic and environmental motivations; emission trading policies bridge the gap between climate change discussion and the strategic and economic settings of stakeholders and industries. The climate change discourse is informed by expert knowledge on the risks provided by natural scientists. The business world draws on knowledge from economic experts on the possibilities of equity by market-based policy instruments. We expect that this field will be dominated by the market mode of governance and a reliance on expert/market knowledge.
3. Strategic Environmental Assessment (SEA): SEA is a process that takes environmental concerns seriously in the decision-making process. Nevertheless we suppose that this field is dominated from the outset by planning rather than environmental attitudes. We expect that this field will be dominated by the hierarchical governance mode and steering/expert/technical knowledge.

To illustrate the potential analytical and hermeneutic value of the GFORS concept I will discuss the implementation of the PM_{10}-directive in Potsdam, Germany.[8] This case is interesting firstly because Germany has an image as a leader in environmental protection and secondly because the air quality measures are associated with non-hierarchical governance modes (for example network involvement).

In its analyses of the cases, the GFORS model follows the logic of the Kooiman governance model and the multi-level governance perspective of the EU.[9] The reconstruction of the discourses on the meta-governance level shows that the 'production' of the PM_{10} directive contains some interesting features. In a first step, natural scientific expert knowledge on fine dust emerges somewhere in the seventies. These European and global discussions on issues such as acid rain acted as the first filtering processes (see Figure 5.2 above) for the implementation of rudimentary air quality policies. In a second step – since the 1980s – this expert knowledge (and the first legislation) became more relevant in a governance action arena for two reasons:

- PM_{10} had (and still has) effects on flora and fauna.
- PM_{10} had (and still has) effects on the health of Europe's citizens.

It is important to stress that the directive was mainly formulated for the second reason. The EU wanted to increase the life expectancy of Europeans in an efficient way. After this knowledge formation, the PM_{10} case entered the action arena and became a relevant directive.

The PM_{10} directive was influenced and induced by the WHO Clean Air guidelines. The first PM_{10} directive in 1996 and daughter directives indicate this (97/101/ES, 99/30/EC). These directives regulate the exchange of information of air quality and set limits on particulate pollution. Moreover, the Sixth Environmental Action Programme (EAP) establishes a broader strategy on air pollution to involve '[a] review of the implementation of air quality directives and effectiveness of air quality programmes in the Member States; improving the monitoring of air quality directives and effectiveness of air quality and the provision of information to the public, including by indicators; priorities for further actions, the review and updating of air quality thresholds and national emission ceilings and the development of better systems for gathering information, modelling and forecasting' (European Commission, 2001: 245: 6). Besides, it particularly emphasises technical knowledge to guide the measures taken. One of the further products of scientific discourse is the realisation that $PM_{2.5}$ should also be banned (see Fahrner, 2007).

Implementation of the PM_{10} directive in Germany is part of a larger public debate. It foresees features like local action plans and 'environmental zones' in the city centres. Nevertheless, implementation at local level happens in a 'business as usual' mode (see Haus and Zimmermann, 2007). The Potsdam experience is in this sense that of an average city. The action arena comprises actors that interact in hierarchical, market (for example chamber of industry) and networks modes (for example environmental NGOs). These actors jointly devised an action plan for Potsdam in order to fulfil the directive – no more and no less.

The first findings of this constellation are of limited innovative potential. From the GFORS perspective the important features of the PM_{10} implementations are the governance modes of the action arena, involved actors and knowledge forms. Their interplay produces potential effects on sustainability:

- Despite the broad involvement of different actors, the dominant governance mode is hierarchical through the top-down effect of PM10-legislation.
- Surprisingly, there is a hierarchy of the involved knowledge forms. Scientific and expert knowledge dominate the process as guided by the forces of administrative and institutional knowledge. Knowledge forms of the 'everyday life' domain are less relevant and reduced to a subordinate role. The high level of technical expertise (simulation/models) produces a kind of reflectivity particular to the field of science and expert knowledge.
- But there is a detectable change in the way air quality management and control is handled at municipal level. The pressing need to adapt and readjust at the local institutional level (from a reactive to a proactive stance) can be understood as a learning process. Participatory approaches have little impact on opening up the action arena towards more deliberative modes of problem solving. The action arena was developed to an instrument for the exchange of information on the new regulations between the administration and a wider public. Sustainability is detectable in the sense that the PM_{10} regulation is part of (a vision of) a strategy of sustainable urban development, but not at actually embedded in institutional routine.

5.4   REFLECTIONS: FROM GFORS TO EPI AND BACK

What can we learn from the initial insights of this case? EPI plays a minor role in the local implementation process of PM_{10} removal in Potsdam. This contrasts with the way these directives were drawn up. Bearing in mind that fine dust is first and foremost recognised as a health problem, nevertheless this view plays almost no role in the implementation process at the local level. From this general point of view the implementation process seems to be less sustainable than expected. We can conclude that the PM_{10} case is an average regulatory policy which is typical for environmental issues. The integration of environmental policy in other policy fields remains relatively poor despite the fact that the local administration integrates experts form different fields. The process is seen as an implementation of an environmental policy (or more precisely of a stipulated action plan from the higher level) with no points of contact to other policy fields. It becomes a more or less routine EPI, or EPI under 'duress'.

Nevertheless there are signs of innovations; we can detect, for example, the involvement of new actors such as environmental NGOs and new forms of problem-solving mechanisms like the action plan. Interestingly, this involvement does not necessarily seem to make the outcomes more sustainable.

This sceptical analysis of the outcomes could lead to the following hypothesis: EPI occurs at different levels of the EU's multi-level system and at different points of a policy process. The PM_{10} case shows environmental policy integration at the metagovernance level and limited integration at the implementation level.[10] This leads to the conclusion that EPI should be discussed not only at different levels of governance, but also at different stages in the policy processes. The GFORS focus is not so much on the policy areas as on the knowledge forms that are involved in this area.

These crucial insights, emerging through our conceptual work, allowed us to provide a different and more nuanced understanding of policy outcomes. We understand policy outcomes as aggregated effects of governance and knowledge in the context of how to address sustainability within particular regional and local situations. Sustainability, from this position, is thus more about experience-based learning processes and their implications for causal assumptions, while institutional change and the generation of new knowledge are more concerned with causes and effects. Given this, our view is that policies developed to promote sustainability will be partial and ineffective unless they effectively incorporate a range of knowledge forms on the first and second order governing. Sustainability itself seems to fit better as a 'Leitbild' at the meta-governance level.

Moreover, with regard to those actors directly and indirectly involved, our theoretical framework suggested that evaluative processes have the potential to produce learning and reflective knowledge which can in turn result in institutional change. In some way, a widespread inclusion of different knowledge forms and their interaction in a governance arena 'may generate a need for new forms of government' (Jordan et al, 2005: 493). But this is far away from the focus of this chapter.

NOTES

1. I would like to thank my colleagues Alessandra Goria, Sonja Fahrner, Mic Hale, Hubert Heinelt, Eva Reisinger and Karsten Zimmermann for their support and comments.
2. This chapter is based on Atkinson et al. (2010).
3. EPI could be seen as a policy principle, governing process and outcome (Sgobbi, 2007: 13). This threefold bias makes it (EPI) slippery.
4. One interesting issue is a perceived 'absence' of knowledge in planning or policy reality. This is an interesting constellation in some of the case studies (particularly in the eastern European countries) in the GFORS project. The fundamental challenge is that this

perception leads to a lack of awareness about environmental problems. The 'absence of knowledge' leads to a marginalisation of relevant knowledge forms. In our case studies the EU is the 'back door'. Even an instrumental implementation of EU regulations involves an institutional dynamic that overcomes traditional procedures supporting the 'absence' of knowledge. This dynamic will drive incremental policies changes that give more emphasis to knowledge sources and KnowledgeScapes (for more critical stances towards non-knowledge see Beck, 2007).

5.   Lafferty (2004: 200–201) suggests a suitable operationalization for this kind of approach. He defines three criteria for measuring sustainability: comprehensiveness, aggregation and consistency. These criteria could be used for adjustment. Nevertheless this should not imply a final and for all definition for measurement of sustainability. But these criteria could help to make different cases comparable.

6.   It is hard to deny that this concept prefers the network modes of governance. Networks focus on problem solving and are predestined to shape governance arrangements.

7.   I owe these insights to my colleague Eva Reisinger who is working on the Potsdam case study.

8.   Potsdam is the capital city of the federal state of Brandenburg (East Germany) with about 150,000 inhabitants and with a special problem constellation concerning air pollution and different sources of air pollution. These problems are connected mostly with the nearby federal capital, Berlin.

9.   Kooiman (2002) distinguishes between three governing orders: meta, first and second order. Meta-governance is the area for symbolic and fundamental discussions on policies and their regulative rules. The first order of governance is oriented towards the 'world of action' and the second order of governance is oriented toward institution building and creation of policy programmes.

10. The other two fields could be interpreted in the same way. For example, the member state level plays an important role in the implementation of the emissions trading scheme. Thus we can expect that the EPI at the local level will be relativity low. From a GFORS perspective it also depends on the different knowledge forms that a process includes; if, in a policy field like emissions trading, the expert or market knowledge dominates local implementation of the scheme, than you will hardly find really environment-friendly implementation. Market logic will transfer the sustainability issue to a cost–benefit–relation, to the detriment of environmental issues.

REFERENCES

Atkinson, R., G. Terizakis and K. Zimmermann (2010), 'Introduction', in R. Atkinson, G. Terizakis and K. Zimmermann (eds), *Governance, Knowledge and Sustainability: The Challenge of Integration and Policy Development*, London, Ok and New York, USA: Routledge (forthcoming).

Beck, U. (1986), *Risikogesellschaft. Auf dem Weg in Eine Andere Moderne*, Frankfurt/M.: Suhrkamp.

Beck, U. (2007), *Weltrisikogesellschaft. Auf der Suche Nach der Verlorenen Sicherheit*, Frankfurt/M.: Suhrkamp.

European Commission (2001), *Communication from the Commission: The Clean Air for Europe (CAFE) Programme: Towards a Thematic Strategy for Air Quality*, COM(2001) 245.

Fahrner, S. (2007), *Governance on Particulate Matter*, GFORS working paper No. 7, http://www.gfors.eu/28.0.html.

Fischer, F. (2000), *Citizens, Experts, and the Environment. The Politics of Local Knowledge*, Durham and London: Duke University Press.

Haus, M. and K. Zimmermann (2007), 'Die feinstaubproblematik als governanveherausforderung für die lokale umweltpolitik?', in K. Jacob, F. Biermann, P.O. Busch and P.H. Feindt (eds), *Politik und Umwelt*, Wiesbaden: VS-Verlag, pp. 243–61.

Heinelt, H. (2000), 'Nachhaltige entwicklung durch "Agenda 21" – prozesse. politikwissenschaftliche fragen und überlegungen zur debatte', in H. Heinelt and E. Mühlich (eds), *Lokale 'Agenda 21' – Prozesse. Erklärungsansätze, Konzepte, Ergebnisse*, Opladen: Leske + Budrich, pp .51–66.

Heinelt, H., T. Malek, N. Staeck and A.E. Töller (2001), 'Environmental policy: The European Union and a paradigm shift', in H. Heinelt, T. Malek, R. Smith and A.E. Töller (eds), *European Union Environment Policy and New Forms of Governance: A Study of the Implementation of the Environmental Impact Assessment Directive and the Eco-Management and Audit Regulation in Three Member States*, Ashgate: Aldershot, pp. 1–32.

Heinelt, H., G. Held, T. Kopp-Malek, U. Matthiesen, E. Reisinger and K. Zimmermann (2007), *Governance for Sustainability*, GFORS working paper No. 2, http://www.gfors.eu/28.0.html.

Kooiman, J. (2002), 'Governance: a social-political perspective', in J.R. Grote and B. Gbikpi (eds), *Participatory Governance. Political and Societal Implications*, Opladen: Leske + Budrich, pp. 71–96.

Jordan, J., K. Rudiger and A. Zito (2005), 'The rise of "new" policy instruments in comparative perspective: Has governance eclipsed government?', *Political Studies*, **3**(53), 477–96.

Lafferty, W.M. (2004), 'From environmental protection to sustainable development: the challenge of decoupling through sectoral integration', in W.M. Lafferty (ed.), *Governance for Sustainable Development*, Cheltenham, UK and Northampton, MA, USA: Edward Elgar, pp. 191–220.

Lafferty, W.M. and E. Hovden (2003), 'Environmental policy integration: Towards an analytical framework', *Environmental Politics*, **3**(12), 1–22.

Matthiesen, U. (2005), *KnowledgeScapes. Pleading for a Knowledge Turn in Socio-Spatial Research*, IRS working paper, Berlin.

Nullmeier, F. (1993): 'Wissen und Policy-Forschung. Wissenspolitologie und rhetorischdialektisches Handlungsmodell', in A. Héritier (ed.), *Policy-Analyse, Kritik und Neuorientierung*, Politische Vierteljahresschrift. Sonderheft 24, Opladen, Germany: Westdeutscher Verlag:, pp. 175–96.

Ostrom, E. (1999), 'Institutional rational choice: an assessment of the institutional analysis and development framework', in P.A. Sabatier (ed.), *Theories of the Policy Process*, Boulder: Westview Press, pp. 35–71.

Ostrom, E., James Walker and Jimmy Walker (1994), *Rules, Games and Common-Pool Resources*, Ann Arbor: University of Michigan Press.

Rydin, Y. (2007), 'Re-examining the role of knowledge within planning theory', *Planning Theory*, **1**(6), 52–68.

Sgobbi, A. (2007), *EPI at National Level – a Literature Review*, EPIGOV Papers (draft), Berlin: Ecologic – Institute for International and European Environmental Policy.

WCED (1987), *Our Common Future, Report by the World Commission on Environment and Development*, Oxford.

Willke, H. (1992), *Ironie des Staates*, Frankfurt/M.: Suhrkamp.

WWF (2007), *How Green is the Future of EU Cohesion Policy? A WWF Scorecard Analysis of the Regional Fund Programming 2007–2013*, Brussels.

6. From G-FORS to EPIGOV: Which Governance Modes for EPI? The Case of Strategic Environmental Assessment in Spatial Planning

Carolina Pacchi and Davide Zanoni

6.1   INTRODUCTION

The EU Commission's 6th Research Framework Programme has funded two main projects aimed at analysing the relationship between environmental policy integration and governance modes: EPIGOV – Environmental Policy Integration and Multi-level Governance; G-FORS – Governance for Sustainability.

In order to coordinate existing research and to disseminate results through the different work teams, we tried to create a bridge between the theoretical and empirical approaches adopted. Starting from the G-FORS side, we relate the analytical model developed for the study of governance for sustainability to the EPIGOV common framework, and present some preliminary research findings to better understand the effectiveness of different modes of governance used to promote environmental policy integration (EPI).

In the chapter we present results from the G-FORS Italian case study related to the Strategic Environmental Assessment (SEA) of the Province of Milan Master Plan (process of adaptation 2003–2007). This case fits well in the G-FORS analytical model, but it could also be useful in the light of the EPIGOV research questions, because it concerns an articulated policy process split into different phases and because the implementation of SEA passes through different conceptual definitions and governance arrangements as the process evolves. In particular, it is possible to follow the evolution of an implementation through the change of regulative framework (the Regional Law 12/2005 introduced mandatory SEA for plans and programmes in Lombardy) and cultural perspective (from a process that just involved institutions and technical experts to a decision-making process that aimed to be more open). The chapter firstly introduces the main concepts of the G-

FORS and EPIGOV theoretical frameworks, focusing on environmental policy integration and governance mode definitions (Section 6.2). We then present the SEA case study following the empirical approach adopted in G-FORS, describing the action arena in terms of policy domain, rules, actors and interaction modes throughout the different phases of the planning process (Sections 6.3–6.4). The chapter afterwards tries to discuss some EPIGOV questions, in particular to evaluate to what extent integration analysed in the SEA case study corresponds to the EPIGOV concept of environmental integration and to relate the governance modes prevailing in the contest to the modes considered and described in EPIGOV (Section 6.5). The chapter concludes by proposing some hints on the effectiveness of different governance modes in promoting a broader environmental integration in the policy-making process (Section 6.7).

Governance for Sustainability (G-FORS) is a three year research project funded by the 6th FP priority 7 (Citizens and Governance in a Knowledge-Based Society – The Implications of European Integration and Enlargement for Governance and the Citizen). The G-FORS STREP develops an analytical model for the study of governance for sustainability, focusing on the synergy between new governance modes and different forms of knowledge, taking into account the rapid changes in the knowledge society. For this purpose, G-FORS identifies a range of different forms of knowledge and analyses how these different forms of knowledge may interact in the context of particular governance arrangements to produce 'reflexive knowledge' and contribute to a more legitimate understanding of sustainability.

The project then empirically tests this new model through case studies examining EU policies in the field of air pollution control and environmental planning and their implementation at domestic level. These areas have been chosen because they involve different governance modes in a multi-level context that illustrate the positive interactions and potential tensions between certain governance arrangements, different forms of knowledge and sustainable development.

The empirical research is useful to assess how the engagement of a range of actors in new complex multi-level governance arrangements can be activated to tackle any future threats of 'democratic deficit', and to promote participation and sustainable development. In particular, G-FORS will demonstrate the key economic, social and political roles of sub-national actors.

The fundamental objective of the G-FORS project is captured by the following questions: how do certain governance modes impact upon the effectiveness and legitimacy of policies aimed at sustainability objectives by using and generating different types of knowledge? How can they help to organize the boundary-crossing of non-scientific everyday (local) knowledge with steering and expert knowledge?

According to the analytical model, based on Ostrom's IAD approach (1999), a governance mode refers to an action arena in which actors interact in a certain way leading to specific policy objectives. Their behaviour in the action arena depends firstly on three external components: given attributes of the physical world (type of policy, scope of the plan, spatial conditions of the policy problem); attributes of the community (dominant policy style, culture of trust) and rules in use structuring actors' interaction (authority, boundary, information rules).

These components, linked to features of the policy, the community and the rules (formal and informal) in action, 'shape' the actor constellations (arena) and the governance arrangements. Actors enter into the arena according to specific boundary rules that attribute more or less formally their roles in the process, bringing different knowledge forms (expert, steering, local) but also private interests.

6.2   EPIGOV AND G-FORS CONCEPT

The EPIGOV and G-FORS theoretical frameworks differ to a significant extent in terms of definition of concepts and background assumptions. The first intends to develop an analytical model for the study of governance for sustainability, the second serves as a point of reference for the discussion within the project and it is a clear template to coordinate research activities; therefore their relative scope and extent are not fully comparable. Nevertheless they both are aimed at providing analytical tools to evaluate the effectiveness of governance modes – prevailing in specific contexts – to improve environmental policy integration. For this reason, we found it interesting to attempt to create a link between these frameworks, in order to better understand the approaches and to find a common ground.

EPIGOV defines Environmental Policy Integration (EPI) as the integration of environmental concerns into other policy areas: this is perceived as the most important instrument to achieve sustainable development, even if only the environmental component of sustainability is considered. Full integration is achieved if sectoral policies respect long-term environmental sustainability. The level of integration depends on the status attributed to environmental issues in a given policy-making process, the availability of relevant information and the political will or ability to include results from environmental assessment into the policy.

The point to be stressed is that environmental integration represents a particular way of addressing coordination problems between sectors within the political system: environmental and other sectoral policies are seen as sub-systems of the political system. The integration is seen primarily as an internal (in-house) process, referred only to the public administration domain, resources and actors.

The G-FORS perspective on environmental integration towards sustainability is based on the coordination between the political system and other societal systems, or in other words, the integration is seen as an internal and an external process. Institutional changes are grounded on learning processes by the actors involved in the process and the respective knowledge forms. These actors belong to different societal systems and thus they outnumber the public institutions (departments or multi-level administrations) responsible for policy making.

The G-FORS conceptual framework is based on three main concepts: governance, knowledge and sustainability. The concept of sustainability used in the model is broader than environmental sustainability, because it includes economic and social concerns, but it also goes beyond the static definition of sustainability based on threshold values (sustainable development means systemic equilibrium which has to be kept stable by under-running critical thresholds), substantive criteria and indicators to be monitored.

The fundamental research idea is that sustainability is a dynamic and relative concept to be analysed in a certain governance (but also political, social, economic) context, and that in particular it is highly dependent on local knowledge. Sustainability and thus environmental policies cannot be defined only through a top-down procedure led by technical experts and steering knowledge holders: there is a gap to be closed using knowledge forms that may arise from local actors and their even contradictory perspectives, in terms of future developments, external effects and contextual implications of policy actions.

Therefore sustainability is considered a dynamic and learning process, in which all local actors (political, social and technical) should coordinate to build a common view of the local context, to imagine future scenarios, to mobilise different knowledge forms and to commit to long-term objectives.

In this way, the policies adopted to foster sustainability should gain legitimacy (the participation of external actors may influence the process and the final decisions, through the collection of different points of view), effectiveness (actors involved are more willing to facilitate the implementation of plan and the risk of conflicts is lower) and transparency (institutional settings and processes are transparent and political actors are accountable).

The knowledge-based approach to sustainability starts from a move to find out which knowledge forms are essential to governance for sustainability: an innovative approach to sustainability entails a shift from regulative to more interactive and dynamic patterns of governance, and therefore, together with regulative instruments, public actors have to create institutional mechanisms to produce and exchange knowledge (infra administrative sectors, infra societal sectors, infra tiers of government) as they are asked to promote policies for sustainability which incorporate both expert and local knowledge.

Coming back to the EPI concept, the G-FORS framework also refers to sustainability as an issue of policy integration and inter-sectoral coordination (Lafferty, 2003): this implies that policies or programmes should reflect environmental, economic and social concerns which should find their way into policies via different forms of knowledge. Nevertheless the difference is that the knowledge base should be opened to external input because the variety of types of knowledge may lead to a more complete range of points of view taken into account and able to influence the policy process.

The other part of the two frameworks to be considered refers to governance modes. In the literature, the term governance is frequently used as an alternative to traditional government, which is understood as top-down decision making and command-and-control enforcement, while governance instead entails less hierarchical policy-making and more involvement of non-state actors. More in general, it is used to indicate changes in institutional arrangements of action coordination (Newman, 2001) and political contexts in which the role of government in the process (of governance) is much more contingent (Pierre, 2000; Stoker, 2000).

EPIGOV adopts a broader concept of governance which includes traditional government as one of several modes of governance. This is because both traditional government and other modes of governance may be used to promote EPI. Specifically, the framework considers two concepts of governance that could be relevant for the research approach, even if the first seems more coherent with the EPI concept: modes of governance are different continuous (or established) political processes of setting explicit goals for society and intervening in it in order to achieve these goals (Kohler-Koch, 2006); a state-centric perspective, focusing on the 'steering' capacity of the state and its institutions (the state usually sets goals for society, integrating environmental concerns into sectoral policies). Alternatively they refer to different conceptual or theoretical representations of the co-ordination of social systems (Pierre, 2000); a society perspective in which private and public actors interact creating networks and partnership that may have important implications for policy-makers dealing with EPI.

The second concept is nearer to the G-FORS perspective on governance and environmental integration towards sustainability, mainly based on the interaction between the political system and other societal systems. In fact, the G-FORS framework uses the term governance to describe the steering capacities of a political system without making any prior assumptions about the institutions and actors actually doing the steering. The model therefore applies a broader concept and extends the typology of governance forms to include public and private, hierarchical, competitive and network forms of action coordination.

The relevant modes considered are: hierarchy or hierarchical governance with the dominance of steering and expert knowledge; networks of public and private actors interacting and reaching a coordination through bargaining (the aim of the actors involved is to defend their position and interests by applying bargaining power and leaving preferences unchanged); and networks relying on arguing for influencing decision making (shared meanings are collectively built and positions developed on empirical evidence and impartial assumptions).

Beside these political modes of governance characterised by their attempts to coordinate societal interactions by binding decisions intentionally, societies are also governed (unintentionally) by the 'hidden hand' of the market.

These governance modes are just ideal types, empirically combined in governance arrangements prevailing in specific policy contexts; there is not a mode of governance more or less appropriate but rather an effective mix of modes and the integration of knowledge forms in order to follow a local-dependent and legitimated approach to sustainability.

The EPIGOV framework instead identifies a higher number of modes of governance (seven typologies) that have been presented in terms of relevant decision-making types, actors and policy-making instruments. These modes are discussed in terms of relevance for EPI and classified according to their effectiveness in promoting cross-sectoral policy coordination (that is environmental integration). There are basis modes which exist despite the specific instruments (for example SEA, IA, reporting) implemented to improve EPI and other modes (EPI modes) specifically employed or derived from the tool in use. However, these modes are more comprehensive than the arena created by the instrument because they include the wider (existing) institutional and political context.

6.3   STRATEGIC ENVIRONMENTAL ASSESSMENT (SEA)

In order to test the hypotheses of the conceptual framework, the G-FORS research project works on the in-depth analysis of a certain number of case studies, in three different policy domains and in nine countries.[1] In particular, the implementation of SEA has been chosen firstly because it is an instrument aimed at implementing a more transparent planning process through the involvement of the public and the integration of environmental considerations into proposed plans and policies, and secondly because it is implemented across the EU.

The purpose of SEA is to ensure that environmental consequences of a given plan are identified and assessed against local priorities, during its development and before its adoption. An SEA can be described as a systematic process for integrating environmental considerations into strategic decision-making processes, in which environmental authorities and the public can give their opinion and results can be integrated and taken into account in the course of the planning procedure.

This would help to move towards the goal of sustainable development, not only in terms of policy outcomes but also through innovations in procedures and institutional arrangements which allow reversibility and experimental action, in order to better coordinate and, if possible, integrate the three dimensions of sustainability.

The extent to which SEA is able to go beyond traditional planning processes by effectively integrating a range of social, economic and environmental factors to influence the decision-making process remains to be seen, and becomes therefore one of the important research questions. Environmental assessment can help to transfer knowledge and to foster cooperation across policy fields, but it does not necessarily ensure an effective use of knowledge or the enhancement of governance for sustainability, unless this knowledge base is integrated into the whole plan making process. In general SEA processes could be conceptualised in two main types: SEAs that proceed parallel to the planning process, and that evaluate the possible outcomes and impacts of plans; and SEAs that are strictly integrated into the planning process, and that start before the planning process itself.

We expect that, especially in this second case, SEA can contribute to integrate, in a more effective way, the three dimensions of sustainability, creating an appropriate EPI mode of governance.

6.4   CASE HISTORY

The G-FORS Italian case study concerns the Strategic Environmental Assessment (SEA) of the Province of Milan Master Plan (PTCP). PTCP is not a land-use plan, but rather a general plan that gives some overall rules for the transformation of the areas, then defined in more detail in Local Land Use Plans (PGTs). The PTCP in force was approved in October 2003, but after the issuing of the new regional Planning Law (Regione Lombardia, 2005), it has to be adapted to the new regulative framework through a reframing process, according to the regional guidelines. In November 2005, the Provincial Council approved the 'Action programme and first indications for the adaptation of the PTCP in force' (Provincia di Milano, 2005) and has formally started the upgrading procedure. The overall planning process, started in 1999 with the planning of the PTCP 2003, can be divided in four main phases:

1999–2004
> Phase 1 – PTCP 2003 planning and implementation

March 2005–July 2006
> Phase 2 – Institutional and procedural setting for the adaptation process

July 2006–July 2007
> Phase 3 – Adaptation process for the PTCP 2003

Sept 2007–ongoing
> Phase 4 – Fine tuning and approval revised PTCP

The Province of Milan experimented with a test strategic appraisal of the Master Plan in 1999 and a more structured implementation of strategic environmental assessment (Valutazione Strategica – VaSt) for the new Plan in 2003, although at the time it was not yet mandatory. These former initiatives, although quite articulated and comprehensive from a technical point of view, foresaw neither stakeholder involvement nor articulated public participation procedures, apart from the direct involvement of local authorities (inter-institutional cooperation). Nevertheless they can be considered as useful experiments in terms of environmental integration, because external experts have been involved in the planning process and some efforts to increase the knowledge base have been undertaken.

For the adaptation of the Plan in force (Phase 3), the Province Planning Department launched in parallel an SEA process and a public consultation strategy (Forum), that started in autumn 2006 and ended in spring 2007, with the aim of ensuring the overall sustainability of the new interventions and of enlarging, at the same time, the knowledge base and the possible consensus about the main planning issues.

According to the SEA Directive and to regional guidelines, we considered planning and the strategic environmental assessment as just one process, trying to identify the actual level of integration in terms of governance modes and learning mechanisms (plan contents, knowledge generation). This approach allowed us to better understand the differences between the process in theory, as it is described in the guidelines and in the Regional Planning Law, and the effective implementation of the provisions aimed at improving the planning process through environmental assessment and the interaction with a range of different stakeholders from inter-institutional cooperation with local authorities to public participation aimed at diffused interests.

6.5 RESEARCH FINDINGS FROM THE CASE STUDY

6.5.1 External Components: Type of Policy, Scope of the Plan, Rules

The PTCP subjected to strategic environmental assessment can be considered in broad terms as a regulatory policy. As stated before, PTCP gives some general objectives and overall rules to manage and to transform the areas; these rules have to be connected to supra-municipal interests and be consistent with the regional planning framework. This means that the Plan is intended to have a coordinating function between different tiers of government because the spatial issues to be addressed cross the administrative borders. The Plan also includes some binding provisions which prevail on local planning and have to be defined with broad consensus and accuracy, in particular those concerning agricultural areas and indirectly urbanisation permits.

The most important vertical relationship with other government levels is the one with Local Authorities, in order to review the land-use plans (PGTs). When a PGT presents a definition of agricultural areas that contrasts with the binding provincial provision, the City Council has to conform to the provincial plan. This is the reason why the cooperation between levels of government may be crucial in preventing conflicts that could limit the effectiveness of the provincial plan itself.

Given the regulatory nature of the policy, as far as some areas are concerned, the role of the Province in planning is closely related to an effective cooperation with the Municipalities and with the Region. Due to the relative weakness of the Province *vis-à-vis* these other government levels and in the absence of a multi-level governance framework able to define shared guidelines and to uniform tools and procedures, provincial planning could turn out to be a political failure. In other terms, planning at the intermediate level may show limits in implementing a strategic coordination role.

The rules in use forming the context variables and in particular the action arena refer mainly to authority rules that specify the actors that take the final decision on the plan, boundary rules that indicate the actors (private and public) to be consulted in order to take the decision and information rules that specify the forms of knowledge and the expertise needed to elaborate the spatial plan and to carry out the environmental appraisal.

In this case, the action programme and first directions for the upgrade of the PTCP in force (Provincial Resolution n. 460/05) provides a preliminary analysis of the issues related to the adaptation of the Plan and defines the structure, procedures and general rules. The responsibility of the process is attributed to the D.G. Planning and Land Use which has to develop the plan, to coordinate a technical inter-departmental committee and to assign specific tasks to an external experts panel. Therefore the rules in use assign a leading role to the provincial authority which defines the overall process, in terms of stakeholders to be invited, experts to be involved and knowledge to be collected; above all authority rules give much of the decision-making power regarding which inputs from consultation procedures are to be taken into account finally.

This means that formal rules design an open arena, in which a range of different stakeholders actors may participate in the planning process and the interaction between different actors may lead to an extended knowledge base including the local perspective. Nevertheless in practice the rules in action, that is the informal rules used by the more powerful actors, shaped a different arena with hierarchical governance forms, as will be further examined below.

6.6   ACTORS AND ACTION SITUATION

The action arena in which the Milan PTCP SEA process takes place is a highly complex and differentiated one. While a large part of the planning and assessment processes take place within the public administration, there is also interaction with a number of other actors, some of whom play a major role, but most a very marginal role. In terms of the EPIGOV framework, there is a significant concentration of activities within the public administration structure, even if this does not directly mean that the prevailing governance mode is hierarchical. In fact, the 2005 Regional Planning Law foresees network governance as a means of coordination not just at the same governance level, but also between different levels: in particular, this is true for provinces, that are an intermediate governance and planning level between regional governments and Local Authorities.

The most important actors in the process are essentially the Province of Milan and the Municipalities. A powerful debate between the two levels of governance marks the process in a prevailing way, because the relevant decisions concerning the management of the territory arise from their interaction. The PTCP framework gives access to stakeholders (interested public, third sector, civil society) but it is rather a consultation on strategic objectives, aimed at informing and building general consensus within the community, than an effective participation in the policy-making process. In practice, however, the most important decisions (for example agricultural area boundaries, infrastructures) are taken through specific concertation activities with municipalities and other key actors. In the background the Region carries out a relevant role, because the architecture of the process and the definition of the specific rules in the elaboration of the plan arise from regional law, and its passible reformulations. The action arena changes significantly throughout the process, from the rule setting to the implementation phase, and it can be considered overall a quite complex one (see Table 6.1).

We have in fact different kinds of actors (politicians, technical bureaucracies, general interest groups, special interest groups) and different levels (from the national to the local one). In particular, the process is quite closed and limited to governmental actors in the very first (and, possibly, also in the very last) phases, while it is more open in the central phases, which correspond to the consultation (based on arguing) with the general public and to the concertation (based on bargaining) with Local Authorities. It is important to underline the strong difference between these last two governance tools.

6.7   GOVERNANCE MODES

According to the G-FORS model, the patterns of interaction prevailing in the action arena are the result of a certain mix of 'pure' governance modes described in the framework (hierarchy, bargaining networks, arguing networks, market). In the Strategic Environmental Assessment (SEA) of the PTCP adaptation process, a hierarchical governance arrangement seems to be prevailing over market or network governance forms, even if there are formal procedures for inter-institutional cooperation, stakeholder involvement and public participation.

As stated before, there is a strong hierarchical influence in the plan-making process, and the idea of planning based on public participation seems to be more rhetoric than substance. The prevailing of a hierarchical mode of interaction can be found in the low degree of openness of the plan toward some of the actors to whom the formal model attributes an important role in the process. The Province was in fact forced to consider the requests of other organised actors, firstly the Municipalities, but also Regional Parks and agriculture associations. This means that the disposals of the plan are mostly top-down towards public actors who have played a substantive role through participation in the formal consultations and during the inter-institutional negotiation (for example roundtables, Conference of the Municipalities, Shop for the Municipalities). Moreover the provincial planning must be consistent with the Regional Territorial Plan and the plans of the Regional Parks.

Governance for the Environment

Table 6.1   Action Arena PTCP-SEA (2006)

	Politicians	Technical Bureaucracies and Experts	General Interest Groups	Special Interest Groups
International/ National		Po Basin Authority		
Regional		• Region Lombardia Planning Dept. and Agriculture Dept. • ARPA Lombardia (Environmental Agency) • Regional Parks		
Provincial	• Commissioner for Planning • Unione Province Lombarde • Local Authorities Permanent Conference	• Province Planning Dept. • Other Provinces (Varese, Como, Lecco, Bergamo, Lodi, Pavia, Novara) • Law Consultants • Planning Consultants • Mobility Consultants • SEA Technical Experts • SEA Process Experts	• Environmental NGOs • Third Sector	• Agriculture Associations • Other Economic Interests
Local	• 11 Municipal Roundtables • 188 Majors • Major of Milan	• Municipal Planning Dept. • Local Parks	• Environmental NGOs • Research Institutions and university • Local/ Community Organisations	Businesses

The plan also seems to be closed to other actors formally involved in the planning and appraisal process. First, regarding the consultants for strategic environmental assessment whose work would have to be broadly considered and to be integrated in the plan: according to the empirical evidence, it does not seem that the environmental dimension has had an important weight in their planning choices, so that the Environmental Report (final delivery of the SEA) is critical against the plan.

Moreover, the Province took into account only a few outcomes of the public consultation process (Forum for the government of the metropolitan territory). The consultation of local actors is an integral part of the SEA and it is also provided in the new Regional Planning Law, which considers the involvement of economic and social actors as a basic element in the new approach to spatial planning. However, the outcomes of the participation process are unclear, above all in terms of input to the planning process: the debate on objectives, actions and indicators of the master plan has supplied innovative elements and knowledge, only partly granted by the provincial officers. Moreover, the alternatives and their evaluation have not been submitted to the actors during the Forum and not entirely considered in the final draft of the Plan. Therefore it seems quite difficult to consider the relation between social actors and rule makers (Province) like an effective participated planning with interactions based on a bottom-up approach.

Forms of networks (arguing and bargaining) are integrated in the decision-making process at two different levels and several arenas have been created by the Province, with different weights and aims. The first type is the bilateral interaction with Municipalities which it is based on bargaining and becomes an effective place for dealing with some policy decisions with direct effects on the plan. The second type is articulated in at least three different arenas: public participation (Forum), inter-institutional roundtables and SEA working groups with external consultants

They are based on arguing, with knowledge exchange and creation, but their effectiveness in shaping the plan is questionable.

In the first case, during some bilateral encounters with almost each single Municipality, the Provincial Planning Department opened up a negotiation (bargaining) in which every Municipality tried to defend the right of managing its land and the Province tried to defend more general interests. The stake in the game is clear, as are the role and interest of every actor in the arena; we can say that a bargaining network prevails by definition, thanks to the rules and the functions defining the arena itself.

A quite different mode of interaction prevails in the Forum opened to diffused interests (economic and social actors), but also in the working groups and in the inter-institutional roundtables. In these cases, the Province involved actors in the planning process with an arguing mode of interaction, even if the stake in game was not clear enough. The Province has presented itself to the public putting forward the definition of objectives and actions, thus raising high expectations among the actors; they were convinced of being able to take part in a dialectic process of objectives and actions redefinition, in which they could propose new points of view, diverse knowledge types and different interests. At the end of the day, the Forum has been an arguing network but partly deprived of its meaning and original function, because the integrations and modifications formally brought by local actors have not been considered much in the plan.

The first network is therefore an effective place for dealing with some policy decisions that could touch the interest of some key actors (Municipalities); the second is an exercise of participation not really aimed at discussing planning proposals (as many actors believed) but rather aimed at creating 'preventive' consensus (in order to avoid or to reduce observations after the adoption of the plan) and diffusing information on the planning activities in course.

The most interesting of the three networks, from a governance point of view, is the one formed by 11 inter-institutional roundtables formed by groups of Municipalities; here the Province interacts with Local Authorities on a strategic level, not dealing with specific land-use issues and individual requests, but trying to shape future scenarios in an effort to plan in cooperation.

EPIGOV questions

A step forward in the analytical discussion on EPIGOV and G-FORS frameworks could be the attempt to use some findings drawn from the case study in order to answer the EPIGOV research questions: in particular to evaluate to what extent environmental integration analysed in the SEA case study corresponds to the EPIGOV concept of EPI and to relate, as far as possible, the governance modes prevailing in the specific contest to EPI modes. These questions are related to the main issue to be addressed, that is which mode (basic/existing) or EPI mode is more effective in fostering environmental integration? SEA is considered an instrument or tool to improve EPI (Jacob and Volkery, 2006) and its application to the planning process of the Province has partly transformed the existing governance mode into a mode specifically oriented to environmental policy integration.

The G-FORS' focus on integration is broader than the EPI approach, both in terms of content (sustainability versus environmental) and process (external versus internal). But anyway we can advance some considerations on the level of integration between SEA and the plan procedure in order to evaluate if the application of the tool (SEA as EPI initiative) to the institutional context has really created a new governance mode potentially conducive to EPI.

From a theoretical point of view SEA is seen as an element strictly related to the planning process itself, as a cyclical process that gives feedback on the planning decisions rather than an ex post evaluation of the final plan.

Nevertheless, in the specific case we studied, SEA seems to proceed parallel to the planning process, as a different plan or an additional review of the options proposed. The team of experts in charge of SEA has not been involved in the preliminary drafting of the plan rules (there is also a low coordination of the planning department with other sectors and environmental agencies) and the consultation with the general public and to the concertation with Local Authorities remained two distinct 'sub-arenas' with different capacity to influence the planning process. Moreover the appraisal of planning alternatives have not been submitted to the public consultation and the final plan is influenced only marginally by the environmental assessment.

Therefore, the level of effective integration (content) is quite poor despite the fact that an appropriate governance structure has been created (process). In this case, the will of the policy makers (more the departmental officers than the politicians), in spite of the rhetorical commitment, seems oriented to protecting the traditional planning 'core' activities, while at the same time trying to convince the public opinion of their environmental integration objective.

Following the G-FORS categories, the governance modes prevailing in the local context could be considered a mix of hierarchy and networks (bargaining and arguing): the Milan PTCP process is dominated by public actors (planners and politicians) but the plan formulation is influenced by bargaining and to a lesser extent by arguing (public consultation/participation?) in formal networks. These typologies are quite similar to Knill and Lenschow's modes (2005) which include in particular hierarchy and communication. Hierarchy is described as in the G-FORS model, while communicative governance relies on deliberation and learning in networks. Nevertheless the emphasis on participation by non-public actors is low and the main network actors are officers and experts.

Given the presence of the public consultation process, it could be more appropriate to make a reference, at least formally, to the network governance mode, in which local actors are called on to participate in the planning and assessment process. Even if not directly considered in the EPIGOV framework as a necessary condition to the integration (state-centric perspective), the involvement of local actors may serve different purposes with respect to EPI. A broad stakeholder participation may help to define a sustainable development scenario in a preliminary phase, to discuss the plans' proposal with the affected groups and to rely on local knowledge to perform SEA. As argued by Foxon et al. (2004) stakeholder participation in sustainable innovation policy is necessary to establish politically, economically and technically viable strategic options.

Broadly speaking, the governance modes in the SEA of the provincial plan are EPI modes, or better they relate to some EPI modes considered by the EPIGOV framework. The governance structure is appropriate to cross the boundaries of sectoralisation, considered the main obstacle to EPI, but this is not enough. The problem of the effectiveness (in fostering integration) cannot be reduced to two dimensions: EPI modes on the one hand and environmental integration on the other. The relationship between these dimensions is influenced by other variables, other softer or hidden boundaries such as knowledge gap, cultural attitude, political or internal officers' will. In this sense, it is important to stress that a broader analytical approach may be useful to detect these aspects and dimensions. What emerges from this discussion is that it is difficult to show that certain modes of governance are inherently more conducive to EPI than others unless some other variables are considered.

6.8   CONCLUSIONS

The process of SEA and PTCP planning entails different levels of negotiation with public and institutional actors, a public participation process and the employment of resources from external experts and consultants. If therefore we limit the appraisal to these aspects, that is the structure of the process and the procedures developed, we can say that the governance mode, stemming from the application of the SEA procedure to the planning process, has been conceived purposely in order to favour environmental integration. It would appear to lie within an EPI mode.

However, this does not seem enough to fully understand the effective integration of the environmental dimension into the spatial plan. Reducing and crossing sectoral boundaries, described as the main obstacle to integration, is certainly a first order condition, necessary, but not sufficient. A useful way to go beyond is to consider other variables and other dimensions, such as: the patterns of interaction and the type of actors involved; the inclusion of local knowledge in consultation procedures alongside expert and steering knowledge, and also the forms of knowledge effectively spent in the action arena; the extension of the knowledge base and learning process within the administration (creation of reflexive knowledge); and substantive integrations to the plan arising from external (to the public administration) actors, providing more localised insights into the environmental effects of sectoral plans but also scenarios and development tracks in terms of sustainability.

In practice, it is necessary to looking inside the processes and deconstruct them, in order to understand what happened during the interaction between actors, but in particular to understand what passed through, which flows and types of knowledge, and then what finally remained. On a higher, more strategic level the inclusion of such new governance practices in parallel to more traditional hierarchical structures may allow the reframing of the local planning policy, and thus a better integration of environmental concerns and local knowledge into the policy-making and consultation procedures.

NOTE

1. Case studies: UK, Polish, Dutch, Greek, Hungarian, German, Swedish, Italian, Norwegian. The EU SEA Directive has been implemented in the Italian law by legislative decree 29/04/2006 'Environmental Consolidation Act' which sets out a comprehensive framework for environmental assessments, defining new procedures for EIA and SEA. At the local level, regional legislations, in particular those focusing on planning, have to be revised in order to incorporate environmental assessment procedures.

   The Lombardy Region has already introduced the strategic environmental assessment for provincial and municipal plans with the approval of the Planning Law (Regione Lombardia, 2005). Then the Regional Council approved general guidelines for the strategic environmental assessment of plans and programmes, which represent the regional transposition of the SEA Directive 2001/42/CE.

   The guidelines give instructions on: the integration between the planning process and the appraisal activity (tight cooperation between policy makers and assessment experts coupled with a transparent and participatory approach to decision making); the scope of application of the environmental assessment (regional, provincial and local plans); the consultation process to allow a broad public participation.

REFERENCES

European Commission (2001), *Directive 2001/42/EC of the European Parliament and of the Council of 27 June 2001 on the assessment of the effects of certain plans and programmes on the environment.*

Foxon, T., Makuch, Z., A. Mata, et al. (2004), *Towards a sustainable innovation policy – Institutional structures, stakeholder participation and mixes of policy instruments*, paper presented at the IDHP Berlin Conference on the Human Dimensions of Global Environmental Change 'Greening of Policies – Interlinkages and Policy Integration', Freie Universität Berlin, December 3–4, 2004.

Heinelt, H., G. Held, T. Kopp-Malek, U. Matthiensen, E. Reisenger and K. Zimmermann (2006), 'Governance for sustainability', downloadable at http://www.zit.tu-darmstadt.de/cipp/tudzit/custom/pub/content,lang,1/oid,778/ticket,guest [last accessed: January 2010].

Homeyer, I. (2006a), *Environmental Policy Integration and Modes of Governance – State-of-the-Art Report*, EPIGOV Paper No. 2, Ecologic-Institute for International and European Environmental Policy Berlin.

Homeyer, I. (2006b), *EPIGOV Common Framework*, EPIGOV Paper No. 1, Ecologic-Institute for International and European Environmental Policy Berlin.

Jacob, K. and A. Volkery (2006), 'Institutions and Instruments for Government Self-Regulation: Environmental Policy Integration in a Cross-Country Perspective', in

Martin Jänicke and Jacob Klaus (eds), *Environmental Governance in Global Perspective. New Approaches to Ecological and Political Modernisation*, Berlin: Freie Universität Berlin, pp. 239–61.

Knill, C. and A. Lenschow (2005), 'Compliance, communication and competition: patterns of EU environmental policy making and their impact on policy convergence', *European Environment*, **15**(2), 114–28.

Kohler-Koch, B. and B. Rittberger (2006), *The 'Governance' Turn in EU Studies*, ARENA, Centre for European Studies, University of Oslo.

Lafferty, W. (2003), 'From environmental protection to sustainable development: the challenge of decoupling through sectoral integration', in W. Lafferty (ed.), *Governance for Sustainable Development*, Cheltenham, UK and Northampton, MA, USA: Edward Elgar, 191–220.

Newman, J. (2001), *Modernising Governance*, London: Sage.

Ostrom, E. (1999), 'Institutional rationale choice: An assessment of the institutional analysis and development framework', in P.A. Sabatier (ed.), *Theories of the Policy Process*, Boulder, CO: Westriew Press, 35–71.

Pierre, J. (2000), 'Introduction: understanding governance', in J. Pierre (ed.), *Debating Governance: Authority, Steering, and Democracy*, Oxford: Oxford University Press, pp. 1–10.

Pierre, J. and G.B. Peters (2000), *Governance, Politics and the State*, New York, USA: St. Martin Press.

Provincia di Milano (2003), *Piano Territoriale di Coordinamento Provinciale (PTCP)*, approval by the Provincial Council, C.P. n.55/2003.

Provincia di Milano (2005), *Piano di azione e prime indicazioni per l'adeguamento del PTCP vigente*, Provincial Resolution n. 460/05.

Regione Lombardia (2005), *Legge regionale per il governo del territorio n°12*, 11 March 2005.

Stoker, G. (2000), 'Urban political science and the challenge of urban governance', in J. Pierre (ed.), *Debating Governance*, Oxford: Oxford University Press, pp. 91–109.

7. A Systems Theoretical Perspective on Greening EU Regional Policy

Philipp Schepelmann

7.1 INTRODUCTION

Functional differentiation is a process which dominates modern societies. With global communication amplified and accelerated by information and communication technologies, this will increase exponentially in spite of antagonistic movements (for example by totalitarian or fundamentalist ideologies). Functional differentiation is a profound challenge for environmental policy integration, because a consensus about what relevant environmental problems are and how they could be prevented or solved is more and more unlikely.

A constituting feature of functional differentiation is the functional selection of information. Only the information relevant to the function of a differentiated system is selected. Any other information is unnecessary noise, which decreases the functionally defined efficiency of a system and thus needs to be suppressed.

Environmental policy integration does not rule out the suppression of information. The communication of every social system is based on the selection of information. If it were not to select information it would be limitless and thus identical with its environment (universal). Incompleteness by selection of information is therefore constitutive for every social system.

The suppression of information will become dysfunctional 'blindness' if the suppressed information is related to risks which are needed to maintain the integrity and reproduction of a system. Nevertheless, from a system theoretical point of view the possibility of jeopardizing survival due to ecological unfitness does not sufficiently motivate adaptation.

7.2 RESPONSIVE BEHAVIOUR OF SOCIAL SYSTEM

Environmental policy integration (EPI) in EU Regional Policy requires intensive communication between policy sectors (horizontally, for example between economic and environmental ministries) and between the multiple levels of governance (vertically, between local, regional, national and European levels). Therefore, social systems and their communication deserve further contemplation. Horizontal and vertical communication between social systems can create substantial problems, because rational communication, learning and adaptation cannot necessarily be assumed. Stakeholders are often representatives of system rationalities which do not have the primary social function of generating and processing ecological knowledge. Their communication is not primarily scientific but economic, political, juridical, ethical, and so on. These system rationalities can block the processing of scientific information about their environment and consequently the motivation for EPI. Thus, environmental policy integration (EPI) can be interpreted as a communication problem.

A prerequisite of environmental policy (integration) is the perception of social risks which are connected to the destruction of ecological functions. Social systems tend to ignore environmental problems, which results in a state that Hans-Jochen Luhmann (2001) refers to as 'blindness of society'.

Luhmann has studied a number of scandals and man-made catastrophes which had negative impacts on man and nature although they could have been avoided by taking precautionary action. He explains how social systems tend to isolate and suppress warnings and writings on the wall. According to him a central reason for this is the societal division of labour. 'Apparently the blindness of society is connected to the blindness of the expert for cross-cutting issues' (ibid., p. 13, own translation). He sees a pattern of ignorance which is fuelled by the desire not to be responsible for the 'greater good' and to concentrate on a core competence.

This can have the consequence of suppressing warnings and alarm. Luhmann illustrates this with the example of the BSE crisis. Apparently, decision-makers did not insist on a thorough problem analysis and solution, because they were afraid of being held responsible for the negative economic repercussions on the European beef market. Luhmann describes the twilight zone of uncertainty and irresponsibility that characterizes precautionary policy. Can precautionary interventions against policies driven by powerful economic interests be justified, if their negative impacts have not yet materialized?

The European Environment Agency has issued an impressive collection of examples, which illustrate that the apparent irrational suppression of risk information is part of the rationality of modern society. The documentation 'Late lessons from early warnings' (EEA, 2001) is a history of suppressed precaution in the light of division of labour and dominant economic rationality.

The extent of the problem might become apparent if one is to name examples of successful precautionary action of social systems in the light of environmental evidence. If the reader might take a moment to name examples of collective (not individual!) precautionary action, it will most likely result in recognizing that precautionary action is exceptional, but not the rule. These exceptional cases of precautionary action are usually based on the experience of damage, but not on the processing of ex ante assessments (for example flood prevention).

The apparently widespread pattern of suppressing environmental information indicates a general behaviour of social systems, which has been described by Niklas Luhmann in his sociological systems theory (1981, 1989, 1994). Sociological systems theory is highly relevant for environmental policy integration, because it explains the following patterns of social behaviour:

- the tendency of social subsystems of selection of information, delineation, and closure; as well as
- the conditions for environmentally relevant communication.

Niklas Luhmann (1990) describes the perception and processing of environmental risks by modern societies as 'ecological communication'. His theory defines the 'blindness of society' as a constituting system property, because any system can only exist if it delineates itself against its environment. Systems demarcate borders between inside and outside. Thus they constitute themselves (inside) and their environment (outside). Social systems do this by means of communication. According to Luhmann society is the totality of all relating communications. 'Society is nothing but communication, and by continuous reproduction of communication by communication it delineates itself against its environment and other systems. This way evolution builds up complexity' (Luhmann, 1990, p. 24, own translation).

Niklas Luhmann explains the perception by social systems with their so-called resonance. Resonance is based on the fact that systems can only react to their environment according to their own structure. The structure and thus the resonance of a social system are determined by their functional differentiation. Functional differentiation describes the development of systems within systems (subsystems), that is the differentiation of a society into social sectors. The differentiation is called functional, because the identity of the subsystem is defined by its function to the overall system (society). Functional differentiation is autopoetic. The individuals reproduce each other by networks and delineate themselves from their environment by means of communication. This distinguishing communication is happening by a functionally adapted coding of reality. Differentiated systems perceive reality not 'holistically', but only its functionally important aspects based on a system-specific coding. The selection of information results in a higher order and cohesion within the system as well as the ability to reproduce. Examples for such a functional differentiation are the increasingly complex development of law and the specialization of scientific communities including their specific languages (Stichweh, 1979).

The differentiation of society increases the selectivity of perception and in consequence decreases the possibility of a response towards (unspecific) environmental information. Thus, the systems theory by Niklas Luhmann offers an explanation for the abovementioned 'blindness of society' described by Hans-Jochen Luhmann (2001) or the 'institutional unwillingness' mentioned by Glasson and Gosling (2001) in the context of environmental impact assessment. Niklas Luhmann denies the simple but tempting precautionary notion that there are facts on which society has to react, in order to avoid damage. Niklas Luhmann rather asks in which scheme facts are recognized, which desired states relate to a perception and how expectations can be met by what appears in relation to them as reality. Obviously information about physical limits to or negative impacts of a desired project, programme or policy is intelligence, which is not necessarily welcomed by decision-makers and managers.

Systems theory itself is an act of observation of a functionally differentiated scientific system. Evidently, this observation happens from a point of view with its own systemic context (system science). Luhmann refers to such an observation of a system by another system as cybernetics of second order. Without cybernetics of second order a scientist cannot understand why 'important' scientific information often does not meet 'appropriate' social response. He will not be able to realize that scientific information (for example about negative impacts of climate change) has within the context of many social systems no value at all. Cybernetics of second order is relevant for understanding the limited willingness among different policy areas to integrate environmental requirements. They are often not motivated to do so, because systems cannot see what they cannot see. It explains that in spite of or even because of the large number of specialists, expert groups, agencies and a substantial growth of scientific knowledge about ecological risks it is more and more unlikely that society as a whole can control special interests that drive ecological self-destruction.

Functional differentiation is a process which dominates modern societies. With communication amplified and accelerated by information and communication technologies, this will increase exponentially in spite of antagonistic movements (for example by totalitarian or fundamentalist ideologies). Functional differentiation is a profound challenge for environmental policy integration, because a consensus about what relevant environmental problems are and how they could be prevented or solved is more and more unlikely. Since the 1990s a social movement has rallied around the sustainability paradigm. This could be interpreted as a counter-reaction against functional differentiation by attempting to harmonize economic, ecological and social coding (Valentin and Spangenberg, 2000). Numerous round tables, advisory councils and Local Agenda 21 groups have formed.

The Cardiff process on environmental policy integration of the EU could be seen as an administrative counterpart of this social movement by trying to balance antagonistic sectoral interests under the roof of sustainability. As we now know, more than 20 years after the publication of the Brundtland Report the success of the sustainability movement has been limited. Also the Cardiff process can be considered as having been overruled by the special interests of different administrative sectors (Schepelmann et al., 2000; Kraemer, 2001).

Based on these experiences any strategy for environmental policy integration is bound to fail, if the concerns formulated by Niklas Luhmann are not properly addressed by the following considerations.

Every social system constitutes itself by selection of information, but the suppression of ecological communication can become life-threatening, if the suppressed information is needed to maintain the integrity and reproductive capacities of a system. Yet, the risk of ecological unfitness (and thus extinction) does not necessarily cause social systems to adapt:

> Ecological self-destruction is therefore indeed a possibility of evolution. Risky situations do not only occur because a high degree of specialization turns out to be unfit when the environment changes.
>
> It is also a possibility that a system impacts as much on its environment that it can no longer exists.
>
> The primary objective of autopoetic systems is always the continuation of autopoiesis disregarding its environment, and therefore, the next step is typically more important than caring for the future, which is not attainable, if autopoiesis is interrupted.

After this explanation Niklas Luhmann (2001, p. 39, own translation) points out the central problem:

> To the degree to which technical interventions alter nature resulting in negative impacts for society, not less but more intervention competence needs to be developed. However, this competence needs to be applied according to criteria, which integrate social rebound effects.
>
> The problem is not causality, but the selection criteria. The question which emerges from this is twofold:
>
> Is technological competence sufficient for a selective behaviour, which means: will there be enough freedom from natural constraints? And:

is the communication competence in society sufficient for operationalizing the selection?

The first question whether environmental policy integration would leave enough freedom from nature has been answered positively by different authors (Schmidt-Bleek, 1994; von Weizsäcker, 1998; Carley and Spapens, 1998). It is the logical prerequisite and optimistic foundation of environmental policy integration. The second question is still largely unanswered and leads to the central challenge of environmental policy integration: Do we know enough to improve the communication competence of social systems for environmental concerns? How can this improvement be operationalized?

In this chapter we cannot answer the question whether the knowledge about ecology is sufficient for sustained social development. Logically, this question cannot be answered *a priori*. We will rather show that improving the communication competence of social systems can not only be operationalized, but even measured and compared.

7.3   THE ANALYSIS OF SOCIAL RESPONSE

The description of EPI as an improvement of the communication competence of social systems requires a definition of social systems. Niklas Luhmann has primarily described primary systems of society such as economy, law, science or religion. Policy is usually only referred to in total as 'the political system'. This general description of policy is too general for EPI analysis, because EPI focuses on the integration of differentiated subsystems of the political system (for example agricultural policy, transport policy and so on). The functional differentiation of the primary political system is analogous to the functional differentiation of the primary system of science as described by Stichweh (1979). According to him the scientific disciplines are diverging[1] although they are all serving the identical primary social purpose of gaining knowledge. Analogously, all policies have the primary function of preparing or executing collective binding decisions (Krause, 2001).

The necessity of environmental policy integration arises precisely when functionally differentiated political systems execute in parallel contradicting decisions (for example when different ministries promote at the same time fossil fuel-powered locomotion and CO_2 reduction). In such a conflicting case it is evident that different policy areas (for example transport and environment policy) meet different societal functions. Although this has not been sufficiently described by social system scientists, it seems that not only the function, but also other social system properties such as output, media, codes and programmes are different. In some cases single policy areas can be overlapping (for example energy and transport policy), but each can be described as operative systems with a differentiated and limited social function. We can therefore describe policy areas as functionally differentiated subsystems of what Niklas Luhmann referred to as the political system.

Social systems theory tends to rule out the option that differentiated social systems can improve their communication competence. Luhmann himself has practically excluded this possibility (Metzner, 1993). He justifies his pessimistic view by arguing that communication in social systems is principally different from nature and that it increasingly eliminates influences from its environment. Thus, society would only be able to learn from shocks that environmental requirements need to be integrated. Unfortunately, environmental shocks often occur when ecosystems have reached the point of no return (Luhmann, 1990).

Examples which justify the pessimistic assumption of societal 'blindness' towards environmental risk information are numerous and seem to be the rule (EEA, 2001). Although sociological systems theory does not offer pragmatic solutions for this problem, it helps to understand EPI as a communication problem. The phenomenon of functional differentiation as described by sociological systems theory is generally undisputed (Schimank, 2000), but for formulating pragmatic policies it is not very helpful. This tendency towards a pessimistic description of society's disintegration might have contributed to widespread rejection of social systems theory. Nevertheless, even in systems theory there is a concept which does not only stress the difference of systems, but which could be seen as the nucleus of possible convergence and integration.

Social systems usually shut themselves off against environmental disturbances (noise). They are 'blind' towards information which is not directly useful for its self-organization (*autopoiesis*). Nevertheless, even operative closed communication systems respond to their environment. Under certain circumstances environmental incidents can irritate and disrupt operations of the system. If the system is rocked hard enough (which depends on the soundness of the system structure) the system starts 'swinging'. Niklas Luhman describes this condition as resonance.

Sociological systems theory describes exclusively communication. An environmental incident is pure communication, which has its source outside the (communication) system in question. Therefore, resonance is not caused by ecological processes, but by the societal communication reflecting these processes. Societal communication about ecological processes is what Niklas Luhmann (1990) describes as ecological communication.

7.4   OPERATIONALIZING RESONANCE

Apparently, ecological communication indicates communication competence which is the prerequisite of EPI. Nevertheless, in Luhmann's publication on ecological communication this notion remains rather abstract.

Therefore, the use of environmental indicators will be used as an operationalization of ecological communication. Thus we have a more concrete hypothesis: policies can increase the communication competence for EPI by using environmental indicators or even shorter: environmental indicators can support EPI.

Environmental indicators are usually generated by environmental policy systems. For other than environmental policy they are external controlling measures (environmental incidents). According to Luhmann, systems can only perceive environmental incidents – and in consequence increase their communication competence – in compliance with their own structure. This reaction of a system's structure to environmental indicators is what we refer to as resonance.

How could we describe or even measure resonance with environmental indicators? Resonance within social systems cannot be recorded like the physical phenomenon by measuring the frequency of a resonator. Instead of a quantitative measurement, the empirical evidence of societal 'vibrations' is a qualitative description of EPI strategies, measures and institutions. For this purpose, a relevant indicator needs to be chosen. The indicator should represent a problem where sufficient knowledge of causal problem chains exist for assuming political salience (for example CO_2 equivalents as an indicator for the problem of global warming). The plausibility of a societal differentiation according to the problem should be preliminarily assessed on a meta level. If societal resonance can be assumed, it can be tested whether and how functional differentiation on the different levels of governance (international, national, regional, and so on) takes place.

In summary: the abstract concept of ecological communication can be operationalized by means of environmental indicators. Societal resonance with these indicators and the problems which they represent can be measured by describing problem-specific functional differentiations (for example which have the function of achieving causally related environmental objectives) and their actions on the different governance levels.

It needs to be emphasized that resonance is not similar to acceptance. According to Luhmann (1990) resonance is a neutral phenomenon which can result in the amplification, distortion or buffering of environmental information. In any case, it is an interpretation of information in a system-specific code.

There are also cases in which resonance does not lead to acceptance, but to ignorance or even resistance. Benz and Fürst (2002), for example, stress that specific policy networks might behave conservatively by hindering structural adaptation. An analysis of negative resonance, resulting in resistance rather than acceptance, would probably be a policy-relevant application of the resonance concept, but in this chapter we would like to concentrate on positive resonance as the societal ability to plan and implement target-oriented action. We would like to emphasize that this approach is not a methodology for appraisal or evaluation of environmental policy but a methodology for assessing and comparing the maturity of policies to influence factors and causalities which are supposed to be represented by an environmental indicator.

7.5 METHODOLOGY

Societal resonance with indicators means that a network of stakeholders establish a policy which is functionally related to the indicators, respectively the political objective which they represent (for example the indicator CO_2 equivalent for the objective of reducing greenhouse gas emissions).

The degree of resonance will be quantified by relating empirical evidence of functional differentiation to the different phases of the policy cycle (Figure 7.1). The degree of resonance with an indicator is expressed by the number of phases which have been reached by a matching policy. Low degrees of resonance are realized in a specific policy, for example when only the early phases of problem analysis and target setting have been reached. In contrast to that, a mature policy expresses a maximum degree of resonance, by having gone through all phases of the policy cycle.

The analysis of resonance requires an understanding of the meta and meso level of society. Esser et al. (1996) have managed to integrate elements of industrial and innovation economy with industrial sociology before the background of the steering discourse of policy networks in political science. While values and concepts on the meta level drive and motivate successful regional development, the active target-oriented intervention happens on the meso level. This understanding has been successfully tested in the analysis of regional policy in NRW (Meyer-Stamer 2000).

The internet has proven to be a useful tool for resonance analysis on the meso level of social networks. A central objective of meso policies is the creation of internal and public relations of governmental and non-governmental actors in order to develop a functional differentiated social system (policy network). For this purpose the internet has become an indispensable tool. In developed democracies governmental institutions seem to maintain different public–private platforms for supporting public relations, information exchange and networks of excellence. There is no systematic overview on the variety of regional policy networks, but there seems to be an increasing ecological functional differentiation on the meso level, which is also reflected by increasing internet communication.

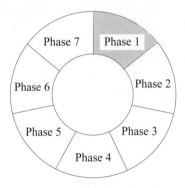

| Phase 1: problem analysis |
| Phase 2: target setting |
| Phase 3: development of options |
| Phase 4: choice of options |
| Phase 5: implementation |
| Phase 6: evaluation |
| Phase 7: optimization |

Figure 7.1   Policy Cycle (Clockwise Order of Phases)

Before stakeholders learned to use the internet for extensive electronic networking the research for collecting evidence for the functional differentiation according to the requirement of each environmental policy theme would have been done by interviews with governmental and non-governmental stakeholders and the screening of formal and informal publications (brochures, working papers and so on).

This would have been a laborious and time-consuming task. The evidence would often be incomplete or lagging behind the quick changes in formal and informal networking of stakeholders. In societies where the use of the electronic communication is advanced, internet search-engines can be very useful in detecting formal and informal networks. The validity of the information can be corroborated by interviews with stakeholders and governmental officials. So far, a distortion of information by the internet could not be detected.

Nevertheless, it needs to be considered that internet research also filters information, because it only allows consideration of information available on the internet. The research presented in this chapter supports the assumption that political networks or initiatives which do not use the internet do not meet sufficiently their function of public relations and networking, because the internet has become indispensable for these purposes. Therefore, we may say that networks which are not mentioned or represented on the internet can be regarded as being negligible.

The information on the internet is usually constantly updated. This is an important advantage of this source of information. The drawback is that information is often extremely volatile. Already during the research for the response analysis presented in this chapter (between December 2002 and May 2003) some of the content was removed from the internet or replaced. The volatility of this methodology reflects the changing reality that it wants to analyse: meso policies are usually complex processes of searching and learning. They are often influenced by spontaneously changing political notions, priorities and stakeholders. The analysis of resonance can therefore only reflect currents in society which can change, increase, decrease or disappear.

The amount of information found on the internet usually reflects the degree of differentiation. While information about complex policy objectives such as reduction of transport or waste volumes is present on numerous websites, much less information is available on relative specific policies such as the reduction of particle emissions.

This chapter will not allow analysing and explaining policy fields in great detail. Nevertheless, the suggested internet-based methodology will allow a sufficiently representative overview of the degree of differentiation in society concerning a specific political objective represented by an indicator. Therefore, the societal responses are not portrayed in total, but outlined according to their most important features in order to give an impression about the degree of regional functional differentiation.

7.6   THE CASE OF NORTH RHINE-WESTPHALIA

North Rhine-Westphalia (NRW) is situated in the Western part of Germany sharing borders with Belgium and the Netherlands. It has over 18 million inhabitants, generates about 22 per cent of Germany's gross domestic product and comprises a land area of 34,083 km² (13,158 square miles). In terms of population size and economic output the westernmost federal state of Germany (*land*) is comparable to Australia and thus larger than most EU Member States. Due to the large scale of the region, conclusions might not only be relevant for regional policy but also for national EPI.

The following sections describe the analysis of resonance in North Rhine-Westphalia with the EU structural indicators. This does not suggest that EU structural indicators are generally appropriate for controlling purposes in regional policy. We will present the examples of resonance with the indicator 'energy intensity' (Figure 7.2) and the indicator 'municipal waste volumes' (Figure 7.4). They represent two cases from both sides of the resonance scale. While regional resonance with the indicator 'energy intensity' is rather high, resonance with the indicator 'municipal waste volumes' is low.

7.6.1 Structural Indicator 'Energy Intensity'

Resonance in NRW
North Rhine-Westphalia is most important for German energy production. Almost 30 per cent of the electricity is produced in NRW. More than 80 per cent of the electricity production is based on lignite and pit coal. In its climate strategy the ministry of economy states that NRW is 'energy-oriented like no other region in Europe' (MWMEV, 2001, p. 16).

Consequently, there is an extraordinarily dense meso structure

> with a network of technology centres with transfer facilities to industry, economy and trade. The perception of energy technologies as technologies of the future is therefore a distinctive feature of the innovation profile, which is characterized by an adaptive energy policy.
>
> The technological and industrial aspect of energy policy in NRW is manifested among others by an increasing number of enterprises, which develop innovative technologies and components and services for innovative energy transformation and use. (MWMEV, 2001, p. 17)

Phase 1: Problem analysis
In NRW energy efficiency can be considered as being a broadly accepted objective among stakeholders of society, politics and economy. From an economic perspective an efficient use of energy makes sense. It is neither possible to identify the phase of problem analysis in space and time nor to connect it to a single institutional setting. Problem analysis for preparing the NRW policy of improving energy efficiency must therefore be interpreted as being implicit. Although the objective of increasing energy efficiency is broadly accepted in NRW, the setting of a quantitative target is debatable (for example increasing energy efficiency by Factor 4 according to Weizsäcker et al., 1995). In the European Union the rate of increasing energy efficiency is currently at 0.6 per cent per year. With the action plan for energy efficiency[2] the European Commission hopes to increase this rate to 1 per cent annually. Furthermore, the Commission has hoped to fully exploit the potential for saving energy which is estimated for 2018 at 18 per cent of the energy use of 1998.

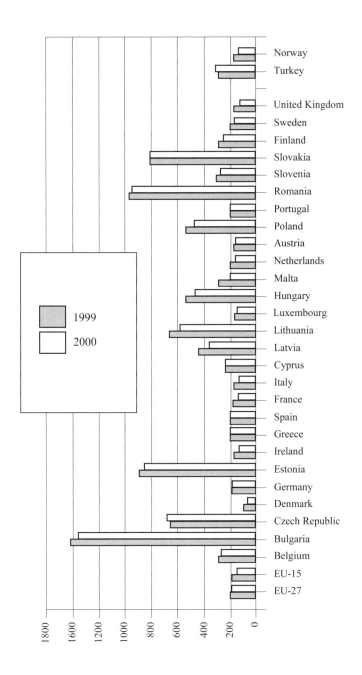

Figure 7.2   Structural Indicator Energy Intensity

In NRW there was no particular time during which a target for energy efficiency was set. Insofar as there was no target-setting there was consequently no optimization phase, which is usually coupled with a specific target (Figure 7.3). In spite of the missing target, Germany shows high ranking in the EU's spring reporting. This indicates that a non-quantified objective of using energy efficiently is effectively met. Again, it seems that improving energy efficiency is an implicit objective of the NRW government's energy policy.

Identified phases in the policy cycle. Phase 3: development of policy options; phase 4: choice of options; phase 5: implementation and phase 6: evaluation.
The rich meso structures of NRW produce continuously options for energy policy, which are selected, implemented and evaluated in market-related activities. In addition and connected to the market a number of governmental initiatives support – among other objectives – the improvement of energy efficiency of economic processes, for example:

- the so-called land initiative 'NRW future energies' (Landesinitiative Zukunftsenergien NRW);
- energy-related research and technological development;
- the programme 'rational use of energy and regenerative energy sources' (REN-Programme);
- the energy agency NRW;
- energy-related programmes of the consumer protection agency NRW,
- the efficiency agency NRW;
- the action programme 2000+ 'municipal framework energy in NRW', the initiatives Communal Label, KommEN;
- the energy saving directive;
- the campaign 'Climate protection in private households and offices';
- the agreement with the housing sector 'Coalition for climate protection';
- the power plant modernization programme NRW;
- the market place for absorption heat pumps NRW;
- the stakeholder network 'fuel cells'.

All these initiatives have in common that they contribute to decreasing the energy intensity of the NRW economy. They are often measures of research and technological development (RTD), of consultancy and of classical industry policy. Often RTD and consultancy is coupled with stakeholder networks. The initiatives cannot be portrayed in detail.

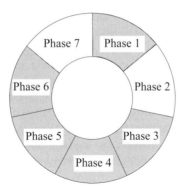

Phase 1: problem analysis
Phase 2: target setting
Phase 3: development of options
Phase 4: choice of options
Phase 5: implementation
Phase 6: evaluation
Phase 7: optimization

Figure 7.3   Resonance in NRW (in White the Phases not or Partially Identified)

Therefore, only a few of the most important elements, which are mutually supportive, will be mentioned in order to illustrate resonance of policy networks with the EU structural indicator 'energy intensity'. Even more regional energy-related activities can be found, if resonance with the related objective of CO_2 reduction is considered (Schepelmann, 2005).

Programme Rational Use of Energy (REN)
In 1987 the NRW government established the programme for the rational use of energy and use of renewables (Rationelle Energieverwendung und Nutzung unerschöpflicher Energiequellen, REN). The programme has an annual budget of about 50 million EUR. Since its creation more than 42,000 projects have been funded with about 435 million EUR. The objective is to

use potentials for industry, technology and energy production which are offered by a rational use of energy and renewable energies. This objective is met in cooperation with stakeholders from industry, science and public administrations.

The REN programme consists of a bundle of legislative measures, consulting and financial support actions. The activities include the support for research, development and technological demonstration projects as well as the removal of administrative hurdles. These activities are accompanied by public campaigns, for example, the campaign 'energy consultancy 2000+'. In this campaign different chapters of the consumer agency NRW offered energy consultancy on the rational use of energy to consumers.

Land initiative for future energies NRW (http://www.branchenatlas.nrw.de; http://www.energieland.nrw.de)

In 1996 the *land* initiative for future energies NRW (Landesinitiative Zukunftsenergien NRW) was founded primarily with financial support of the REN programme. The initiative is an exercise of horizontal policy integration in itself with participation from different ministries.

The activities ranged from applied research (supported by the Ministry for Education, Science and Research), technological development and demonstration (Ministry for the Economy, Energy and Transport) and introduction to the market (Ministry for Urban Construction and Living, Culture and Sports as well as the Ministry for Environment and Nature Protection, Agriculture and Consumer Protection). The initiative is a strategic platform for future energies, but also a forum for consultation, a framework for action as well as a clearing house for information, contacts and cooperation.

The *land*'s initiative is meant to accelerate innovation in NRW by mediating cooperation and strategic alliances as well as the introduction of new technologies, products and services nationally and internationally.The initiative tries to target the whole NRW meso landscape.

In particular, the following stakeholders are considered:

- Industry and SMEs, crafts and construction;
- Energy producers and plant construction companies;
- Research and science;
- Consultancy agencies and engineering offices;
- Building and construction management.

More than 3,000 experts are coordinated in working groups on the following subjects:

1. export and trade;	10. water energy;
2. building and construction;	11. hydrogen power;
3. biomass;	12. cogeneration;
4. solar thermal technology;	13. energy storage;
5. absorption heat pumps;	14. photovoltaics;
6. sectoral energy concepts;	15. geothermal energy;
7. fuel cells;	16. wind energy;
8. energy-related services;	17. power plant technology.
9. firedamp;	

Particularly innovative or significant projects have been further developed into so-called 'lead projects'. Criteria for their selection have been:

- Good prospects of technological or economic success,
- Benefits to the economy (investments, employment),
- Benefits in terms of saving energy, climate or environmental protection.

Lead projects according to these terms are, for example, a solar cell production site (Gelsenkirchen), an energy park (Mont Cenis in Herne), about 50 solar-powered settlements in NRW, the test field for inland wind energy generation (Grevenbroich), a number of wind energy plants, a fuel cell bus and the use of waste heat from an aluminium rolling mill for heating purposes of a settlement (Neuss).

Additional criteria have been developed for the building and construction sector. Here, companies are requested to develop holistic solutions for ecological construction. Integrated planning processes need to meet high standards for energy efficiency with the participation of the building's end-user. The design is considered as well.

The activities of the *land* initiative for future energies in NRW is accompanied by public relation activities. An annual conference of the land initiative provides information about the latest technological developments and the progress of the working groups. The *land* initiative is also represented at national and international fairs. Public relations are also supported by editing the NRW atlas for future energies with a corresponding database and a magazine.

Energy agency NRW (http://www.ea-nrw.de)
In 1990 the Ministry of Economy created the energy agency NRW. The agency is an information centre actively promoting and broking help for improving energy efficiency and the use of renewables.

The target group is primarily small and medium-sized enterprises.

Furthermore, the agency informs municipalities, engineers, architects, craftspeople, NGOs, the churches, parties and other associations. For industry and municipalities the agency is the contact point for all questions related to energy contracting.

7.6.2   Structural Indicator 'Municipal Waste Volumes'

The EU structural indicators targeting municipal waste management are pressure indicators on waste volumes. They indicate the pressure exerted on the environment by the mass of waste which is collected in a municipality, disposed of through landfill or incinerated. The unit is kilograms per capita and year. OECD and Eurostat define municipal waste as wastes which are collected by municipalities or on their behalf. About 70 per cent of municipal wastes originate from households

The collected household waste often includes wastes from shops, and private and public offices. The OECD and Eurostat classification of municipal wastes comprise paper, cardboard, paper products, plastics, glass, metal, organic wastes and textiles.

The EC Directive 2150/2002/EC will be the basis for harmonized waste statistics in the European Union. In 2003 the only German data available referred to 'generated municipal waste' and 'incinerated municipal waste' for the year 1998. German data of the category 'collected municipal waste' and 'municipal waste deposited through landfill' were not available for the EU spring report of 2003. Except for Greece and Sweden all other EU Member States were able to provide data at least for their collected wastes in 1999 (Figure 7.4). According to the structural indicators about 500 kg municipal wastes are collected per capita. Concerning deposition through landfill, only Germany and Greece were not able to produce 1999 data. The estimated average amount of deposited waste per capita in the EU is almost 300 kg. About 100 kg wastes per capita have been incinerated.

Resonance in NRW
Resonance in NRW with the indicators on municipal wastes is a special case (Figure 7.5), which sheds light on the considerable difficulties of governing material flows and waste streams.

Waste management is to a large extent the responsibility of the NRW municipalities. The *land*'s government is primarily monitoring municipal waste streams and their disposal by public and private companies. Although turnover and employment in this sector is considerable, the NRW government does not apply a sectoral policy comparable to the energy sector.

Nevertheless, NRW has developed policy approaches of resource management, which could contribute to a reduction of municipal wastes.

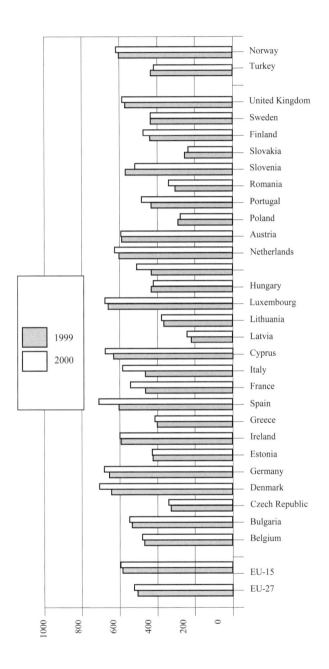

Figure 7.4   Structural Indicator 'Generated Municipal Waste'

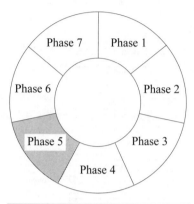

| Phase 1: problem analysis |
| Phase 2: target setting |
| Phase 3: development of options |
| Phase 4: choice of options |
| Phase 5: implementation |
| Phase 6: evaluation |
| Phase 7: optimization |

Source: http://www.bvse.de/home.html; http://europa.eu.int/comm/environment/natres/index.htm.

*Figure 7.5   Resonance in NRW with the Indicators on Municipal Wastes
(in White the Phases not or Partially Identified)*

The EU spring report 2003 did not quantify Germany's municipal waste
volumes, which meant that already the Eurostat yearbook on regional
statistics did not contain data about NRW municipalities. This is remarkable,
because there is data on all other NUTS 2 regions in the EU (Eurostat 2002).

Complete waste accounts in NRW were made in 1993 (LUA, 2000).
According to these statistics, about 6.4 million tons of an overall mass of
about 74 million tons originated from public waste treatment, the remaining
67.6 million tons from industry. According to the environment agency in
NRW the share of landfilled wastes from households decreased while the
share of recyclable material increased. This seems to be good news. A closer
look at the gross household waste volume in NRW (all wastes from

households) reveals a more differentiated situation. In 1997 there had been less waste to be disposed of than in 1994, but the sinking waste volumes resulted from increased recycling rates which grew during the same period from 2.2 million tons to 3.1 million tons. In total there was not a significant reduction of household wastes. If we assume that the indicator 'gross waste volume' is comparable to the Eurostat indicator 'collected municipal waste', then the NRW per capita generation of household waste varies in NRW municipalities between 400 and 500 kg per capita.

The importance of the NRW waste sector has been described by Landsberg (2001). Similar to the energy sector the waste sector has an outstanding position in Germany. Large German waste companies have their headquarters in NRW (for example Remondis, AGR, DSD). In 1996 almost 60 per cent of the turnover and employment of the NRW environmental sector was generated by the waste sector.

Altogether the structure of the waste sector is rather opaque, it is in a process of economic concentration and characterized by diverging interests. There is no 'land initiative waste' which could contribute to higher transparency. Scientific literature on the development and governance of the waste sector in NRW is rare.

According to the German constitution, the legislative competence on waste management is on the federal level. By issuing the circular economy legislation (Kreislaufwirtschaftsgesetz) the federal government shifted the emphasis of waste legislation from deposition towards recycling. In particular the recycling quotas for example for glass, aluminium and paper, proved that the legislation had an impact on consumption and production patterns in Germany. The federal legislation was complemented by legislation on the regional (*länder*) level. Since 1999 NRW has a new waste legislation that regulates the responsibility of public waste management especially in municipalities.

Also on the EU level there is development of relevant legislation, for example in the area of electronic wastes and integrated product policy (IPP). The Thematic Strategies on the Prevention and Recycling of Waste and the Sustainable Use of Natural Resources indicate an increasingly integrated view of material flows and waste management.

These concepts are based on the assumption that saving inputs will result in the overall efficiency of a productive system, which will ultimately result in smaller outputs. In contrast to that, increasing use of wastes by recycling and waste incineration could be counterproductive to input minimization strategies. This can happen if companies develop a commercial interest in using or treating (increasing) volumes of waste. In North Rhine Westphalia this seems to be the case.

In recent years cases of fraud and corruption indicate a significant need for regulation in the waste sector of NRW. The federal association for secondary raw materials and waste management (BVSE) published a press communiqué which used clear language on the waste management in NRW. The BVSE organises about 600 SME of the waste sector with an overall turnover of about 10 billion EUR and about 50,000 employees. About 130 of the SMEs are based in NRW. In a press statement dated 3 July 2002 the BVSE president, Hans Jürgen Cieron, contradicted a statement by former NRW Prime Minister Wolfgang Clement. After detention of a number of his social democratic party colleagues Clement said in a TV interview that he regarded the criminal actions in NRW as being common practice of the sector. Cieron commented that increased networking between municipal policy-makers and business would foster corruption. These networks would grow funded by BVSE's SME constituency and the tax payer. Already in an earlier press communiqué dated 20 June 2002 he stated that no other regional government in Germany would mix public with private interests as much as the NRW government.

After a number of scandals the NRW government set up the task force 'anti-corruption' for shedding light on the waste business in NRW. After a short period the final report of the task force was removed from the internet, due to legal pressure from the accused. The final report explains (Innenministerium NRW, 2003, p.17, own translation):

> In recent years the situation of the waste sector has changed considerably. At the beginning of the 1990s a waste management crisis was expected. Nowadays, significant over-capacities need to be acknowledged. Next to decreasing waste volumes the circular economy legislation is responsible. The changing conditions of waste legislation have contributed to a new situation; especially new structures for final disposal and responsibility have emerged. Until then, a public waste sector based on public interest had been protected with monopoly rights. Suddenly and for the first time in their history they were confronted with market competition and the resulting need for cost reductions.

According to the task force this changing situation gave rise to inscrutable public–private structures.

With the aim of governing these structures municipal representatives have been delegated into the controlling bodies of these new public–private companies, but according to the task force (Innenministerium NRW, 2003, p. 31):

> The lack of technical understanding of the municipal representatives was in stark contrast to the know-how of their private counterparts.

After a while the municipal waste management in NRW got out of control. Eventually, private interests partly dominated public interests, especially during preparations of tender procedures (Innenministerium NRW, 2003, p. 43):

> The revision of waste treatment during the 80s and beginning of the 90s required new concepts of waste incineration, re-use and disposal for meeting the political objectives of the municipalities. Since the necessary technical know-how was often not available in their administration, the municipalities adopted waste treatment concepts of their private counterparts. This created dependencies among administrations and political decision-makers, which raised significant doubts concerning their neutral position.

Altogether it seems that regional structures in NRW are hardly capable of resonating with the objectives of decreasing municipal waste volumes.

Especially in the municipalities there seem to be deficits among elected and official representatives to undertake a transparent and independent problem analysis, target setting, the development of options and a selection of measures. Consequently, there is no interest in an evaluation or an optimization of measures for effectively decreasing municipal waste volumes.

Implementation (http://www.munlv.nrw.de/sites/arbeitsbereiche/boden/ murlhtml/index_org.htm; http://www.efanrw.de; http://www.wupperinst. org/Projekte/Umwelt/u1.html; http://www.lua.nrw.de)
Even though other phases of the policy cycle are lacking, the NRW government promotes measures which could influence the volumes of municipal waste. As discussed above there is evidence that data on municipal waste volumes could not be provided for the EU spring reporting with EU structural indicators, since the NRW data was missing. This was also indicated by the lack of NRW data in the Eurostat yearbook on regional statistics (Eurostat, 2002).

Next to the unexplainable lack of NRW data, conventional waste management in NRW does not seem to resonate positively with the political aim of reducing municipal waste generation.

Neither waste treatment nor recycling industries have an interest in minimizing municipal waste streams. In any case, they could only contribute to this objective in a limited way as they are at the end of the product life. Resonance with indicators aiming at the reduction of municipal waste volumes can rather be expected in structures which have a broader material flow agenda.

According to Bringezu (2002) there are three intervention points for a material flow policy

1. Resource extraction and imports;
2. Consumption and production;
3. Waste management.

The EU addresses these three intervention points of material flow policy (input, consumption and production, output) with three connected strategies:

1. The Thematic Strategy for the Sustainable Use of Natural Resources (COM (2003) 572);
2. The Integrated Product Policy (COM (2003) 302);
3. The Thematic Strategy for Prevention and Recycling of Waste (COM (2003) 301).

Approaches of material flow policy developed in the 1990s (for an historical overview see Hinterberger and Schepelmann, 1998). Parts of it have been adopted by the European Commission with the Thematic Strategies of the 6th Environmental Action Programme.

For creating an appropriate data base for material flow accounting Eurostat has developed a methodological handbook (2001) for national statistical services. The central indicator for accounting direct material input (DMI) has been put on the list of sustainable development indicators for priority development.

Efficiency agency NRW (www.efanrw.de)
The efficiency agency (Effizienzagentur, Efa) is a central institution which contributes to decreasing waste volumes primarily by means of an integrated product policy (IPP).

The regional ministry for Environment, Nature Conservation, Agriculture and Consumer Protection (MUNLV) established Efa in 1998. Efa is a clearing house primarily for SME on all questions concerning IPP.

The agency explores opportunities for saving natural resources and offers counselling for realizing these (cost-) saving potentials by broking corresponding services and funding opportunities. In relation to the objective of reducing municipal waste volumes it needs to be stressed that the activities of Efa target primarily commercial wastes. Further reductions might be achieved by eco-efficient products.

In summary, we can conclude that the material-flow-related economic structures in NRW have evolved rather asymmetrically. While end-of-pipe waste management has a very large turnover and employs many people, the preventive policies targeting consumption and production patterns are still in their infancy.

7.7 RESONANCE ANALYSIS AND MODEL OF GOVERNANCE

The focus of this chapter has been the integration of ecological communication into EU Regional Policy, which represents a classical case of environmental policy integration (EPI). We have operationalized ecological communication by means of the environmental indicators of the EU structural indicators. Thus, we have described the integration of environmental indicators in the context of the social and economic development policies of the system which is commonly referred to as EU Regional Policy.

Systems theory suggests that policy integration is rather unlikely, because the 'mega trend' in society is functional differentiation rather than (policy) integration. The evolution of the political systems seems to correspond to this overall societal development. Thus the focus is on policy, but as a reflection of societal disintegration, that is functional differentiation.

The standard mode of operation of non-environmental policy systems seems to be a filtering of environmental information, because it is not relevant for their autopoiesis. In other words, the successful development of a non-environmental policy system usually does not require ecological communication. Even the opposite can be the case: conflicting environmental information can be interpreted as 'noise', which keeps the system from efficiently fulfilling its primary function. For example, a conventional transport policy will be disrupted by information which conflicts with traditional policy means of building infrastructure for fast (usually fossil-driven) locomotion. The central problem of EPI is that environmental information can get in the way of established policy systems. In this case environmental communication is 'noise' which needs to be reduced for the benefit of the primary function of a (non-environmental) policy system.

The concept of policy integration works against the general logic of functional differentiation of the political system. It often assumes the possibility of integrating antagonistic policy systems. The evidence presented in this chapter suggests that the system of EU Regional Policy can successfully integrate ecological communication. The integration of environmental objectives in EU Regional Policy is not complete or consistent, but it occurs to different degrees, depending on a number of circumstances which vary from case to case. This chapter has proposed criteria and a measure for analysing and comparing degrees of policy integration: for analysing the degree of EPI the chapter has introduced the concept of resonance. This concept is based on sociological systems theory which explains why in spite of the substantial growth of scientific knowledge about ecological risks it is more and more unlikely that society as a whole can control special interests that drive ecological self-destruction. Under certain circumstances environmental incidents can irritate and disrupt operations of social systems. If internal operations of a system become sufficiently distracted by 'noise' the system becomes more and more inefficient and starts to reorganize itself into being able to receive communication from its social environment. Niklas Luhmann (1990) describes the ability of a social system to receive impulses from the environment as resonance.

We have operationalized ecological communication by means of environmental indicators of the EU Structural Indicators. The measure for resonance has been operationalized by means of the policy cycle.

Thus, resonance (and EPI) can be corroborated if there is empirical evidence for one or several phases of the policy cycle corresponding to the political objectives, which are represented by an (environmental) indicator. The degree of resonance (EPI) corresponds to the number of phases realized within a political system. For example, a given environmental indicator can be CO_2 (equivalents). The political objective which is represented by this indicator is the reduction of greenhouse gas emissions. If a policy system is developing a climate protection strategy it can usually be shown that the system has undergone the phases of agenda as well as target setting and is now in the process of developing and choosing its options (for CO_2 reductions). The documentation of these activities in the context of the policy cycle is the empirical evidence for resonance.

The methodology of resonance analysis was tested in the framework of EU Regional Policy in the German region of North-Rhine Westphalia (NRW). The indicators represented seven different environmental policy target areas of the EU Structural Indicators. The overview in Figure 7.7 shows that resonance with environmental indicators in the NRW region has been varying. A complete policy cycle could only be established in the area of nature conservation. The resonance with all energy-related indicators (GHG-emissions, energy intensity, use of renewable energy) was also quite high. The lowest degree of resonance could be found in the environmental policy areas' reduction of waste and road traffic.

In the contemporary governance literature there is a tendency to categorize modes of governance. However, for interpreting the empirical evidence presented in this chapter, the added-value of the different categorizations of modes of governance is not clear yet.

Börzel (2006) sets out to identify new modes of European governance, which according to Börzel are not really new but different. They relate to the preparation and implementation of collectively binding decisions, which are 'non-hierarchically imposed' (Börzel, 2006, p. 4) and systematically involve private actors. According to Rosenau and Czempiel (1992 quoted in Börzel 2006) new governace is 'governance without government'.

The findings presented in this chapter do not support the hypothesis of emerging 'new' modes of governance. The case of the NRW energy sector rather supports the conclusion that formal and informal coexistence as well as mutual support of government and non-governmental stakeholders have a long tradition in NRW, especially in the energy sector.

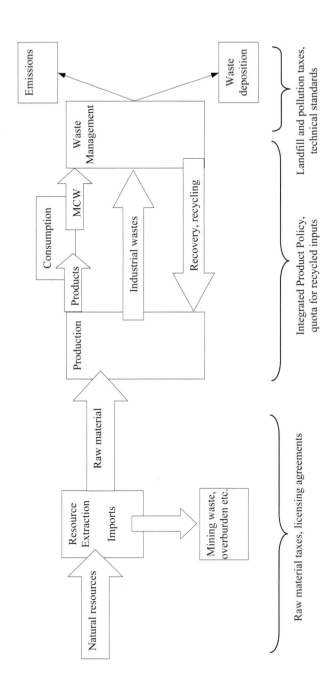

Source: Bringezu (2006)

Figure 7.6   Intervention Point of Resource Policy

Best practice of EPI in EU Regional Policy is certainly not 'governance without government', but a target-oriented organization of state and non-state actors organized by the government.

For explaining resonance and EPI in policy networks it does not seem to be important whether a specific mode is 'old' or 'new'. For organizing environmental policy integration the question is rather how competence and power for preparing and implementing policies is distributed among state and non-state actors and how competence and power relate to each other.

The comparison between the energy and waste sector suggests that target-oriented cooperation between state and non-state actors require time to develop into maturity in a more or less stable legislative and social framework. Obviously, the degree of maturity of these networks does not only depend on the region and its political system, but also on the policy area.

The distinction between prescriptive, communicative and competitive modes (Knill and Lenschow, 2005) would be misleading, if it would have suggested that social systems operate in one or the other mode. Indeed, these patterns are 'ideal-typical' (ibid. p. 114). It rather seems to be the case that a mix of all modes can be found in more or less all social systems.

Complex social systems without negotiation, competition or hierarchy can hardly be found or even conceptualized. The kind of mix seems to be different in the various policy fields. Their appropriateness can probably only be decided on the basis of a case by case analysis.

This also seems to be the case in the classification of Trieb et al. (2005): mixes of coercion, voluntarism, targeting and framework regulation have always been elements of more or less successful governance.

Eberlein and Newman's (2006) differentiation between regulatory, OMC, inter-or transgovernmentalism, market and incorporated transgovernmentalism address modes of governance between EU Member States. Although EU governance sets the framework for EU Regional Policy, it does not seem to influence the success of EPI to a relevant degree on the regional level.

Also the distinction of regulatory and redistributive modes of governance by Majone (1996) as well as Christensen and Laegreid (2006) is not really helpful in characterizing EPI in EU Regional Policy in NRW. A redistributive mode of governance relies on the state budget as a key instrument of policy making. In analogy, EU Regional Policy is mainly characterized by a distribution of Structural Funds. In contrast, the regulatory mode of governance is dominated by fact-based decision-making of more or less independent agencies and experts. In the case of NRW contrasting distributive against regulatory measures does not really make sense, because for promoting EPI distributive measures of allocation of EU Structural Funds is often used for building target-oriented stakeholder networks and agencies, which seem to belong to the regulatory domain of policy-making. Again, a mix of both policy modes can be noted.

Objective	Indicator	Policy cycle
Reducing greenhouse gas emissions	Greenhouse gas emissions (*pressure*)	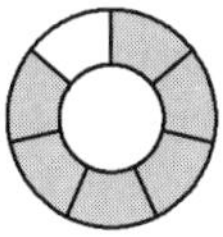
Reduction of energy intensity of economy	Energy consumption per GDP (*driving-force*)	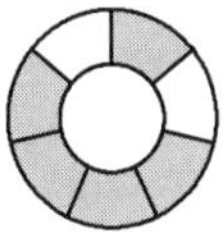
Reduction of traffic volume and share of road traffic	Goods and person transport volumes per GDP (*driving-force*) Share of road traffic in goods and person transport (*driving-force*)	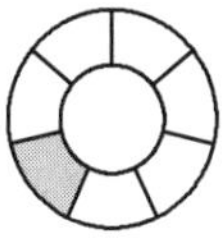
Improving urban air quality	Population exposure to air pollution by ozone and particles (PM 10) percentage of urban population exposed to concentration levels exceeding target values (*state*)	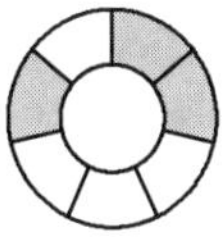
Reducing municipal waste	Municipal waste volumes per capita (*driving-force*)	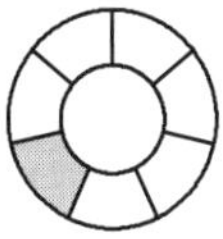
Increased use of renewable energy	Share of renewables in gross energy consumption (*response*)	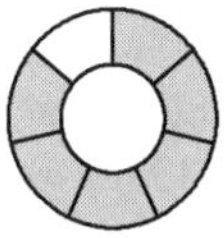
Nature conservation	Share of notified sites (habitat and bird directive) in total surface (*response*)	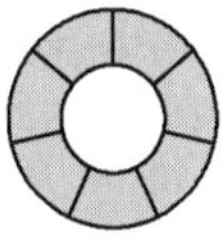

Figure 7.7   Resonance with Environmental Indicators in NRW

Kohler-Koch's (1999) distinction of networks, corporatism, pluralism and statism is also only helpful, if the mix and mutual interaction of the modes are considered. For explaining EPI in NRW, Kohler-Koch's theory could be used to describe how institutionalized and informal bargaining in networks is used to support or to obstruct pluralism and statism.

In relation to Hall's (Hall and Gignerich, 2004; Hall and Thelen, 2006) differentiation of liberal market economies and coordinated market economies, NRW has a clearly coordinated market economy usually described as 'Rhineland capitalism' ('Rheinischer Kapitalismus'). This model became the dominating form of capitalism in Germany after the Second World War. It is sufficiently described in literature (Windolf, 2002).

7.8   CONCLUSION

Understanding EPI in EU Regional Policy requires a precise description of multi-level governance. For example, one cannot explain the resonance of climate policy objectives with EU Regional Policy without an understanding of the vertical integration of climate policy from the international to the regional level. Resonance analysis of climate policy with EU Regional Policy helps to understand the vertical integration of policy including agenda-setting and implementation across the different levels of governance.

Can a description of the different modes of governance at different levels improve this description? On the one hand, it is obvious that EPI in EU Regional Policy requires a good understanding of the interaction between state and non-state actors. On the other hand, a clustering of this interaction in different 'modes' seems to have only limited added value. In the case of the distinction between 'old' and 'new' governance it seems to be counterfactual. It can also be misleading, if the distinction between 'new' and 'old' goes along with value judgements (for example 'new' = good, 'old' = bad).

At this point, most descriptions of governance modes are often too ideal, theoretical or simplistic in order to help distinguish the fine shades of modern governance. For example, definitions of 'new' governance (Börzel, 2006; Rhodes, 1996) usually suggest a modern style of policy-making in which non-governmental actors are involved in the formulation and implementation of polices. These definitions might not sufficiently explain the difference between a cooperative administration (Benz 1994) and corruption. EPI in EU Regional Policy involves decisions about capital-intensive infrastructure (for example in the areas of energy and waste management). Involving corporate non-state actors is not only useful but necessary, but where does participation end and where does manipulation and corruption of governance begin?

Policy-making in the EU is the subject of much debate. The discussions about the EU constitution and the outcomes of the referenda in France and the Netherlands as well as the general debate in some EU Member States suggest that EU governance is often seen as being non-transparent or even corrupt. The evidence collected by the 'Corporate Europe Observatory'[3] seems to support popular prejudice and perceptions. The lack of scientific consideration of the governance discourse in the general public is disturbing and might well be a development requiring careful analysis.

Particularly in transition economies the relations between state and non-state actors might not be mature and stable enough to guarantee environmental policy integration in EU Regional Policy and an efficient allocation of the considerable financial resources connected to it.

In contrast to the crisis of EU governance, EU Regional Policy has supported environmental policy integration in NRW climate and energy policy and other central policy domains. This positive influence is often underrated and deserves closer analysis and appreciation.

For supporting environmental policy integration the current governance discourse is not yet in a position to identify recommendable modes of governance. Instead of a theory-driven debate on good governance, it might be more appropriate to pay more attention to good and bad EPI practice on a case-by-case level. For this purpose the resonance analysis of policy systems with specific indicators has proven to be a fruitful approach. We have seen that different governance patterns emerge depending on the indicator and the corresponding regional policy networks. Case-specific analysis will allow targeted interventions in order to close the gaps in the policy cycle promoting EPI.

7.8.1   Policy Recommendations

EPIGOV sets out to improve environmental policy integration (EPI) at different levels of governance. It aims at identifying modes of governance that are particularly effective or promising. We have seen that in the framework of EU Regional Policy in North Rhine Westphalia (NRW) it is difficult to identify a dominant mode of governance. The examples of successful EPI in the objective 2 regions of NRW regularly show a continuous mix of different modes of governance.

The objective 2 programme is a multi-level governance scheme for subsidising structural interventions of governmental and non-governmental actors. EU Regional Policy sets the stage for cooperation of governments with non-governmental actors in different policy domains central for sustainable industry policy such as agriculture, energy, waste or transport. It is therefore an ideal object of study for the interaction of state and non-state actors in these policy domains.

We have proposed to shift the emphasis of research away from a discussion of rather ideal modes of governance which can in reality only be found in combination. Rather we are proposing an analysis of concrete EPI processes by means of resonance analysis.

This methodology has been introduced and exemplified in this chapter. It has strengths and limitations from which recommendations for future research directions can be derived. The strength of resonance analysis is that it builds on the distinct and consistent theoretical framework of sociological systems theory. Luhmann (1990) offers in his publication on ecological communication a model for understanding why it is so difficult to integrate environmental concerns in social systems. Based on his theory EPI can be defined as a communication problem and the creation of resonance as a solution to the problem.

With Luhmann's theoretical foundation resonance analysis offers a methodology to describe and measure targeted social responses to environmental problems with the policy cycle model. From the problem definition to implementation and evaluation seven phases of integrating environmental concerns in a policy area can be described. The combined analysis of each phase is a detailed description of the role of state and non-state actors in EPI.

In the successful cases of EPI the state defines an environmental problem and sets a political target. After that the regional government organizes participatory forums and agencies to involve relevant state and non-state actors. It is important to note that in these forums the state is rather a facilitator than a decision-maker, because expertise and other resources are to a large extent in the control of semi- or non-governmental actors.

Among the actors a rich variety from more or less state-dependent agencies and companies to representatives of independent corporate interests can be found. Selection, implementation and part of the evaluation of activities are therefore often non-governmentally driven. During the phase of programme evaluation and programming which is specific for EU Regional Policy the state dominates the final phase of a Structural Funds cycle and the preparation and launch of the next programme.

Resonance analysis reveals that successful environmental policy integration does not primarily depend on a specific governance mode, but that the dominance of state and non-state actors depends on a specific policy field and phase in the policy cycle. Resonance analysis allows comparing different policies for a targeted structural intervention.

A weakness of resonance analysis is that it is based on a radically reduced model of society. Sociological system theory reduces society to communication. Systems theory and the derived terminology such as coding, programming and selection is often difficult to grasp, therefore it does not meet general understanding and even less approval. Sociological systems theory is therefore not integrated in the mainstream governance theory and remains challenged, especially by actors-oriented theories. Although resonance analysis also integrates elements of actors-oriented theories, the dominating approach is systemic.

Another drawback of resonance analysis is that it describes and compares only the nature and maturity of political responses to environmental problems. It does not fully allow evaluating policies. Evaluation would require further normative standards, therefore resonance analysis does not allow judgement on the appropriateness of policies. After a resonance analysis it cannot always be said whether EPI delivers environmentally relevant outcomes, because only the necessary but not the sufficient conditions for EPI are analysed.

This means that EPI necessarily requires all phases of the policy cycle, but insufficient policies will result in insufficient outcomes, even if all phases of the policy cycle have been undergone. Another weakness of resonance analysis is that it allows only a phenomenological description of EPI; it can show the maturity of EPI efforts, but it does not explain why some EPI policies are stronger and more effective than others.

Nevertheless, resonance analysis allows telling and comparing the history of specific EPI processes. It allows naming (and shaming) of actors, coalitions and drivers of EPI. Most important, it allows detection of weaknesses and gaps in the policy cycle.

Thus resonance analysis can generate the necessary knowledge to improve targeted and indicator-based EPI processes.

NOTES

1. For example by developing their own functional output, media, programmes and 'languages' (codes).
2. COM (98) 246.
3. http://www.corporateeurope.org/index.html.

REFERENCES

Benz, A. (1994), *Kooperative Verwaltung. Funktionen, Voraussetzungen und Folgen.* Baden-Baden: Nomos.
Benz, A. and D. Fürst (2002), 'Policy learning in regional networks', *European Urban and Regional Studies*, **9**, 21–35.
Börzel, T. (2006), *New Modes of Governance and Enlargement. When Theory Meets Reality*, Interim Report, NEWGOV, New Modes of Governance, Berlin: Free University of Berlin http://www.eunewgov.org/database/DELIV/D12D04_ Interim_Report.pdf.

Bringezu, St. (2002), *Towards Sustainable Resource Management in the European Union*. Wuppertal Papers Nr. 121. Wuppertal: Wuppertal Institute for Climate, Environment, Energy.

Carley, M. and Ph. Spapens (1998), *Sharing the World*. London: Earthscan.

Christensen, T. and P. Lægreid (2005), *Regulatory Reforms and Agencification*, Stein Rokkan Centre for Social Studies, Universitetsforskning Bergen (UNIFOB AS), Working Paper 6–2005, November 2005. Bergen: Universitetsforskning Bergen.

Eberlein, B. and A. Newman (2009), 'Tackling the regulatory dilemma: The rise of incorporated transgovernmental networks', in: I. Tömmel and A. Verdung (eds), *Innovative Governance in the European Union: The Politics of Multilevel Policymaking*, Boulder, CO, USA: Lynne Rienner Publishers.

EEA, European Environment Agency (2001), *Late Lessons from Early Warnings: the Precautionary Principle 1896–2000*. Kopenhagen: European Environment Agency.

Eurostat (2001), *Economy-Wide Material Flow Accounts and Balances with Derived Resource Use Indicators. A methodological guide*. Luxemburg: Office for Official Publications of the European Communities.

Eurostat (2002), *Regionen – Statistisches Jahrbuch 2002*. Luxemburg: Office for Official Publications of the European Communities.

Esser, K., W. Hillebrand, D. Messner and J. Meyer-Stamer (1994), 'Systemische wettbewerbsfähigkeit: neue anforderungen an unternehmen und politik', *Vierteljahreshefte zur Wirtschaftsforschung*, **64**, 186–99.

Glasson, J. and J. Gosling (2001), 'SEA and regional planning – overcoming the institutional constraints: some lessons for the EU', *European Environment*, **11**, 89–102.

Hall, P.A. and Gignerich, W. (2004), *Varieties of Capitalism and Institutional Complementarities in the Macroeconomy. An Empirical Analysis*, Max-Planck-Institut für Gesellschaftsforschung Köln (MPIfG), Discussion Paper 04/5, Köln: Max-Planck-Institut für Gesellschaftsforschung.

Hall, P.A. and Thelen (2006), *Institutional Change in Varieties of Capitalism*, Paper prepared for presentation to the Europeanists Conference, Chicago, March 2006.

Hinterberger, F. and Ph. Schepelmann (1998), 'Resource Productivity and Eco-Efficiency', in FRN (ed.), *Framväxten av idéer om hallbar utvickling*. Stockholm: Forskningsradsnämnden, 42–62.

Innenministerium NRW (2003), *Untersuchungsstab Antikorruption 'Abschlussbericht'*. Düsseldorf: Innenministerium NRW.

Knill, Chr. and A. Lenschow (2005), 'Compliance, communication and competition: patterns of EU environmental policy making and their impact on policy convergence', *European Environment*, **15**, 114–28.

Kohler-Koch, B. (1999), 'The evolution and transformation of European governance', in: B. Kohler-Koch and R. Eising (eds), *The Transformation of Governance in the European Union*, London, UK: Routledge, pp. 14–35.

Kohler-Koch, B. and B. Rittberger, (2006), *The 'Governance' Turn in EU Studies*, ARENA, Centre for European Studies, University of Oslo, ARENA Seminar Tuesday 23 May 2006, Oslo: University of Oslo, www.arena.uio.no/events/seminarpapers/2006/KohlerKoch_May06.pdf.

Kraemer, A. (2001), *Results of the 'Cardiff Processes' – Assessing the State of Development and Charting the Way Ahead*. Study commissioned by the Federal Ministry for Environment, Nature Conservation and Reactor Safety. Berlin: Ecologic.

Krause, D. (2001), *Luhmann-Lexikon*. Stuttgart: UTB.

Landsberg, A. (2001), 'Nachhaltige Entwicklung und Umwelttechnologien in NRW und Schottland', in: Ministerium für Wirtschaft und Mittelstand, Energie und Verkehr des Landes Nordrhein-Westfalen, MWMEV (ed.), *Partner in der Strukturpolitik*, Düsseldorf: MWMEV.

LUA, Landesumweltamt NRW (2000) *Umwelt NRW. Daten und Fakten*. Düsseldorf: Landesumweltamt NRW.

Luhmann, H.-J. (2001), *Die Blindheit der Gesellschaft. Filter der Risikowahrnehmung*. München: Murmann.

Luhmann, N. (1981), *Politische Theorie im Wohlfahrtsstaat*. Analysen und Perspektiven, Bd. 8/9. München: Olzog.

Luhmann, N. (1989), Politische Steuerung: Ein Diskussionsbeitrag. *Politische Vierteljahresschrift*, **30**, 4–9.

Luhmann, N. (1990), *Ökologische Kommunikation*. Kann die moderne Gesellschaft sich auf ökologische Gefährdungen einstellen? Opladen: Westdeutscher Verlag.

Luhmann, N. (1994), 'Die Gesellschaft und ihre Organisationen', in H.-U. Derlien, U. Gerhardt and F.W. Scharpf (eds), *Systemrationalität und Partialinteresse*. Festschrift für Renate Mayntz. Baden-Baden: Nomos.

Majone, G. (1996), *Regulating Europe*, London, UK: Routledge.

Metzner, A. (1993), *Probleme sozio-ökologischer Systemtheorie*. Natur und Gesellschaft in der Soziologie Luhmanns. Opladen: Westdeutscher Verlag.

Meyer-Stamer, J. (2000), *Meso-Laboratorium Nordrhein-Westfalen*. Beobachtungen zur Struktur- und Standortpolitik in einer altindustriellen Region. INEF Report Nr. 47. Duisburg: INEF.

MUNLV, Ministerium für Umwelt- und Naturschutz, Landwirtschaft und Verbraucherschutz des Landes Nordrhein-Westfalen (2004b), *NRW 2015*. Ressourcen nutzen – Regionen stärken. Bericht des Zukunftsrates NRW. Düsseldorf: MUNLV.

MWMEV, Ministerium für Wirtschaft und Mittelstand, Energie und Verkehr des Landes Nordrhein-Westfalen, Hrg. (2001), *Handlungsfelder und Maßnahmen der Klimaschutzpolitik in Nordrhein-Westfalen*. Düsseldorf: MWMEV.

Rhodes, R.A.W. (1996), 'The new governance: governing without government', *Political Studies*, **44**(4), 652–667.

Rosenau, J. and E.O. Czempiel (1992), *Governance without Government. Order and Change in World Politics*. Cambridge, UK: Cambridge University Press.

Schepelmann, Ph. (2005), *Die ökologische Wende der EU-Regionalpolitik*. Die regionale Resonanz von umweltpolitischen Indikatoren des Lissabon-Prozesses der Europäischen Union. Hamburg: Dr. Kovac.

Schepelmann, Ph. (2000), *From Helsinki to Göthenburg*. Evaluation of environmental policy integration in the European Union. Study commissioned by the Federal Ministry for agriculture, forestry, environment and water. Sustainable Europe Research Institute (SERI), Vienna: SERI.

Schimank, U. (2000), *Theorien gesellschaftlicher Differenzierung*. Opladen: Westdeutscher Verlag.

Schmidt-Bleek, F. (1994), *Wieviel Umwelt braucht der Mensch?* MIPS – Das Maß für ökologisches Wirtschaften. Berlin: DTV.

Stichweh, R. (1979), 'Differenzierung der wissenschaft', *Zeitschrift für Soziologie*, **8**, 82–101.

Trieb, O., H. Bähr and G. Falkner (2005), 'Modes of Governance: A Note Towards Conceptual Clarification', *European Governance Papers (EUROGOV)* No. N-05-02, http://www.connex-network.org/eurogov/pdf/egpnewgov-N-05-02.pdf.

Valentin, A. and J. Spangenberg (2000), 'A guide to community sustainability indicators', *Environmental Impact Assessment Review*, **20**, 381–92.

von Weizsäcker, E. (1990), *Erdpolitik*. Darmstadt: Wissenschaftliche Buchgesellschaft.

von Weizsäcker, E. and A.B. Lovins (1998), *Factor Four*, London, UK: Earthscan.

Windolf, P. (2002), 'Die Zukunft des Rheinischen Kapitalismus', in: J. Allmendinger and Th. Hinz (eds), *Organisationssoziologie, KZfSS-Sonderheft 42*, Wiesbaden, pp. 414–42.

8. Environmental Policy Integration in the UK

Duncan Russel and Andrew Jordan

8.1 INTRODUCTION

The United Kingdom (UK) is widely regarded as having a very coordinated system of government, especially in relation to the management of foreign policy (Metcalfe, 1994: 285; Bulmer and Burch, 1998; Jordan, 2002a: 37). Its so-called 'Rolls-Royce' coordination system was created to ensure the constituent parts of government 'speak with one voice' (Bulmer and Burch, 1998; Jordan, 2002a: 37). More recently, under Tony Blair the UK has made a concentrated effort to pursue more joined-up government across a range of other cross-cutting issues, such as sustainable development, social exclusion, race and gender (Cabinet Office, 1999; Pollitt, 2003). The UK also has a long history of trying to achieve greater environmental coordination; it was actually one of the very first EU Member States to develop a national environmental policy integration (EPI) system (Jordan and Schout, 2006). Crucially, its pursuit of EPI significantly predates the EU's efforts and it has been a strong advocate of European level EPI within the various organs of the EU (Jordan, 2002a: 41). Additionally, the UK has been a leader in the development of different mechanisms to achieve greater coordination (for example environmental cabinet committees and policy appraisal).

Given this apparently supportive context, it is not entirely surprising that the Organisation for Economic Cooperation and Development (OECD) (2001, 2002) recently applauded the UK for its innovative approach to EPI. In this chapter, we try to arrive at a more detailed assessment of the UK's performance. Overall, we find that the implementation of EPI in the UK is far from perfect (see also Jordan (2002a) and Ross (2005)). Indeed, there seems to be a puzzling disparity between the UK's evident ability to act in an internally coordinated manner on general matters like foreign policy and on a more narrowly focused policy coordination challenge such as EPI.

The remainder of this chapter unfolds as follows. First, a historical overview is given, including a summary of the key factors that led to the adoption of EPI as a formal policy goal in the late 1980s. Then, we describe the main elements of the UK's EPI system and explore how well they have performed. The main theme of this section is that performance has failed to match initial expectations. Next, we discuss where the UK's EPI system might be breaking down and some of the potential reasons for this. Finally, we conclude by drawing some transferable lessons for other jurisdictions seeking to pursue EPI.

8.2   HISTORY

The evolution of the UK's EPI system can be broken down into three distinct periods. The first of these (1970–90) relates to the time when the environment was initially recognized in government as a distinct policy problem meriting a separate department to oversee it. Crucially, though, beyond the setting up of the Department of the Environment as the world's first such department, there were very few real attempts at EPI. The second period (1990–97) is marked by the Conservative's first attempt to establish a national EPI system within central government. Significantly, EPI was not established as a legal or constitutional principle but largely as an administrative process supported by guidance (for example DoE, 1991) and managed by the environment department. The primary focus was on integrating environmental considerations specifically into the policies of other sectors. Crucially, there were no set criteria for the level of integration to be achieved.

   The final period (1997–2005) saw the election of a Labour government and, under a more widespread programme for more concerted cross-cutting action across government, the strengthening of the UK's existing EPI tools and mechanisms, as well as the introduction of several new ones. Notably, a transition from EPI to something more akin to sustainability policy integration occurred during this period.

8.2.1   1970–90: National Environmental Policy in the Doldrums?

The UK government first gave the environment principled preference in the late 1960s at a time of heightened public concern (Osborn, 1997: 4). As a result, the Department of the Environment was born in 1970 (Painter, 1980). Its creation arguably represented the UK's first attempt to pursue environmental coordination, as it was essentially a 'super ministry' which housed the functions of the former Ministries of Housing and Local Government, Transport, and Public Buildings and Works (ibid.) under one roof. In the same year, the ruling Labour government produced the UK's first national environmental strategy in the form of a White Paper (Her Majesty's Government, 1970). Crucially, it made no mention of cross-governmental responsibility for the environment or to EPI, and generally generated very little attention within or outside government. The Labour Party was swept from power by the Conservatives later that year. In 1974 a significant piece of environmental legislation, the Control of Pollution Act, was produced (Osborn, 1997: 4). However, it was also more concerned with old-style environmental regulation than integration, and was never fully implemented (Jordan, 2002a).

In the late 1970s and early 1980s, the UK's progress on environmental policy largely stagnated (Rose, 1990; Jordan, 2002a: 43). By the 1980s, its record was so poor that it was dubbed 'the Dirty Man of Europe' by national and European environmental pressure groups (Rose, 1990). During the 1980s, pressure from the EU's environmental policies and high-profile environmental degradation, such as the destruction of the ozone layer and acid rain, once again led to increased public concern over the environment (Jordan, 2002a: 42). Against this background, and following the publication of the landmark Brundtland report on sustainable development, the Conservative government (now under Margaret Thatcher), rushed out a response entitled 'Sustaining Our Common Future' (DoE, 1989). This report sought to claim that the UK was already implementing sustainable development through its extensive body of environmental legislation. It summarily dismissed the need for changes to the machinery of government, arguing that 'the concept of collective responsibility[1] inherent in the British system of government' would suffice (DoE, 1989: 13).

8.2.2   1990–97: Environmental Policy under the Conservatives

Following her speech on the environment to the Royal Society in September 1988 and the unprecedented success of the Green party in the 1989 European elections (Osborn, 1997: 5), Thatcher sought to improve the UK's environmental relations with other European member states. She appointed the young, Europhilic, media-friendly MP, Chris Patten, to be her new environment minister (Jordan, 2002a: 44) and gave him the task of producing a new and much more comprehensive White Paper on the environment (DoE, 1990). In contrast to the government's previous stance on sustainable development and the environment, the new White Paper outlined a comprehensive cross-governmental approach, signed up to by all departments. It sought to re-orientate the machinery of government to 'integrate environmental concerns more effectively into all policy areas' as early in the decision-making process as possible (ibid.: 230). So was born the UK's – and, arguably, also the world's – first national EPI system.

Crucially, the UK system was primarily, although not exclusively, an administrative-orientated system, which was led by the Department of the Environment. Specifically, it harnessed existing coordination mechanisms to establish: an Environment Cabinet Committee (it was, in fact, an extension of the committee that had drawn up the White Paper) to pursue cross-departmental environmental coordination; an inter-ministerial network of Green Ministers to oversee the delivery of the White Paper within their respective departments; and a process through which the White Paper would be regularly reviewed and its targets revised. In addition, it announced a cross-sectoral procedure for conducting *ex-ante* environmental policy appraisal (EPAs) to assess the potential impacts of different policy options. EPA was supported by guidance published by the Department of the Environment (DoE, 1991).

Furthermore, the White Paper also contained a whole annex on green budgeting. Subsequently, on top of the existing differential on unleaded petrol (established in 1987, which set the duty on leaded petrol at a higher rate), the Conservatives introduced three revenue-raising, market-based instruments aiming at better internalizing environmental costs: a landfill tax in 1996; a fuel duty escalator of gradual annual increases in VAT on vehicle fuel in 1993; and indirect tax on domestic fuel in 1993 (Helm, 1998: 11; Jordan et al., 2003: 187). In 1994 the Conservative government also produced a sustainable development strategy (Her Majesty's Government, 1994), making the UK one of the first countries to do so following the 1992 United Nations-sponsored Rio summit (Sustainable Development Commission, 2004: 9). Notably, the commitment to EPI in the White Paper was not particularly forceful, with a preference for guidelines rather than a rigid set of rules to be followed in all cases (DoE, 1990: 231) or a legally binding principal.

Why, though, did the UK choose this particular approach to EPI? There are arguably several reasons. First, the UK has a tendency to deal with environmental policy problems by changing its machinery of government (Weale et al., 2000: 176). Second, as mentioned above, UK central government already had strong coordination mechanisms for policies connected to international and EU affairs (Bulmer and Burch, 1998: 48). Thus, the 1990 White Paper arguably sought to build in a more explicit environmental dimension into the government's work. Third, the policy style of pollution control in the UK had traditionally evolved around the principle of cooperation and discretion in the setting and application of standards. This tacit and informal way in which policy has traditionally been made in the UK has been described as an example of 'club government' (Weale et al., 2000: 181). As such, it was potentially easier for the UK to tweak the machinery of government, rather than impose tighter environmental standards and planning targets on business. Crucially, it also did not disturb the policy status quo or the working practices of the various sector departments. Finally, the content of the 1990 White Paper also reflected the strong input of Patten's external advisors, such as David Pearce, who was a strong advocate of cost–benefit analysis and market-based environmental instruments.

8.2.3   1997–2007: Environmental Policy under Labour

Shortly after being elected in 1997, Tony Blair pledged at a high-profile United Nations (UN) conference (Rio+5) to 'make the process of government green'. He added that:

> The environment must be integrated into all our decisions, regardless of sector. [It] must be in at the start, not bolted on later.

This commitment was very much in line with his government's demand for more joined-up and evidence-based policy making (Pollitt, 2003; Cabinet Office, 1999). It can also be seen as a continuation of efforts that he made while in opposition, to court the green vote. Under Blair's leadership, the new Labour administration injected fresh impetus into the UK's EPI system by significantly strengthening the existing tools and mechanisms and adding new ones (Jordan, 2002a). For instance, the political profile of the Environment Cabinet Committee was augmented by placing it under the chairmanship of the Deputy Prime Minister (Jordan, 2002a: 47). In 2005, it was given added clout by the addition of energy to its brief; even more importantly, the chair was taken over by the Prime Minister (EAC HC 698, session 2006–2006, para. 17). Moreover, the status of the Green Ministers' network was raised by making it a sub-committee of the Environment Cabinet Committee (Ross, 2005: 29). It was also given responsibility for producing an annual report on the progress made by government departments on EPI and sustainable development. These reports have tended to be rather anodyne accounts of the progress made, but some difficulties have been explicitly acknowledged, notably with respect to policy appraisal (see below) (Green Ministers' Committee, 2001: para. 3.7).

One of Labour's first acts in power was to combine the environment and transport departments into one super-ministry, called the Department for the Environment, Transport and Regions (DETR). In 2001, this was changed again, when transport was hived off and agriculture, fisheries and food was added. This new department was named the Department of the Environment, Food and Rural Affairs (DEFRA), and, like its predecessors, is primarily responsible for leading the UK's EPI system. In addition, a special cross-departmental integration unit, the Sustainable Development Unit (SDU), was established within the DETR (later housed in DEFRA) to support the Green Ministers, to promote best practice and report on progress made by other departments (Jordan, 2002a: 46; Ross, 2005: 29).

The Labour government also founded two independent bodies to examine EPI and sustainability in the UK, namely: a Parliamentary Environmental Audit Committee (EAC) and a Sustainable Development Commission (SDC) to act as an independent advisory body to the government and the devolved assemblies on sustainable development. The EAC was established in the House of Commons towards the end of 1997 (ENDS, 271: 3–4). Its principal task is to scrutinize and report on how EPI and sustainable development is implemented across government (Jordan, 2002a: 46; Ross, 2005: 38). Over time, the EAC has increasingly received more assistance from the far better resourced National Audit Office.[2] The SDC was established in 2000 and currently comprises 14 commissioners. In the 2005 Sustainable Development Strategy (Her Majesty's Government, 2005: 154), the Commission was given a stronger watchdog role, which involves monitoring the government's progress on sustainable development. Moreover, in 2005 responsibility for producing the annual reports on the progress made by government departments on EPI and sustainable development was removed from the Green Ministers and handed to the Commission (ENDS, 372: 8).

Procedures for policy appraisal were initially strengthened by Labour, through the issuing new supplementary guidance on EPA best practice by the DETR (1998). However, more recently, EPA was dropped in favour of a more integrated form of appraisal known as RIA. This is akin to sustainability appraisal and, unlike the rest of the UK EPI system, is managed by the Cabinet Office.[3] In addition, strategic environmental assessment (SEA) is also in the process of being rolled out for regional and local-level programmes and plans in line with an EU Directive.

One of the central elements of Labour's more purposeful and integrated approach was publication of a new sustainable development strategy in 1999 (Her Majesty's Government, 1999). The strategy essentially detailed priorities for a more sustainable future, including reducing social exclusion and improving energy efficiency, and so on. It was supported by the publication of 15 headline indicators to measure progress on sustainability (Jordan, 2002a: 47). The strategy was recently updated in 2005, promising a more robust departmental reporting system, a more explicit focus on sustainable consumption issues and climate change, and so on (Her Majesty's Government, 2005). The UK's sustainable development indicators were also expanded to cover 68 areas.

Labour's application of green budgeting can essentially be broken down into two areas. First, on the revenue side it involved expanding the range of market-based environmental instruments introduced by the Conservatives.

Labour added a vehicle excise escalator in 1999, which placed lower taxes on smaller cars and lorries, and an aggregates tax in 2002 (Jordan, et al., 2003: 187–9). In 2001 the unleaded petrol differential was replaced with a ban on leaded petrol. Second, to improve the strategic planning of expenditure priorities, a two-yearly cross-departmental spending review was introduced in which all departments have to bid to the Treasury for their upcoming spending allocations (Russel, 2005: Ch. 6). Essentially, it aims to align future spending programmes with the government's core priorities (EAC HC 92, session 1998–1999, para. 2). As part of the process, the Treasury agrees Public Service Agreements (PSAs) with each department, which stipulate specific policy targets[4] (Russel, 2005).

While the spending review is not specifically an EPI mechanism, it has been partially used to foster cross-cutting consideration of sustainable development issues. For instance, in the 1998 and 2000 reviews the Deputy Prime Minister and the Treasury asked departments to consider sustainable development in their spending plans (EAC HC 92, session 1998–1999, para. 11; HC 70, session 2000–2001, appendix). In the 2002 and 2004 reviews, a more systematic sustainable development reporting process was introduced to support each department's bid (Russel, 2005: Ch. 6). Moreover, Public Service Agreements are mentioned in the latest Sustainable Development Strategy (Her Majesty's Government, 2005: 165) as a possible means to enforce the government sustainability commitments.

Overall, EPI under Labour has gradually evolved to be something more holistic and akin sustainable development policy integration. In 2002 the government claimed the change 'signal[ed] the government's commitment to practice what [it] preach[es] by considering the full range of economic, environmental and social impacts of the government estate and [the] policy making process' (Green Ministers, 2002: 5). This re-orientation is very much reflected in the gradual addition of more sustainability-oriented elements to the UK's EPI system, for example the Sustainable Development Unit, the UK Sustainable Development Strategy and sustainable development indicators. More recently (in 2002), the government has refocused the EPI reporting process towards sustainable development in government, and (in 2005) re-branded the Green Ministers as Sustainable Development Ministers (EAC HC 698, session 2006–2006, para. 17).

8.2.4   The UK's System and Modes of Governance

So, in all, the UK appears to have adopted a blend of governance modes in its EPI system, which can be broadly categorized under Knill and Lenschow's

(2005) typology of hierarchy, competition and communication. It might be argued that the primary thrust of the UK's approach to EPI is geared towards more hierarchical forms of governance as represented by the Environment Cabinet Committee, the Green Ministers, the Sustainable Development Unit, and the integration of sustainable development into the Treasury's spending review process. All of these, to varying degrees, seek to manage environmental coordination and minimize the degree of discretion sectors have. That said, the UK's green revenue-raising initiatives (for example the fuel duty escalator) are probably more akin to competition, as they seek to integrate the environment into targeted areas of the market. Furthermore, other parts of the UK's EPI system best fit with the communication mode of governance, as they seek to bring stakeholders together and/or facilitate learning. For instance: the application of policy appraisal to sectoral policies is supposed to generate information on environment-related policy spillovers for stakeholders to coordinate around; the SDC and the EAC both provide a forum for non-governmental groups (for example experts, businesses, non-governmental organizations) to comment on the UK's performance on EPI; and the Sustainable Development Strategy allows for sectoral learning through reporting against the sustainable development indicators.

8.3   EPI IN PRACTICE

This short historical overview suggests that, at least on paper, the UK's EPI system is indeed innovative. The UK certainly possesses many more EPI tools, mechanisms and processes than most other member states. But, how well have these different elements been implemented? And how well have they complemented one another?

8.3.1   Administrative and Bureaucratic Tools

As indicated above, the UK's earliest attempt at environmental coordination was to combine three existing departments to create a super-ministry – the Department of the Environment – in 1970. More recently, Labour demonstrated a similar if not stronger appetite for administrative reform. However, their longevity and impact have been quite limited. The original Department of the Environment was downsized after only six years in 1976, when transport was hived off. One senior official remembers it being far too unwieldy (Osborn 1997: 4). More recently, Labour's Department of the Environment, Transport and Regions was reformed after just four years (see above). The reasons for its dismemberment arguably have more to do with getting to grips with the 2001 foot and mouth crisis than EPI or sustainability.

According to the EAC, however, this reorganization had a negative impact on the UK's pursuit of sustainable development. It absorbed huge amounts of administrative time, undid a great deal of work that had been done at the interface of environment and transport, and distracted ministers and senior officials from longer-term initiatives like EPI (HC 624-I, session 2003–2004, para. 84). Both the EAC and the SDC voiced their concern about the loss of transport and local planning responsibilities, as these are two crucial aspects of the sustainable development *problematique* (HC 624-I, session 2003–2004, para. 84; Sustainable Development Commission, 2004: 20).

The performance of the Environment Cabinet Committee under both the Conservatives (1990–97) and Labour (1997–2005) has also been strongly criticized, although examining its real impact is made difficult by the cloak of secrecy that envelops its work (HC 426-I, session 1998–1999, para. 10; Ross, 2005: 36). Under the Conservatives, it was criticized for not showing adequate leadership: it met infrequently and only ever in secret (Jordan, 2002). The majority of its time was devoted to resolving major policy clashes or failures (ENDS, 200: 15–17). Moreover, most of its work was done by bilateral negotiations with departments or by correspondence, rather than in face-to face meetings (ibid.). Similarly, under Labour, the Environment Cabinet Committee displayed very little extra leadership. Critics suggest that it met too infrequently to drive the government's pursuit of sustainable development. It was simply not proactive enough in unearthing and dealing with policy conflicts (EAC HC 426-I, session 1998–1999, para. 10; Jordan 2002a).

It is reported that under the Conservatives the political profile of the Green Ministers in Whitehall was low (Jordan, 2002a: 44): they only ever met seven times; even then, many Green Ministers failed to attend, sending lower level deputies instead (CPRE, 1996). Furthermore, the meetings of the Green Ministers tended to focus on green house-keeping rather than substantive policy concerns (ENDS, 246: 26–27; CPRE, 1996: 1; Jordan, 2002a: 44). Under Labour, though, the Green Ministers have taken a more dominant role. For example, they have produced annual reports on EPI and, more lately, sustainable development. In a sense, they have grown into the focal point role that the Conservative administration had in mind for them. The turnout, focus and frequency of the first meetings under the Labour administration appeared much better than under the Conservatives. For instance, in their first meeting 15 out of 19 members attended and the agenda was purposely focused on policy rather than house-keeping issues like office paper recycling (ENDS, 274: 33). Moreover, its improved status as a sub-committee of the Environment Cabinet Committee gives it a 'clear remit to tackle key cross-government sustainable development issues from both a policy and operations perspective and deliver greater progress' (Green Ministers'

Committee, 2001: para. 7.7). However, assessing its performance has become harder as, in its changed state, its operations are governed by the doctrine of Cabinet secrecy (EAC HC 961, session 2002–2003, para. 72).

The SDU has been criticized by the EAC and some academics with regard to its role, status and position in Whitehall (HC 426-I, session 1998–1999; Jordan 2002a: 48; Ross 2005: 39). Concerns have been expressed about its location in DEFRA, which is seen as too peripheral (ENDS, 294: 33–34; Jordan, 2002a: 48; Ross, 2005: 39). Instead, a more appropriate home might be in the Cabinet Office, where Labour originally promised to place it when in opposition (Labour Party, 1994). The Cabinet Office has much more central authority and a remit covering strategic coordination issues (Jordan, 2002a: 48; Ross, 2005: 39). The SDU's work is also potentially undermined by the more high-profile Social Exclusion and Performance and Innovation Units in the Cabinet Office, both of which deal with sustainability related issues (Ross, 2005: 40).

Since their creation, both the EAC and the SDC have actively reported on the UK's progress. According to Ross (2005: 38), many of the EAC's recommendations have been accepted by the government. A recent report by the SDC argues that 'it is evolving into a more effective organisation after a slowish start and now has a significant impact at many levels' (Plowman, 2004: para. 28). Be that as it may, both bodies have helped to open up the working of government to greater scrutiny and external evaluation.

8.3.2   Green Budgeting

On the revenue-raising side of green budgeting, the Conservatives' attempts to use environmentally-orientated market instruments were very fitful. Problems arose when the level of indirect tax on domestic fuel was doubled to 17.5 per cent. This sparked fears about fuel poverty and the government was forced into an embarrassing climb-down (Jordan et al., 2003: 187). Questions have also been asked about the environmental credentials of the fuel duty escalator, with critics suggesting that it was more of a revenue earner than an environmental tax (Helm, 1998: 11).

As discussed above, the Labour administration under Blair have sought to extend the income revenues derived from the environmentally-targeted taxes established by the Conservatives. However, in an attempt to placate fuel tax protesters, the fuel duty escalator was spectacularly suspended in 2002 (Jordan et al., 2003: 187) due to high oil prices. Since then, Labour has been much more wary about introducing new environmental taxes. Crucially, the EAC has frequently noted that very few of the UK's budgetary measures have been independently appraised, making it difficult to establish whether they have been environmentally successful or not (for example HC 547, session 1997–1998; HC 71-I, session 2001–2002; HC 216, session 2004–2005). Overall, the SDC (2004: 21) claimed that the use of environmental taxation is one area where 'the government has clearly failed to put the environment into the heart of government'.

In relation to spending, Labour has been seemingly more innovative in its attempts to integrate the environment and sustainable development considerations into strategic planning. That said, the actual performance of its spending review process in this respect does not appear to have been an overwhelming success. Reports suggest that the 1998 and 2000 spending reviews showed no evidence of the environment or sustainable development being integrated into departmental spending plans (EAC HC 92, session 1998–1999, para. 28; Russel, 2005). Even when departments were required to produce a sustainable development report (as in the 2002 review), their quality was poor (many seemed to have been written long after the spending priorities had been decided) (Russel, 2005: Ch. 6). Moreover, thereafter the requirement to conduct separate reports for the next (2004) review was downgraded to a voluntary activity; the Treasury argued that sustainable development considerations should be integrated into individual departments' submissions. The EAC has criticized the paucity of environment targets in the PSAs produced by the 2002 and 2004 reviews (HC 261, session 2004–2005: 33–6). For instance, in the 2004 review, only ten out of 124 departmental targets were environmental, of which six were set by or with DEFRA (ibid.). Although each PSA normally states who is responsible for the delivery of individual targets (James, 2004), they are framed in such general terms that they are effectively little more than mission statements.

8.3.3 Strategies And/Or Strategy Developing Processes

While the profile of the Conservative's sustainable development strategy seems to be relatively low, it did, however, provide 'a framework for shaping some of the first moves towards sustainability up to 1997' (Sustainable Development Commission, 2004: 9). Labour's 1999 Strategy (Her Majesty's Government, 1999) was supposed to be more wide ranging than its predecessor (Sustainable Development Commission, 2004: 9). However, while acknowledging that the strategy had positive elements, the EAC (HC 624-I, session 2002–2003) argued that it 'had not driven environmental progress [as was] originally envisaged' (para. 44); 'traditional socio-economic concerns still largely dominate[d] policy making' (para. 40). Both the EAC and the SDC have acknowledged that the development of sustainable development indicators has been a significant step forward in the UK's pursuit of sustainable development. However, the SDC claimed they failed to provide a sufficiently broad indication of the UK's performance

(EAC HC 624-I, session 2003–2004, para. 69). It is too early to comment on the 2005 Sustainable Development Strategy and its expanded set of indicators. However, the SDC regards them as an improvement on what had gone before them (Sustainable Development Commission, 2005: 1).

8.3.4   Policy Appraisal System

Overall, it appears that the use of appraisal and particularly environmental policy appraisal has been rather limited and generally of poor quality. Under the Conservatives, analysis of parliamentary questions revealed that, when asked by MPs, no department could provide any evidence that it was actively using the guidance on environmental policy appraisal (Young, 2000: 252). In 1997, a Department of the Environment-commissioned report into the use of EPA was published, which concluded that there was room for a 'more comprehensive systematic consideration of the environmental impacts of policy' (DETR, 1997: 32).

Labour's performance on EPA has also fallen short of what it promised (DETR, 1998), with even the Green Ministers (2001: para. 3.7) admitting that the overall performance was 'somewhat disappointing'. Russel and Jordan (2007: 9) were only able to uncover 65 published EPAs for the period 1997–2003, 47 of which had been conducted by DEFRA or the Department for Transport. Not only did the output of EPAs appear to be limited, but there were also questions raised over their quality. For instance, the EAC has noted that they 'varied greatly in their coverage of environmental issues' (HC 426-I, session 1998–1999, paras 47–48), while Russel and Jordan (2007: 10) found that very few fulfilled all nine best practice criteria (DETR, 1998) inherited by DEFRA. The majority appeared to be simplistic *ex-post* assessments to 'green proof' unsustainable policies (Russel and Jordan, 2007: 10–11). Therefore the pattern of EPA production appeared to be very sectorized, and not as strategic or cross-cutting as one would expect of an EPI initiative.

Given this apparent failure of EPA to make significant inroads into departments' policy-making processes, it is perhaps not surprising that stand-alone EPAs were recently discontinued in favour of more integrated RIAs. However, far from improving the situation, this move might well marginalize environmental issues further, as RIA has traditionally concentrated on reducing regulatory burdens on business. Indeed, the EAC has been so concerned about this that they recently recommended that the government 'considers restructuring the present RIA procedures by inserting a new higher tier... [to] separately identify economic, environmental and social impacts' (HC 261, session 2004–2005, para. 55). In response, the government promised that the National Audit Office would examine RIAs for their coverage of sustainable development issues (Her Majesty's Government, 2005: 155). In their first report on this issue, the National Audit Office (2006) found the coverage of sustainability issues in the RIAs that it sampled to be limited which seemingly adds weight to the aforementioned the fears that more integrated RIA may not pick up environmental issues.

8.3.5 Strategic Environmental Assessment

The UK's opposition to SEA at policy level is longstanding. It opposed the European Commission's initial attempts to make extend the EIA Directive to policies (Jordan, 2002b: 185). As a result of UK efforts, the SEA Directive is squarely aimed at plans and programmes. The UK does not advocate the use of SEA in its policy appraisal guidance (for example DETR, 1998). Nonetheless, the UK has conducted at least one SEA at policy level: the Ministry of Defence's Strategic Defence Review which may well be one of the most comprehensive EPAs conducted under the Labour administration (Russel, 2005: 163).

8.4   SUMMARY DISCUSSION

Overall, the UK has innovated, has been a pathfinder and has an extensive and growing toolbox of mechanisms. Despite this, however, the evidence presented suggests that it has not been uniformly effective. Indeed, some of the elements have been spectacularly ineffective and some have been very weakly implemented. Moreover, even though it has been in existence for 15 years, the UK's EPI system appears to have not significantly improved the state of the UK's environment. For instance, in a recent environmental performance review on the UK, the OECD (2002: 19) remarked:

> there is considerable margin for further environmental progress, as the UK…has not yet achieved a number of its environmental objectives and still presents an deficit of environmental infrastructure (e.g. waste and waste water treatment infrastructure).

Having said this, though, there are some recent developments that might improve the UK's performance in the future. For instance, there appears to be more central leadership, manifest by the Prime Minister's decision to chair the Environment Cabinet Committee and the Cabinet Office's supervision of integrated RIA. Moreover, there have been other positive developments such as the 2005 Sustainable Development Strategy (see above) and the 2003 Energy White Paper (DTI, 2003), which had a strong environmental component. Aside from these developments, the UK government undoubtedly has failed to 'to grasp the over-arching nature of sustainable development' (HC 517-I, Session 1997–1998, para. 1). As the SDC comments, the EPI 'machinery and … instruments, although desirable in themselves, have not yet been used consistently across [central departments] and not vigorously enough to deliver rapid enough change [for sustainable development]'. This section goes on to explore some of the possible reasons for this state of affairs. The UK's EPI system appears to command support at the highest political levels. Indeed, Tony Blair made three major environmental speeches during his tenure as Prime Minister, in which he has stressed the importance of placing the environment at the heart of policy making. But why does the UK's EPI system appear to be breaking down?

Table 8.1   The Metcalfe Scale of Coordination

Level 1
Independence: each department retains autonomy within its own policy area irrespective of spillover effect on associated departments/areas.
Level 2
Communication: departments inform one another of activities in their areas via accepted channels of communication.
Level 3
Consultation: departments consult one another in the process of formulating their own policies to avoid overlaps and inconsistencies.
Level 4
Avoiding divergence in policy: departments actively seek to ensure their policies converge.
Level 5
Seeking consensus: departments move beyond simply hiding differences and avoiding overlaps/spillovers to work together constructively through joint committees and teams.
Level 6
Conciliation: neutral (possibly central) bodies are brought in or are imposed upon conflicting departments to act as mediatory body. The onus, though, is still on the ministries to reach agreement between themselves.
Level 7
Arbitration: sometimes disagreement and conflict are too strong for voluntary approaches to overcome; therefore, the central or neutral actor plays a stronger role.
Level 8
Setting common parameters: parameters are predefined which demarcate what departments can and cannot do in their own policy making arenas.

According to Schout and Jordan (2005: 215), a good flow of information between departments within the course of daily policy making is an essential condition for EPI. One reason why the administrative and bureaucratic elements of the UK's EPI system may be struggling to make an impact is that they do not appear to have enough information on potential environmental spillovers to chew on. One might argue that this lack of supply has a lot to do with the poor implementation of policy appraisal

One way in which to elaborate this point is to use the Metcalfe scale of coordination (Table 8.1). Essentially, his scale can be seen as 'a flight of steps in which qualitatively different components of coordination are added from the bottom-up' (Metcalfe, 1994: 281), that is it conceptualizes coordination as a *cumulative* process. Consequently, the mechanisms for higher levels of coordination require the existence and proper functioning of the lower ones (ibid.). With regard to the UK's EPI system, level one could be represented by a situation in which all departments accept some responsibility for environment (see above). Levels two to three relate to a situation in which the production of policy appraisals, or sustainable development reports in the spending reviews, provide data on policy spillovers that can be shared between cognate and central departments. However, given the poor implementation of EPA and the sustainable development reports in the spending review process, coordination all too easily breaks down at level three. Consequently, the higher level coordination bodies such as the Sustainable Development Unit (levels three to four), the Green Ministers' Committee (levels five to six), the Environment Cabinet Committee (levels six to seven) and, in the case of the spending reviews, the Treasury (Levels four to seven) have little information to work with. Indeed, the Environment Cabinet Committee's main task is to resolve interdepartmental conflicts, but with no information on policy spillovers it seems to be starved of work.

Overall, therefore, the UK's use of grand, sustainable development strategies or the setting sustainable development related PSAs (level nine) is arguably not satisfactorily supported by the lower level mechanisms. Moreover, the higher level committees do not appear to be proactively putting political pressure on the lower levels to raise conflicts to their attention. Consequently, cross-sectoral coordination simply does not get going. Of course the problem is more complex than simply failure to communicate information on environmentally related spillovers. For instance, why has the demand for such information at the top of the UK government failed to trickle down and stimulate greater cross-sectoral communication?

Aside from former Prime Minister Tony Blair's three major environment speeches, the EAC (HC 517-I, Session 1997–1998; HC 363-I, session 2001–2002), Jordan (2002a: 40), and Russel and Jordan (2007: 12–14) have pinpointed the lack of sustained high-level leadership as a contributory factor. This issue is particularly pertinent with regards to DEFRA, which supervises the main elements of the UK's EPI system. It has a relatively lowly status in Whitehall (ENDS, 356: 33–34). It cannot, for example, compel the sectors to implement EPI in the same way that the prime minister or his core executive can. In the absence of determined central leadership, the other departments find it all too easy to ignore EPI (Jordan, 2002a: 53). The lack of high-level political support is reflected in the distribution of resources devoted to the various implementing mechanisms.

The EAC suggests that 'little in the way of staff resources' is devoted 'to the sustainable development agenda' in Whitehall (EAC HC 961, session 2002–2003, p. 3). And while there are 137 Whitehall staff involved in sustainable development out of an overall total of around five hundred thousand civil servants, 93 of them are concentrated in just three departments (EAC HC 961, session 2002–2003, pp. 13–14), namely international development, foreign affairs and DEFRA. In some departments only one or two officials have been responsible for sustainable development with little in the way of training on sustainable development issues for other staff (Russel and Jordan, 2007: 12, 14), which exacerbates the low levels of political attention and leadership.

Finally, while UK non-governmental organizations have provided strong political support for EPI, very few regularly scrutinize the government's pursuit of EPI (Jordan, 2002a: 42). This is not to say that non-governmental organizations have not engaged with the UK's implementation of EPI. For instance, a small pressure group, the Green Alliance, has attempted to regularly track the UK's implementation of EPI since the mid 1990s, and larger groups such as Friends of the Earth have frequently given both oral and written evidence to EAC investigations. However, the Green Alliance is very small with a low profile (Jordan 2002a: 42), and the larger groups have tended to give it only passing attention. They find it easier to campaign on higher profile issues like climate change and genetically modified organisms than dry, complex machinery of government concerns like EPI. Therefore, there is relatively limited external pressure on the UK to internalize environmental protection by developing and implementing a comprehensive EPI system.

8.5 CONCLUSIONS

At the beginning of this chapter, we identified two apparently conflicting descriptions of the UK's EPI system: the OECD applauding the advanced machinery of coordinative governance, and others doubting EPI performance in practice. In this chapter we have sided with the second view and sought to demonstrate that the UK's system is not nearly as effective as is sometimes claimed. The implementation of EPI is actually quite sectorized, with its individual elements not working as well as envisaged.

The mismatch between the OECD's positive review of the UK's EPI system and the present more negative account is partly a function of the level of analysis adopted. For instance, the OECD's (2001, 2002) assessments tend to rely upon self-reporting by the government. They also involve a largely superficial description of the component parts, rather than a more detailed assessment of how the individual elements function individually and in combination.

Moreover, this chapter has built upon previous studies by: discussing the latest developments in the UK's EPI system; covering a broader number of EPI elements and exploring the relationship between them; and examining the important role that information flows might play in promoting environmental coordination. Overall, our analysis adds weight to the claims made by other authors (for example Richardson and Jordan, 1979: 26–8; Richards and Smith, 2002: 9, 22) that decision making in the UK is in fact highly departmentalized, that is unless it is in the direct interests of departments to cooperate (for example EU and foreign policy issues) or there are strong central controls (for example on economic matters where the Treasury has a strong guiding hand). 'Departmentalism' describes a situation when policy makers operate in vertically-configured departments, thinking and acting in terms of 'their' department's interests instead of more horizontal objectives, such as EPI (Richards and Smith, 2002: 22). It is associated with so-called 'turf wars' when departments compete over policy competencies.

For example, Richards and Smith (2002: 9) argue that the 2001 foot and mouth crisis led departments to 'automatically slip … into the role of defending [their] own sector's interests, rather than considering the larger picture'. This situation is seemingly to be found in relation to EPI and can arguably leads to policy chaos (Richards and Smith, 2002: 9, 22). There are, however, areas in which departments have successfully worked together, especially when it is in their interests to do so. For example, joint planning programmes for rural affairs were created between the Ministry of Agriculture, Fisheries and Food and the DETR, before the creation of DEFRA (Perri 6, et al., 2002: 25). Accounts of departmentalism, however, imply that effective cooperation is the exception not the rule, with critics arguing that UK central government is 'more suited to coordination and integration in theory than in practice'.

Crucially, the UK appears to embarking on a new phase of EPI with a dedicated focus on climate change. For instance, a cross-departmental Office of Climate Change was recently established in DEFRA in 2006 to provide analysis and help departments develop climate friendly policy and to input into the government's climate strategy (DEFRA, 2006). It is clear, however, that to be more successful, such new EPI dives should reflect on the past performance of the UK's EPI system. What lessons then can be drawn from the UK's experience? First, as the OECD implies (2001, 2002), having a variety of EPI elements to pursue coordination at different levels is a necessary but an insufficient condition for greater EPI. The various component parts have to work individually and in combination. In this chapter, we have shown that policy appraisal and some of the administrative innovations do not support one another as strongly as the OECD assumes. Second, an effective supply of information on potential policy spillovers is very important to the success of an institutionally-based EPI system such as the UK's. In particular, the reliability of lower-level coordination mechanisms to produce information on policy spillovers is vital for preventing the breakdown of institutional and bureaucratic elements higher up the Metcalfe scale.

Moreover, the various coordination mechanisms process and tools need to link into one another; simply creating coordinating machinery (such as committees, common strategies and adjudication devices) without adequate grounding at lower levels can easily leave them rootless and unused. The practical implication of this point is hugely important: 'the more basic but less glamorous aspects of the policy coordination process' are vital (Metcalfe 1994: 288). It implies that the underlying capacities (the mechanisms to exchange information, consult and arbitrate and so on) need to be in place *before* political energies are invested in setting strategic objectives, creating committees and defining mission statements. This is a point which does not come easily to politicians looking for a media grabbing headline or a quick fix.

Third, by only focusing on whether sufficiently configured coordination mechanisms are in place ignores the fact that political processes related to departmentalism can derail EPI initiatives. It is therefore vital that departmental officials are adequately stimulated and incentivized to engage with environmental coordination initiatives in order to build their capacity to think beyond the confines of their department's sectoral interests.

This could be done, for example, by integrating EPI goals into job descriptions and making involvement in environmental coordination initiatives favourable for career development. Moreover, in contrast to the Metcalfe scale, which suggests that coordination builds from the bottom up, sustained active central leadership (by the Prime Minister and Ministers of State, and so on) is crucial to create a demand for EPI within the sectors to prevent the lower level mechanisms from breaking down, especially when the environmental department is relatively low down in the government hierarchy.

Thus rather than a bottom-up cumulative model of coordination as suggested by Metcalfe (1994), coordination might be seen as system of mutual interdependence between more bottom-up communicative and hierarchal measures. As Peters (1997: 52) observes, leadership is a vital ingredient to override departmental sectoral interests in the pursuit of cross-cutting goals.

However, central leadership has a tendency to ebb and flow (Ross, 2005: 47), depending on the level of pressure and scrutiny from environmental non-governmental organizations, public interest and the salience of other rival issues which compete for the attention of senior decision makers (for example terrorism). Thus, in the UK the implementation of EPI has 'foundered on the rocks of interdepartmental wrangling ... as a succession of governments has seen no political reason to promote it' (Jordan, 2002a: 36).

Acknowledgements

A version of this work also appears in: Jordan, Andrew and Andrea Lenschow (eds) (2008), *Innovation in Environmental Policy? Integrating the Environment for Sustainability*, Cheltenham, UK and Northampton, MA, USA: Edward Elgar.

NOTES

1. Namely, the convention that all members of government jointly accept responsibility for decisions made in cabinet regardless of their personal views.
2. The National Audit Office has responsibility for reporting to parliament on the efficiency and effectiveness of public spending.
3. Initially RIA was promoted to assess the impact of a policy on business, charity and the voluntary sector.
4. For example, one of the Department of Trade and Industry's Public Service Agreements is 'to reduce greenhouse gas emissions to 12.5 percent below 1990 levels in line with (the UK's) Kyoto commitment' (HMT, 2004: 31).

REFERENCES

Bulmer, S. and M. Burch (1998), 'Organizing for Europe: Whitehall, the British State and the European Union', *Public Administration*, **76**(4), 601–28.
Cabinet Office (1999), *Modernising Government*, London: HMSO.
CPRE (Council for the Protection of Rural England) (1996), *From Rhetoric to Reality*, London: CPRE.
DEFRA (Department for the Environment Food and Rural Affairs) (2006), *News Release: Office of Climate Change Starts Work*, London: DEFRA.

DETR (Department of the Environment, Transport and Regions) (1997), *Experience with the 'Policy Appraisal and the Environment' Initiative*, London: HMSO.

DETR (Department of the Environment, Transport and Regions) (1998), *Policy Appraisal and the Environment: Policy Guidance*, London: HMSO.

DoE (Department of the Environment) (1989), *Sustaining Our Common Future*, London: HMSO.

DoE (Department of the Environment) (1990), *This Common Inheritance*, London: HMSO.

DoE (Department of the Environment) (1991), *Policy Appraisal and the Environment*, London: HMSO.

DTI (Department of Trade and Industry) (2003), *Our Energy Future – Creating a Low Carbon Economy*, London: HMSO.

ENDS (Environmental Data Services), *ENDS Report*, various issues.

Green Ministers' Committee (2001), *Greening Government: Third Annual Report*, London: HMSO.

Green Ministers' Committee (2002), *Sustainable Development in Government: Green Ministers First Report*, London: HMSO.

Helm, D. (1998), 'The Assessment: Environmental Policy-Objectives, Instruments, and Institutions', *Oxford Review of Economic Policy*, **14**(4), 1–19.

Her Majesty's Government (1970), *The Protection of the Environment*, London: HMSO.

Her Majesty's Government (1994), *Sustainable Development: The UK Strategy*, Cm 2426, London: HMSO.

Her Majesty's Government (1999), *A Better Quality of Life – Strategy for Sustainable Development for the United Kingdom*, London: HMSO.

Her Majesty's Government (2005), *The UK Government Sustainable Development Strategy*, London: HMSO.

Her Majesty's Treasury (2004), *Spending Review: Public Service Agreements White Paper*, London: HMSO

James, O. (2004), 'The UK core executive's use of public service agreements as a tool of governance', *Public Administration*, **82**(2), 397–419.

Jordan, A. (2002a), 'Efficient Hardware and Light Green Software: Environmental Policy Integration in the UK', in Andrea Lenschow (ed.), *Environmental Policy Integration: Greening Sectoral Policies in Europe*, London: Earthscan, pp. 35–56.

Jordan, A. (2002b), *The Europeanization of British Environmental Policy*, Basingstoke: Palgrave Macmillan.

Jordan, A. and A. Schout (2006), *The Coordination of the European Union: Exploring the Capacities of Networked Governance*, Oxford: Oxford University Press.

Jordan A, R. Wurzel, A. Zito and L. Bruckner (2003), 'Policy innovation or "muddling through"? "New" environmental policy instruments in the United Kingdom', *Environmental Politics*, **12**(1),179–200.

Knill, C. and A. Lenschow (2005), 'Compliance, Communication and Competition: Patterns of Environmental Policy Making and their Impact on Policy Convergence', *European Environment*, **15**, 114–28.

Labour Party (1994), *In Trust for Tomorrow*, London: The Labour Party.

Metcalfe, L.M. (1994), 'International Policy Coordination and Public Management Reform', *International Review of Administration Sciences*, **60**, 271–290.

OECD (Organisation for Economic Co-operation and Development) (2001), *Sustainable Development: Critical Issues*, Paris: OECD.

OECD (Organisation for Economic Co-operation and Development) (2002), *Environmental Performance Reviews UK*, Paris: OECD.

Osborn, D. (1997), 'Some Reflections on UK Environmental Policy, 1970–1995', *Journal of Environmental Law*, **9**(1), 3–22.

Painter, M.J. (1980), 'Policy Co-ordination in the DoE, 1970–1976', *Public Administration*, **58**, 135–54.

Perri 6, Leat D., Seltzer K. and G. Stoker (2002), *Towards Holistic Government*, Basingstoke: Palgrave.

Peters, G.B. (1997), *Managing Horizontal Government: The Politics of Coordination*, Ottawa: Canadian Centre for Management Development.

Plowman, J. (2004), *Review of the Roles and Responsibilities of the Sustainable Development Commission and the Sustainable Development Unit* (unpublished report).

Pollitt, C. (2003), 'Joined-Up Government: A Survey', *Political Studies Review*, **1**(1), 34–49.

Richards, D. and M.J. Smith (2002), *Governance and Public Policy in the UK*, Oxford: Oxford University Press.

Richardson, J. and G. Jordan (1979), *Governing Under Pressure*, Oxford: Martin Robinson.

Rose, C. (1990), *The Dirty Man of Europe: The Great British Pollution Scandal*, London: Simon and Schuster.

Ross, A. (2005), 'The UK Approach to Delivering Sustainable Development in Government: A Case Study in Joined-Up Working', *Journal of Environmental Law*, **17**(1), 27–49.

Russel, D. (2005), *Environmental Policy Appraisal in UK Central Government: A Political Analysis*, PhD. Thesis, Norwich: UEA.

Russel, D. and A. Jordan (2007), 'Gearing Up Government for Sustainable Development: Environmental Policy Appraisal in Central Government', *Journal of Environmental Planning and Management*, **50**(1), 1–21.

Schout, A., and A. Jordan (2005), 'Coordinated European Governance: Self-Organizing or Centrally Steered?', *Public Administration*, **83**(1), 201–220.

Sustainable Development Commission (2004), *Shows Promise But Must Try Harder*, London: SDC.

Sustainable Development Commission (2005), *Stepping up the Pace*, London: SDC.

Weale A., G. Pridham, M. Cini, D. Konstadakopulos, M. Porter and B. Flynn (2000), *Environmental Governance in Europe*, Oxford: Oxford University Press.

Young, S.C. (2000), 'The United Kingdom: From Political Containment to Integrated Thinking', in William M. Lafferty, and James Meadowcroft (eds), *Implementing Sustainable Development Strategies and Initiatives in High Consumption Societies*, Oxford: Oxford University Press, pp. 245–72.

9. The Case of EPI in Central and Eastern Europe

Keti Medarova-Bergström, Tamara Steger and Adam Paulsen

9.1 INTRODUCTION

Central and Eastern Europe (CEE) constitutes a unique case for exploring environmental policy integration (EPI) given the social, political, economic and historical context of this region.[1] While this context retains some similarities such as the former presence of a strong centralized regime, it is also diverse. Using existing research on EPI in CEE, this chapter explores EPI in relationship to modes of governance. Ultimately, the chapter builds on current efforts to identify and understand particular aspects or modes of governance that are influential in promoting or inhibiting the EPI agenda.

First, we present the CEE regional context, a definition of EPI and a conceptual framework emphasizing modes of governance. Second, prominent factors in understanding EPI in CEE are summarized and briefly discussed. Third, EPI and governance modes in CEE are explicitly explored. Case examples from Bulgaria and Hungary are used to provide detailed insight into the specific opportunities and challenges for the implementation of EPI in CEE. The chapter particularly engages the transport and energy sectors, as well as the programming of the EU funds for regional development.

9.2 CENTRAL AND EASTERN EUROPE: A REGIONAL PERSPECTIVE

Central and Eastern Europe (CEE) entered a state of democratic and economic transition in the late 1980s, fuelled in large part by the collapsing centralized economy orchestrated mainly from Moscow. The centrally-planned economic model promoted during the communist times was characterized by strictly political top-down priority-setting, 'sectoralization' or 'compartmentalization' of public policy lacking public involvement, the rule of law, transparency and accountability. During the transition period, the CEE countries experienced a significant structural shift to market liberalization and pluralist democracy. In this shift, however, 'not enough attention was devoted to the institutional aspects of transition' (OECD, 1999). Institutional reforms seriously lagged behind the rapid economic changes and newly emerging environmental challenges, as the old 'culture' of public institutions persisted in many ways.

As transition approached, strong environmental movements emerged across Central and Eastern Europe. They ultimately played a significant role in facilitating the political changes and the institutionalization of environmental protection (Steger, 2004a). Several reasons are offered as to why people mobilized around environmental issues at this time ranging from their perceived political neutrality to concrete evidence of the severe deterioration of the environment inspired in large part by the Chernobyl disaster (Steger, 2004b).

The transition to a free market system from a centralized economic system had mixed impacts on environmental efforts (DeBardeleben, 2004). Green Parties were initially formed, but did not have much enduring success (Pavlinek and Pickles, 2000). Economic lobbies may have become stronger and better organized in comparison to environmental interests (Pickvance, 1998). Powerful economic lobbies asserted that economic recovery is especially pressing and environmental concerns should not curtail this effort (Fisher, 1993).

The environmental movements declined as environmental concerns were institutionalized. New public entities, such as Ministries of Environment, were formally established to address environmental concerns. Environmental problems thus increasingly came under the helm of the new environmental authorities. The Ministries of Environment, for example, gained significant power during the transition period and moved towards more environmentally cautious, participatory and open policy-making. These positive efforts, however, did not receive much attention from the other sectoral administrations which remained trapped within narrow sectoral expertise prescribing bureaucratic interventions where 'environmental protection [was] largely considered a by-product of restructuring' (Andonova, 2002) as opposed to providing significant leverage in sectoral decision-making.

The negotiation process for future membership in the European Union (EU) placed the CEE countries in a new policy context that asserted sustainable development as a goal. In the effort to strive towards this ambitious goal, EPI gained increasing attention. Even as public mobilization for the environment waned, environmental institutionalization occurred with great speed.

Considering the particularities of the CEE countries throughout the transition period, we review the basic concepts of EPI and modes of governance. The next section provides a definition of EPI and also examines typologies of governance modes to help us explore EPI empirically in CEE countries.

9.3   EPI AND MODES OF GOVERNANCE

Environmental policy integration stands for the incorporation of environmental objectives in the formulation and implementation of other sectoral policies. Its purpose is to integrate environmental concerns into policy processes and outputs aiming to bring 'substantial policy change in the different domains' (Jacob and Volkery, 2003) by strengthening the environmental dimension of sustainable development in sectoral decision-making. The concept of EPI is particularly important for countries in transition such as CEE countries as it offers an innovative approach to policy-making which assists a nation state in developing integrated policies for sustainable development with an emphasis on environmental protection. One way of considering the implementation capacity for EPI is by looking at the operating modes of governance in which the decision-making processes and the relevant actors are explored (IEEP, 2007). An important goal of this chapter is to consider the relationship between modes of governance and EPI. In particular, it is concerned with how modes of governance in CEE influence EPI.

Governance can be defined as a political process, involving state and non-state actors, for identifying objectives and intervention in bringing societal change (Von Homeyer, 2006). The literature on governance offers a systematic typology of modes of governance based on patterns of decision-making, the types of actors involved and the applied policy instruments. In the context of CEE, the dichotomous models of 'old' and 'new' governance as defined in the EPIGOV framework is especially relevant. 'Old governance' is characterized by explicitly top-down command-and-control policy processes where decisions are made predominantly by one actor – the government (Borzel, 2006) and legislation is the main policy instrument (Von Homeyer, 2006).

This mode of governance can be associated with the previous political regimes in CEE countries and the legacy of the centrally planned, fragmented and closed policy-making system. On the other hand, 'new governance' constitutes another mode depicting a non-hierarchical and participatory policy-making process based on network coordination (Jordan et al., 2003; Knill and Lenschow, 2003; Knill, 2006) as well as deliberation and learning (Von Homeyer, 2006). It is also characterized by the development and application of new environmental policy instruments (Zito et al., 2003; IEEP, 2007).

A similar perspective on modes of governance is presented by Knill (2006) – hierarchy, communication and competition, based on three dimensions: degree of legal binding, flexibility of implementation and public–private relations. However, Knill suggests that the main policy actors are national authorities who apply policy instruments such as indicator development, monitoring, benchmarking and peer-review (Von Homeyer, 2006). While governments have a lead in policy formulation, policy implementation is performed by individual commercial actors who tend to put pressure on government actors and respond to market conditions. The latter type of actors' interaction represents competition as a governance mode. Particularly insightful for understanding governance in CEE countries is coordinated market economy as a mode of governance where commercial actors play a central role (Hall and Soskice, 2001). Importantly, it presents a mode of governance where governments provide and maintain market conditions and institutional arrangements for stakeholder networks in which interactions go beyond pure market competition. During the transition period of economic restructuring such a mode of governance involving the state and the market might be detrimental but in some cases also favourable to EPI.

Trieb et al. (2005) differentiate two additional governance modes based on their properties – voluntarism and targeting which we find relevant to the EPI topic. Voluntarism conforms to the idea of 'management by objectives' where the actors act according to their own discretion in order to implement a set of non-binding objectives. Targeting differs from voluntarism in that it includes detailed and precise prescriptions for how implementation should take place leaving less freedom to implementation authorities. Trieb et al. (2005) also discuss framework regulation as a mode of governance which combines legally binding requirements with flexibility in implementation activities, allowing adaptability to local contexts.

The advantage of utilizing the typologies developed by Knill and Lenschow (2003), Trieb et al. (2005) and Knill (2006) is that these modes of governance are widely manifested in the multi-level system of the EU and nation states. A multi-level system implies political authority which is distributed between different levels of decision-making such as EU, national, regional, local, and so on. Knill and Lenschow (2003) develop a typology of modes of governance encompassing regulatory standards, new instruments, self-regulation and open method of coordination (OMC), which involves three main regulatory mechanisms – coercion, incentive structures and learning. Regulatory standards remain in the definition of hierarchy with an explicit coercive power. New instruments imply that the EU creates incentive structures for flexible procedures established at national levels. Self-regulation involves private actors who develop their own regulatory framework according to their needs and capacities. Learning may occur within communication networks of private economic actors. Essentially, the OMC offers a mode of governance whereby the regulatory incentive is in the jurisdiction of national authorities and the EU only facilitates coordination and learning without exercising control over policy outcomes (Knill and Lenschow, 2003).

The literature on EPI and modes of governance suggests that communication, voluntarism, self-regulation and OMC (herein, referred as 'new' governance modes) appear to be promising in terms of enhancing EPI as they tend to fix the failures of the 'old' hierarchical modes and provide novel steering mechanisms. During the communist regime and even during transition, CEE countries endured highly hierarchical command-and-control governance whereas only recently some elements and properties of 'new' governance can be observed. It is the focus of this chapter to examine some of the legacies of the 'old' governance as well as the opportunities and/or limitations of 'new' governance modes with regards to EPI.

9.3.1 EPI in Maturation

EPI in CEE is in a process of maturation. It is too early to fully engage a comprehensive analytical discussion regarding the degree of EPI as it occurs in CEE. It is more relevant at this stage to analyse some of the social and political forces influencing EPI as well as to assess the opportunities and challenges to further materialization of the concept in practice. Important 'external' and 'internal' factors in this process of maturation include: EU accession, bureaucratic and administrative culture, political commitment and Environmental Assessment (EA).

9.3.2 EPI and EU Accession

The EU negotiations and accession requirements imposed a significant leverage for restructuring in CEE countries pursuing significant policy change, including EPI. Ultimately, the EU accession process contributed positively to: 1) raising attention to environmental problems in sectoral policy-making; 2) the harmonization of national legislation with the EU acquis and the adoption of new policy instruments; and 3) providing financial resources for their implementation.

EPI in CEE is strongly encouraged through the EU accession mainly through the transposition of EU regulations and Directives as well as providing guidelines for sectoral policy formulation for taking the environmental matters into account. The integration efforts were largely materialized through the introduction and application of instruments such as Environmental Assessments (EA). The accession process was a key external factor driving the development and implementation of EIA legislation applicable at the project level, as well as SEA for plans and programmes at national and regional levels in CEE countries. Furthermore, enhanced public participation within EA processes has been driven largely by the requirements in EU Directives and international commitments (for example Aarhus Convention). The governance role of the EU in promoting EPI in CEE is discussed in more depth in the section on EPI and Governance.

This prominent role of EU accession in enhancing the EPI agenda in CEE, however, is not straightforward in terms of its ultimate impacts on the implementation of EPI. While efforts to build EPI are mainly pushed by the EU accession processes, it is largely perceived as 'interference' in domestic policy-making and little 'integration' of sectoral policies occurs in practice. There is, hence, some internal or domestic resistance woven into the fabric of bureaucratic and administrative culture. Interestingly, a closer look at the bureaucratic and administrative culture that emerged from the former socialist system in the following section reveals both inhibiting as well as conducive factors in the promotion of EPI.

9.3.3 Bureaucratic and Administrative Culture

In many ways the former socialist regimes persist in a ghostlike fashion reflected in the rigid bureaucratic procedures and administrative culture found throughout CEE. Rigid procedures and structures can deter new ways of thinking and policy-making thereby constituting a major barrier to EPI. Therefore, EPI often occurs as a piecemeal process resulting in partial actions or single instruments. Another problem with the bureaucratic machine lies in its inability to retain qualified experts. The state administrators programming and operating with EU funds for regional development, for instance, receive double salaries and are sent to numerous professional trainings abroad through twinning projects in other member states. And yet, many of these young professionals, after being well trained, choose to leave the public sector for better salary and career opportunities. The state administration urgently needs to adopt a comprehensive policy for attracting, training and retaining experts in its structures if a fundamental change in the organizational culture of administrations is pursued.

On the other hand, speaking of the old regime's legacies, researchers in CEE have demonstrated some of the so called 'positive legacies' from the centrally planned economies (Ürge-Vorsatz et al., 2005). These usually include: high share of organized modes of transportation, that is urban public transportation, rail passenger and freight transport; concentrated spatial planning which favoured not only the public transportation development but also district heating systems; and integrated settlement planning with regards to utilization of co-generation which was a common practice in the socialist era. The authors suggest that preserving these legacies can be realistic in market conditions and has a potential to 'leapfrog' directly to policies which promote sustainable energy consumption and transport development.

9.3.4 Political Commitment

On a general scale, CEE countries now more than ten years into transition, are hard pressed to consider the environment as having a prominent role in policy-making when economic considerations remain consistently high on the political agenda. Administrative adaptation and corresponding capacity to implement EPI should be strengthened with coinciding political and budgetary motivation and support.

Research on EPI in Hungary and Bulgaria reveals a lack of political commitment and leadership towards integrating environmental objectives in other public sectors (Rezessy et al., 2004; Medarova, 2005). As a consequence, there is no strategic vision for EPI.

Environmental objectives fail to become broad societal objectives, and are simply 'added' to sectoral objectives (Antypas et al., 2004). One reason is that there is a lack of understanding among sectoral administrations of the benefits of integrated policies and the importance of early consideration of environmental concerns in other public policies (Medarova, 2005).

According to Nilsson and Persson (2003) if 'the responsibility for a policy initiative lies with the sector actors, the opportunity for EPI seems stronger than if the initiative lies with environmental actors', which requires strong political commitment of the sectoral policy-makers (Lenschow, 2002).

Given the emphasis on economic development in the region, there is a potential for strengthening political commitment to EPI by demonstrating its non-environmental benefits. For example, energy efficiency measures can be beneficial from environmental point of view, but in parallel it can facilitate economic efficiency and competition. The example of energy efficiency in Bulgaria is discussed later in a separate section. Also, the EU structural funds appear to be another source of political motivation for environmental integration directly through investments in environmental projects but also indirectly through technical assistance for infrastructure development.

9.3.5 Environmental Assessment (EA)

Assessment processes are an important variable affecting the extent of EPI (Nilsson and Persson, 2003). Throughout the CEE countries environmental assessment is perhaps the primary tool for the explicit integration of environmental considerations into projects (EIA), and to a lesser extent programming, planning and policy (SEA). The importance of Environmental Impact Assessment (EIA) as a policy tool at the project level is reflected in the prominent reforms to environmental legislation that took place during the 1990s across CEE. In this context, the application of external practices appeared promising by tailoring them to the existing context of transition (Cherp and Antypas, 2003). Strategic Environmental Assessment (SEA) is also a key tool for EPI in plans and programmes, which, however, only recently became obligatory in these countries with a rather limited application. From a governance perspective, there are two emerging questions with regards to environmental assessments and EPI. Essentially, the lack of broader understanding and operationalization of EPI as a concept among sectoral administrators often narrows down the implementation of EPI to policy instruments such as environmental assessments. Another question which arises is the procedural impact of EAs on the actual 'greening' of sectoral decision-making. The particularities of EAs as a policy instrument in the promotion of EPI are discussed in more depth in the following section.

9.4   EPI AND GOVERNANCE IN CEE

In this section, we discuss some of the manifestations of governance modes in CEE while reflecting on the implications for enhancing and/or inhibiting EPI. Emerging themes are highlighted in terms of decision-making styles, the role of the EU and state actors in promoting EPI, the need for a meaningful environmental discourse and the application of policy instruments. Again, we emphasize case examples from Bulgaria and Hungary which constitute the bulk of our more detailed research so far in CEE countries.

9.4.1   Decision-Making

Research in CEE countries suggests that decision-making styles with regards to EPI are crucial when examining modes of governance and EPI. The decision-making style reflects the structure of policy actors, their norms, values and bargaining power. In CEE countries, two main decision-making styles can be identified – formal and informal. Formal decision-making procedures are strictly stipulated in the legislative system. For instance, in Bulgaria a draft policy proposal is developed by the sectoral administration and then submitted to other sectoral authorities for review. Environmental authorities are among the compulsory authorities that a policy proposal should be consulted with according to the formal requirements. Their comments are 'accepted', 'partially accepted' or 'rejected' by the sectoral administration, which has the final word. Therefore, environmental authorities do participate in the process only by 'fixing up' and 'adding to' a policy proposal in this commentary phase. They do not participate early enough in order to influence the actual formulation of the policy or in general the policy agenda. As a consequence, sectoral policy documents often tend to be rather inconsistent with one another.

The informal decision-making style has a much stronger influence on sectoral policy-making. High level decisions are usually made in political party forums where certain interests of the party in power together with supporting businesses, in an 'iron triangle' fashion, are negotiated and reflected in policy formulations. On the other hand, at an administrative level decisions are often dealt with in intimate networks that depend not only on political party affiliation but also on interpersonal relations in which 'like' and 'trust' form the basis for inclusion in the network (for example 'I know this person well so we work together and cooperate'). Ultimately, these networks mainly consist of state actors.

Essentially, EPI matures in a context of strong political interests orchestrated largely by the political party in power and interpersonal relations. In the transition period, sectoral policy networks gave little priority to EPI but this has changed over the last couple of years. Importantly, during the preparation for the EU structural funding for CEE, more attention was given to new opportunities from investing in environmental infrastructure and exploring new business niches. Therefore, if EPI continues to increase in sectoral decision-making, this informal decision-making style may certainly emerge as more conducive to EPI in comparison to formal decision-making.

9.4.2   The Role of the EU

The EU accession obligations, on the other hand, have been a main impetus for moving the environment from the periphery to having a more central role in sectoral decision-making. The negotiations between the EU and accession countries resulted in priority setting whereby environmental protection was allotted a place. Extensive legal reformation of regulations and the introduction of various economic and information policy instruments were effectively undertaken under the stringent control of the EU which culminated in almost complete harmonization with the EU acquis.

Importantly, while EU-based initiatives promoting EPI give guidance and structure, they may not create sufficient substance regarding the meaning of EPI at the national level. This proposition bears significant importance in terms of EPI having in mind the rigid administrative culture in CEE countries. An emerging question is the extent to which this top-down approach is effective at promoting and implementing EPI. Some authors claim it can be a successful learning experience for accession countries by creating high standards and imposing strict rules (Knill and Lenschow, 2003). However, so far, it has had mixed results in CEE countries, resulting in both positive and negative impacts (Medarova, 2005).

This process, while providing guidance and structure for implementing EPI, fails to nourish an administrative culture capable of comprehending, in its own right, the benefits of integrated policies and the necessary administrative capacity to put forward innovative alternatives and solutions. For instance, the understanding of sectoral administration for EPI is limited to following formal procedures and applying policy instruments rather than engaging proactively in the integration of environmental concerns into the entire policy cycle. Therefore, when national sectoral administrations in Bulgaria and Hungary had to develop further the relevant secondary legislation including concrete targets and timetables, and making budget commitments, they largely failed (Rezessy et al., 2004; Medarova, 2007). Apparently, this top-down 'policy transfer' appears to be incomplete as policies 'suffer from technical deficiencies, lack of political support, implementation and enforcement obstacles' (Ürge-Vorsatz at al., 2004). Fundamentally, such governance mode can be conducive to learning and EPI, but only in the short run. Its similarity to the command-and-control style of the communist era can precondition its failure in the long run or would impede progressive bottom-up initiatives for integration.

9.4.3 Actors: Governments and Intimate Networks

Both decision-making styles and the role of EU in modes of governance for EPI discussed above highlight the importance of the policy actors and their relations as a factor, which needs to be taken into account. Sectoral policy-making has been largely dominated by state actors during transition. Only recently, there are some new forms of actor constellations involving non-state actors. Shortly before accession to the EU, within the programming period for the structural and cohesion funds, 2007–2013, the sectoral policy formulation in Bulgaria was revisited and improved so as to enhance stakeholder participation. Special working groups were established and comprised representatives of the environmental authorities, business and social partners as well as representatives of the environmental community (nominated and elected by the NGOs) (Medarova, 2005).

The working group mechanism for decision-making appears to be an opportunity for EPI as the participants assemble at an early stage of the policy formulation. For instance, in Bulgaria the Working Group for the Operational Programme Transport 2007–2013 was established at the end of 2004 having the aim of conducting the socio-economic analysis of the transport sector in the country, performing a SWOT analysis and identifying the major priorities in the sector (Medarova, 2005). However, after the approval of the Operational Programme the working group will be turned into a monitoring committee. In itself, it constitutes a post-implementation participation mechanism and deprives the participants of providing input in the assessment and selection of investment projects, for instance. The assessment and selection of transport projects for actual funding will be performed by a closed inter-governmental body that can be considered a step backwards in terms of EPI.

In Hungary and Bulgaria, the research shows that there are no environmental units or coordination departments within other sectoral administrations neither do the environmental authorities have separate transport or energy units within their structures. Alternatively, positive examples of institutional arrangements that facilitate EPI occur in the form of inter-ministerial committees and joint working groups whose establishment and effectiveness vary from sector to sector. For instance, in Hungary there is an inter-ministerial committee on energy efficiency which deals with the horizontal coordination, a committee preparing the RES strategy and a third one dealing with the flexible mechanisms under the Kyoto Protocol. Comparatively, no similar coordination mechanism can be seen in the transport sector (Rezessy et al., 2004). However, Rezessy et al. (2004) argue that '[inter-ministerial committees are] often established to meet formal requirements' and hence 'are easily marginalised by higher level of decision-making'.

Lenschow (2002) claims that a fundamental factor for EPI is the 'societal backing' or the 'pressure from below', which calls for diversification of the spectrum of policy actors from the public. In Bulgaria, the research on EPI in the transport sector showed that the major obstacle for improving the cooperation within the stakeholders is the negative attitudes/perceptions they have for each other, which prevents the establishment of any partnership. Authorities are accused of being non-transparent, unwilling to co-operate and unable to absorb any new knowledge for improving their performance. NGOs are accused of being radical, unable to participate in a constructive dialogue and propose viable alternative solutions. Academics are blamed for 'selling' their expertise and unable to deliver objective scientific input into policy-making (Medarova, 2005).

However, environmental NGOs have developed other mechanisms to influence decision-making and deliver 'public pressure' from below, hence becoming an influential policy actor. One mechanism is when environmental NGOs act as 'watchdogs' and report to the European Commission and international institutions for cases of violations of the EU Directives and international environmental conventions. Performing alternative public hearings within the EIA procedure are embraced by the NGOs as another mechanism to voice out local concerns (Medarova, 2005; Medarova and Antypas, 2006). For instance, in the case of the Struma motorway project in Bulgaria, it was felt that the local people were intentionally not invited to the public hearings organized by the authorities. In return, two environmental NGOs organized alternative public hearings which received higher attendance rates. NGOs translated and distributed information-rich packages of documents and raised the awareness of the local people about the environmental and social impacts which could be caused by the realization of this project. Essentially, the research demonstrates stakeholder involvement which is not based on a partnership principle but rather re-active pressure from below via alternative actions and reporting mechanisms, which are legitimized by the local community. However, the NGOs' 'pressure-from-below' might decline as environmental organizations become beneficiaries of the EU structural and cohesion funds. The role of NGOs as critical stakeholders for environmental integration in governmental decision-making can change significantly as the same government decides on who gets financing.

In Hungary, within the energy policy formulation process there is an increasing participation of local administrations (Rezessy et al., 2004). This empowerment of the local authorities in the energy efficiency policies, for instance, is largely due to the long history of successful cooperation between the local and national level in certain policy areas. In other policy areas, such as the programming and implementation of the EU structural funds, the role of the local governments becomes crucial as they are the major beneficiary of the programmes in regional and rural development. Inclusion of local authorities in the policy-making and implementation can have significant importance for articulating local needs and addressing local problems such as the state of the environment and the management of natural resources. Therefore, channelling the EU funds in this direction can have a positive effect for encouraging environmental integration. The main concern stems from the lack of capacity and preparedness of the municipalities for managing the EU funds, and taking the environment into account can be easily dismissed in order to get any financing. Furthermore, the involvement of local stakeholders such as energy associations, businesses for RES development, housing associations, and so on outside of the local government appears to be rather limited (Antypas et al., 2004; Rezessy et al., 2004).

Despite the persistent domination of state actors in sectoral policy-making, there is evidence of novel mechanisms for involving non-state actors in policy formulation and implementation with regards to EPI in recent years. Changing the values and attitudes of the actors towards one another is a major challenge for enhancing EPI. Ideally, non-state actors should be involved early in the policy formulation although they demonstrate higher potential in the implementation phase. Local authorities can bridge policy-making to local needs and legitimize decisions. Environmental NGOs can compensate for the limited capacity of central authorities during implementation and monitoring of policies delivering feedback. Businesses and industries should better position themselves as policy actors for the future materialization of EPI. Their role and interaction is discussed in detail in the following section.

9.4.4   Creating a Meaningful Discourse towards the Environment

In relationship to the gradual inclusion of socio-economic partners in the decision-making networks in CEE countries, further opportunities for EPI emerge. Essentially, a successful strategy for EPI has been developed by creating a meaningful discourse towards the environment looking at it, for example, as an economic opportunity and emphasizing its non-environmental benefits. Such a strategy is closely related to nurturing positive political commitment to the environment and integrating the environment beyond the political rhetoric.

For instance, energy efficiency in Bulgaria is placed relatively high on the energy policy agenda. Its successful integration can be explained by the smart way of marketing it as a market opportunity equal to economic efficiency and creating competitive advantages. In the context of economic restructuring, this seems to be a winning strategy in policy formulation, which can reap environmental benefits along with economic ones giving an opportunity for EPI (Medarova, 2007).

Energy efficiency was placed as a major priority in the Energy Strategy from 2002. In 2004, a Sectoral Short-Term Programme and Goal-Oriented Programme for Energy Efficiency were developed by the Ministry of Economy and a year after a National Long-Term Programme for Energy Efficiency was adopted. It introduced integrated energy planning and placed balanced priority on the economy and the environment. Specific energy efficiency measures were proposed for the industrial and household sectors. Simultaneously, two supplementary documents were adopted – the National Programme for Energy Savings until 2014 and the Three-Year National Action Plan. The latter is an important document as it sets more than 80 energy efficiency targets and measures for the agriculture, building, district heating, industry and transport sectors and involves investments of 5.7 billion leva. The Energy Efficiency Law was adopted in 2004 arranging the legal, procedural and institutional issues related to energy efficiency. Among the most important measures stipulated in the legislation is the establishment of the Energy Efficiency Fund, the introduction of energy audits and labelling schemes, and improved building standards and mandatory energy consumption/efficiency indicators for industrial production processes and products.

These specific measures constitute a major progressive step towards legally binding integration of environmental measures into the energy sector (Medarova, 2007). Moreover, an Energy Efficiency Agency (EEA) was established in 2002, which has an explicit mandate for policy formulation, proposal drafting, implementation and control with regards to energy efficiency. It also has assigned responsibilities to co-ordinate these activities with other ministries and state agencies, local government and NGOs. Essentially, it is considered to be a policy actor which will enhance the co-ordination among all stakeholders (Medarova, 2007).

Such an approach provides a significant incentive base for commercial actors to embrace energy efficiency as important aspect of their restructuring. Creating a meaningful discourse towards the environment has proved to be a winning strategy in CEE countries where the economic agenda is strong in both public and private sectors. Such emerging developments at a national level constitute clear manifestations of the opportunities provided by market modes of governance, which needs to be explored in more detail with regards to EPI.

9.5   POLICY INSTRUMENTS: REGULATION, NEPI AND ENVIRONMENTAL ASSESSMENT

Based on our analysis, EPI in CEE is manifested more strongly as policy instruments and less as a coherent policy process. Regulation and the application of Environmental Assessment (EA) are key policy instruments to promote EPI. It is important to note, however, that while policy instruments have been successfully introduced (albeit to varying degrees), this does not imply effective implementation in practice.

9.5.1   Regulation and NEPI

In this section we group regulation and New Environmental Policy Instruments (NEPI). We consider regulation as a necessary condition for reinforcing NEPI (IEEP, 2007) as the latter are 'a mixed bag of regulatory tools' (Knill and Lenschow, 2003). Both Bulgaria and Hungary have experienced overwhelming legal reforms in terms of developing framework environmental regulations in relation to the EU accession and harmonization of the EU acquis. In essence, the reforms spurred the introduction of market and information instruments for incorporating environmental concerns into the energy and transport sectors such as green taxes, standards, tariffs, subsidies, and so on (Rezessy et al., 2004; Medarova, 2005).

However, research shows inconsistency and incoherence in sectoral policies reflecting some legacies from the communist era of centrally governed economic planning and at the same time the inability to handle the current externally-pushed reforms. For instance, environmentally damaging subsidies for the energy and transport sectors continue in the transition period despite the call for internalization of social and environmental costs via economic policy instruments. In the past, due to heavy subsidizing the costs of energy services were maintained artificially low.

During transition, however, the increase in energy costs was felt strongly by the majority of the population, which consequently fell into the category of 'energy poverty' (Ürge-Vorsatz et al., 2005; Medarova, 2007). In other words, the social factor in pricing energy services still plays a stronger role than the call for a green tax reform. Voluntary instruments, on the other hand, remain less popular provided that industry still prefers to pay sanctions in the form of fines instead of engaging in a proactive greening of its activities.

Introducing new policy instruments for EPI may be assessed as successful as they are easily materialized by regulatory frameworks prescribing certain economic behaviour. Their effective application and impact on sectoral policy outcomes with regards to environmental performance, however, will be questioned in the near future. The situation with the other popular instrument for EPI in CEE countries – environmental assessment – is similar.

9.5.2 Environmental Assessment

With the institutionalization of environmental protection in transition and expansion of the EU came the introduction of environmental assessment (EA) largely in the form of Environmental Impact Assessment (EIA) and Strategic Environmental Assessment (SEA) (Cherp, 2000, 2001a, 2001b). EU accession was a key factor driving the development and implementation of EIA legislation applicable at the project level, as well as SEA development for plans and programmes at the national and regional levels in CEE countries.

EA legislation and practice in the region is modelled heavily on western practices, the development of which was facilitated by the networks of EA specialists throughout the CEE (already international in nature) interacting with Western EA practioners thus facilitating 'flows of information, values, and expertise from East to West' (Cherp and Antypas, 2003).

Internal factors have also contributed to the expansion of public participation provisions in environmental assessment in some countries (for example Hungary and Lithuania) as they developed experience with EA.

Openness also appears to be a key factor where 'empirical evidence from CITs[2] seems to suggest that the success of EA policies depended upon the process by which they were developed, implemented and evaluated' (Cherp and Antypas, 2003).

It is difficult to assess the extent to which EA findings are actually incorporated into decisions (especially policy), where 'in the absence of SEA, only a limited number of alternatives to proposed developments are considered, especially at the strategic level' (Cherp, 2001a). One of Cherp's (2001b) key conclusions is that 'EA has probably failed to reach its goal of promoting cross-sectoral integrated analysis and evaluation of diverse environmental issues associated with planned activities.'

Moreover, EA findings are unlikely to be utilized where the decentralization of decision-making authority occurs prior to local authorities developing sufficient capacity to deal with environmental information. Further, extensive research on EIA and its impact on decision-making suggests that this 'instrument serves merely to modify some of the most environmentally egregious projects, it neither blocks them nor makes them somehow inherently "green"' (Antypas et al., 2004).

9.6   CONCLUSION

The scope of this chapter includes the countries from the Central and Eastern European region. They constitute an interesting case for exploring modes of governance for EPI struggling with the legacy of the centrally planned economic model, predominant also during the transition, and the opportunities stemming from 'new' governance modes. Based on research, conducted mostly in Bulgaria and Hungary, EPI is now a work-in-progress characterized by strong motivation from the EU, the bureaucratic administrative culture of national authorities and the introduction of policy instruments.

The externally orchestrated agenda for EPI includes the successful introduction of regulatory policy instruments and assessment tools such as EIA and SEA, which gave the main impetus for moving the environment from the periphery to having a more central role in sectoral policy-making. The critique of this purely top-down instrumental approach lies in the inability to create substantive understanding and spur conceptual learning for the merits of integrating public policies. Therefore, both Bulgaria and Hungary fail to operationalize the vision of EPI, develop the necessary secondary legislation and procedures and register serious drawbacks when it comes to policy implementation.

Significant variables with regards to governance modes for EPI in CEE countries stem from the particularities in the actors' constellation and the patterns of their involvement during the policy-making processes. The lack of political commitment seriously hinders high-level efforts to steer integration. Even the introduction of more innovative coordination mechanisms such as working groups, typical for the 'new governance' mode, is strongly dominated by state actors where the environmental authorities have little power. The establishment of intimate networks based on 'like', 'trust' or political party affiliation is associated with the formation of closed policy sub-systems, which may impose serious leverage on decision-making compared to formal decision-making procedures.

The research, however, also focuses on finding opportunities for EPI in terms of governance. It suggests that the application of EU and international legislation and practice will be successful only if it is adapted to the local context and its characteristics – for example utilizing the so called 'positive legacies' from the previous regimes. Another strategy includes creating a meaningful discourse towards EPI at a national level underlining its non-environmental benefits in sectoral strategic planning and opening up prospects for modes of governance oriented towards market opportunities.

The chapter also concludes that an important aspect of governance for EPI in CEE countries lies in building the capacity of all sectoral, non-governmental and business actors. The interplay between national and EU levels should in the long run engage in modes of governance which can facilitate deliberation, conceptual learning and market relations such as self-regulation and open methods of coordination. Further research is necessary for studying administrative culture as a key factor for enhancing EPI in CEE countries.

NOTES

1. Herein, by region we mean the countries of Central and Eastern Europe (CEE) which are distinct from the Newly Independent States (NIS) of the former USSR. The Baltic States may also be considered a distinct region of these two groups.
2. CITs – countries in transition

REFERENCES

Andonova, L. (2002), 'the challenges and opportunities for reforming Bulgaria's energy sector', *Environment*, **44**(10), 8–19.

Antypas A. et al. (2004), 'Environmental Policy Integration in Europe: an Overview of Progress and Challenges', Paper prepared for the Hungarian Ministry of Environmental and Water.

Borzel, T. A. (2006), New Modes of Governance and Enlargement. When Theory Meets Reality, Interim Report, NEWGOV, New Modes of Governance, Free University of Berlin, http://www.eu-newgov.org/database/DELIV/D12D04_ Interim_Report.pdf.

Cherp, A. (2000), 'Integrating environmental appraisals of planned developments into decision-making in countries in transition', in N. Lee and C. Kirkpatrick (eds), *Sustainable Development and Integrated Appraisal in a Developing World*, Cheltenham, UK and Northampton, MA, USA: Edward Elgar, pp.165–85.

Cherp, A. (2001a), 'Environmental assessment in countries in transition: evolution in a changing context', *Journal of Environmental Management*, **62**: 357–74.

Cherp, A. (2001b), 'EA legislation and practice in central and eastern Europe and the former USSR: a comparative analysis', *Environmental Impact Assessment Review*, **21**: 335–61.

Cherp, A. and A. Antypas (2003), 'Dealing with continuous reform: towards adaptive EA policy systems in countries in transition', *Journal of Environmental Assessment Policy and Management*, **5**(4): 455–76.

DeBardeleben, J. (2004), 'Understanding the Challenges: the Environment in Eastern Europe', www.ics.si.edu/PROGRAMS/REGION/ees/envircon/DEBARD.htm, consulted January 2004.

Fisher, D. (1993), 'The emergence of the environmental movement in Eastern Europe and its role in the revolutions of 1989', in Barbara Jancar-Webster (ed.), *Environmental Action in Eastern Europe: Responses to Crisis*, New York, M.E. Sharpe, Inc.

Hall, P. A. and David Soskice (eds) (2001), *Varieties of Capitalism: The Institutional Foundations of Comparative Advantage*, Oxford: Oxford University Press.

Institute for European Environmental Policy (IEEP) (2007), 'Environmental Policy Integration and Modes of Governance – A literature review', EPIGOV Paper No. 3, Ecologic – Institute for International and European Environmental Policy: Berlin.

Jacob, K. and A. Volkery (2003), 'Environmental Policy Integration (EPI) – Potentials and Limits for Policy Change through Learning', Paper presented at the 2003 Berlin Conference on the Human Dimensions of Global Environmental Change, 5–6 December, Berlin, Germany.

Jordan, A., R. Wurzel and A. Zito (2003), 'Has Governance Eclipsed Government? Patterns of Environmental Instrument Selection and use in Eight States and the EU', CSERGE Working Paper EDM 03-15.

Knill, Ch. (2007), 'Hierarchie, Kommunication und Wettbewerb: Muster europaischer Umweltpolitik und ihre nationalen Auswrikungen', in Frank Biermann, Per-Olof Busch, Peter Henning Feindt and Klaus Jacob (eds), *Politik und Umwelt*, Wiesbaden: VS Verlag, pp. 223–42.

Knill, Ch. and A. Lenschow (2003), 'Modes of Regulation in the Governance of the European Union: Towards a Comprehensive Evaluation', European Integration online Papers (EIOP) 7 (1) http://eiop.or.at/eiop/texte/2003-001a.htm (24/4/2006).

Lenschow, A. (2002), *Environmental Policy Integration: Greening Sectoral Policies in Europe*, London: Earthscan Publications Ltd.

Medarova, K. (2005), 'Environmental Policy Integration: Policy Process and Instruments for the Transport Sector in Bulgaria', Master of Science thesis, Department of Environmental Sciences and Policy, Central European University, Budapest.

Medarova, K. (2007), 'Environmental Policy Integration in Energy Sector in Bulgaria', Paper prepared for the 4th Dubrovnik Conference on Sustainable

Development of Energy, Water and Environment Systems, 4–8 June 2007, Dubrovnik.

Medarova, K. and A. Antypas (2006), 'Implementation of the Aarhus Convention in Bulgaria: limping towards effectiveness', *Environmental Liability*, **14**(1):13–22.

Nilsson, M. and A. Persson (2003), 'Framework for analytical environmental policy integration', *Journal of Environmental Policy and Planning*, **5**(4): 333–59.

OECD (1999), *Environment in the Transition to a Market Economy*, Paris: OECD.

Pavlinek, P. and J. Pickles (2000), *Environmental Transitions: Transformation and Ecological Defence in Central and Eastern Europe*, London: Routledge.

Pickvance, K. (1998), *Democracy and Environmental Movements in Eastern Europe*, Boulder, CO: Westview Press.

Rezessy, S, A. Antypas and K. Szeker (2004), 'Environmental Policy Integration: Lessons from the Energy and Transport Sectors', Paper prepared for the 2004 Berlin Conference on the Human Dimensions of Global Environmental Change Greening of Policies – Interlinkages and Policy Integration.

Steger, T. (2004a), 'Environmentalism and Democratic Network Governance in Hungary and Latvia', Paper presented at Conference on Democratic Network Governance in Copenhagen, Denmark, 21–22 October.

Steger, T. (2004b), 'Environmentalism and Democracy in Hungary and Latvia', Dissertation. Syracuse University, Syracuse, NY.

Trieb, O., H. Bahr and G. Falkner (2005), 'Modes of governance: a note towards conceptual clarification', European Governance Papers. No. N-05-02.

Ürge-Vorsatz, D., S. Rezessy, and A. Antypas (2004), 'renewable electricity support schemes in Central Europe: A case of incomplete policy transfer', *Energy and Environment*, **15**(4): 699–721.

Ürge-Vorsatz, D., G. Miladinova and L. Paizs (2005), 'Energy in Transition: From the Iron Curtain to the European Union', *Energy Policy* **34**(15): 2279–97.

Von Homeyer, I. (2006), 'EPIGOV Common Framework', State of the Art Report for the Project: Environmental Policy Integration and Multi-Level Governance, Berlin: Ecologic-Institute for International and European Environmental Policy.

Zito, A., C. Radaelli and J. Andrew (eds) (2003), '"New" environmental policy instruments in the European Union: Better governance or rhetorical smoke?, *Public Administration,* **81**(3): 509–606.

10. EPI and Regional Governance in Spain

Josu Mezo and Kenneth Hanf

10.1 INTRODUCTION

This chapter is based on research, currently under way, examining the experiences of four Autonomous Communities in Spain with the institutionalization of the general policy commitment to sustainable development within their respective regional governments.[1] The project is concerned with the measures that have been taken to build institutional capacities to 'do' sustainable development. It is assumed that, among other things, these governments will need to adapt existing or create new institutional arrangements in order to be able to produce and implement policy measures designed to manage the transition of their societies toward more sustainable paths of development. One of the things that these governments need to be able to do is produce integrated policies that are capable of bringing together – coordinating – actions in the economic, environmental and social policy spheres. Consequently, although this research has not focused specifically on capacities for environmental policy integration (EPI), it is clear that the integration of environmental considerations into other sectoral policy decisions and actions is a central part of effective governance for sustainable development.

It could be argued that, to the extent that a government focuses its energies on EPI, it lacks the capacity to formulate and implemented integrated policies for sustainable development. This raises the interesting question of whether there is an important difference between EPI, which focuses on integrating the 'environmental dimension' into sectoral policy making, and SDI – integrated policy for sustainable development – which focuses on the need to integrate three different dimensions with each other. However, as we will see, to the extent that governments tend to reduce sustainable development to 'giving due consideration to the environment' in sectoral decision making, this distinction becomes moot. Moreover, as a leading student of EPI has observed, if we view sustainable development 'primarily as the interaction between environment and economics' it is not necessary to treat 'all three aspects equally when attempting conceptual clarification and operational improvement' (Lafferty, 2002: 2). Consequently, although our primary concern had to do with institutional capacities for managing the transition towards sustainable paths of development, it turns out that, in institutional terms, much of what these Autonomous Communities are in fact doing under this heading looks a lot like EPI.

With the above qualifications in mind, we can consider the information presented below as a brief overview of some of the experiences with EPI at the regional level in Spain as a part of the matrix of capacities for planning and implementing strategies for sustainable development. The information provided allows us to compare the experiences of four important Autonomous Communities: Andalusia, Galicia, the Basque Country and Catalonia. The research looks at the extent to which EPI has been promoted and, more particularly, at the institutional adjustments and procedural innovations that have been made by these regional governments to realize EPI within the policy making and implementation process. The focus of the chapter is on efforts aimed at creating and developing institutional capacities necessary to realize EPI in an institutional context characterized by a high level of institutional fragmentation and sectoral policy making. This research is intended to fill a gap on systematic studies in Spanish regional governance.

10.1.1 Analytical Focus for the Description

We are obviously not the first to point out that the precise meaning and components of Environmental Policy Integration (EPI) have not yet been well defined. Much as Sustainable Development itself, EPI is a general label attached to many different institutions, procedures and activities. The framing of the EPI problem influences the perception of what means are necessary, useful and effective in achieving it (Persson, 2004). Following Jordan and Schout (2006: 63), we find it useful to distinguish between EPI as a principle, as a process and as an output. The latter follows beyond the scope of this work, so we will focus on the first two aspects of the concept.

In this chapter we describe the changes that are taking place in our four Autonomous Communities regarding the efforts and energies invested to create the preconditions for achieving EPI within the policy and institutional context of their strategies for SD. In section 10.2 we will focus on EPI as a policy principle. We will examine to what extent it has been incorporated in public and political discourse and in official policy and planning documents; we will also discuss the rank that EPI has achieved in relation to other political priorities, and the meaning that it is given to it in each Autonomous Community by the relevant political actors. This will show the degree of commitment of authorities and the type of changes that might be expected.

Taking a strong normative stance relative to EPI implies for some scholars assigning 'principled priority' (Lafferty and Hovden, 2003) to environmental concern *vis-à-vis* the other dimensions of sustainable development.[2] Giving special normative weight to environmental considerations in a decision can be justified in terms of the instrumental rationality of this procedure: according to this view, a decision is more rational when it avoids costs and realizes benefits that can only be achieved if environmental aspects are taken into account early on in the decision making process (Jordan, 2002; Peters, 1998; Underdal, 1980).

Consequently, the 'principled priority' approach acknowledges the role of the environment objectives as guiding principles in setting policy agendas and policy content in non-environmental sectors. Lafferty and Knudsen (2007) suggest that this strong interpretation is also a pragmatic response to the fact that the balanced understanding of EPI, which has been central to the concept of sustainable development, has not worked thus far.[3]

As for EPI as 'the process through which non-environmental sectors consider the overall environmental consequences of their policies and the active and early steps taken to incorporate them into the policy making at all relevant levels of governance' (Jordan and Schout, 2006), this would result in new administrative practices and cultures that must be institutionalized in order to protect them from the menace of being reversed by countervailing forces originating in the external environment (EEA, 2005). Several attempts have been made to develop a catalogue of institutions, mechanisms, procedures and practices that favour or embody EPI (see, for example Jacob et al. (2008), Jordan and Schout (2006) and Lafferty (2004)), but general agreement on such a list has not yet been reached. Therefore, we have adopted a simple classification of instruments, based on a distinction between institutions and procedures, which we will link, where relevant, to these classifications.

Thus, the third section analyses how the idea of EPI has been translated into institutions, both within the relevant departments and across them, with advisory bodies, inter-ministerial coordinating bodies and other institutional changes. The main obstacles to overcome in striving to achieve EPI are sectoral compartmentalization and the power struggle among competing interests, views and paradigms.

The problem spans the entire policy spectrum of governmental and administrative practice, and arises as a consequence of the divergence between policy problems that are increasingly interdependent on one hand and the extensive and growing fragmentation of the decision system on the other. Sectoral specialization is predicated on considerations of efficiency and cost effectiveness, but can easily end up yielding suboptimal results as departments develop turf mentality (environment vs. the sector) and engage in a competitive struggle to defend their interests, satisfy their clients and increment their resources.

Finally, in section 10.4 we present information on procedures and processes like sustainable development strategies, monitoring processes (as a composite term for the combination of indicators and accountability mechanisms), public participation and strategic environmental assessment (EPI procedural factors). The interplay and performance of all these elements, among others, have been treated in the literature as necessary (but not sufficient) conditions for achieving EPI. Great importance is understandably attached to the decision-making rules and styles defining the position of environmental concerns in the policy process. Decision rules specify the constellation of actors involved in the policy arena (who is in, and who is out) and how the decisions are taken (right of advancing policy proposals, agenda-setting power, timing of participation by environmental department and agency) while decision styles refer to the modes of interactions among actors, that is, whether agreements are reached by mediating conflicting interests through bargaining or by collaborative problem solving (Nilsson and Persson, 2003). Both determine the degree of openness of the policy process to consultation and participation of external actors and have a direct bearing on the potential for learning.

The concluding section is intended to shed more light on the emerging regional modes of governance for EPI.

10.2   THE COMMITMENT TO EPI IN SD DISCOURSE

SD has become an extremely attractive idea that promises the possibility of harmonizing economic development, social progress and environmental protection. The realization of this broad idea will require new forms of governance that are able to transcend the traditional sectoral division of labour between government departments. It is thus commonly agreed that EPI must be part and parcel of any attempt to achieve or at least approach SD. Both EPI and SD require, then, important transformations of the political and administrative systems than can only be brought about by a strong political commitment at the highest level. Normally political commitment can be expressed in different ways (proclamations, statements, legal text, and so on). Political will is also determinant in the attempts to resolve the issue of trade-off by, for example, brokering compromises and solutions in order to compensate the political losers of greening measures (Lenschow, 2002). A common tool for ensuring effective translation of a commitment into concrete action is a formal policy framework for EPI or SD in the government as a whole. In relation to EPI, a strategy for sustainable development is commonly seen as such an overall framework (OECD, 2002, in Persson 2004). We will discuss the regions' attempts to pass their SD strategies more carefully in section 10.4.1, but at this point we want to point out how prominently the goal of integrating environmental objectives into non-environmental policies appears in the political and governmental discourse about SD in the four regions, and in particular in their regional strategies for SD, when they exist, and how the potential conflict with more traditional ideas about economic development and social advances was solved.

The regional government of Andalusia (Junta de Andalucía) was very explicit when it stated, in the Andalusian Sustainable Development Strategy (EADS, its acronym in Spanish) that sustainability for Andalusia means necessarily the progressive reduction of the gaps that separate the region from Spanish and European averages in income, activity and unemployment rates (Junta de Andalucía, 2002: 28). In fact one could say that closing those gaps is the main legitimatizing argument for the regional government of Andalusia. Therefore, its concept of SD does not allow for changes in the overarching position of the objective of growth in terms of classic indicators of development (income and employment). In particular, concerns that might put in question the viability of the actual development model and the quest for achieving European-level standards of life are completely avoided. Consequently, in the Andalusian case environmental concerns are clearly seen as subordinate to other classic economic development priorities.

In the case of the Basque Country, the government has even more clearly adopted an environmentally focused concept of SD. In 2001 the president of the Basque Government and all members of his cabinet signed a solemn *Agreement on the Sustainability of the Basque Country* (Gobierno Vasco, 2001), which centred mainly on environmental aspects of sustainability and declared EPI to be one of its six governing principles. One year later the government approved the Basque Environmental Strategy for SD (Gobierno Vasco, 2002), which from its very title made clear that it was not a holistic SD strategy, but rather an environmental strategy. Its first pages argued that traditionally all governments have paid much more attention to social and economic matters, so an attempt to achieve a balance between these two concerns and environmental objectives requires a strategy that is focused on the latter.

The Strategy was accompanied by an Environmental Framework Programme (2002–2006), which listed five necessary conditions for SD, the first of them being, precisely, the 'integration of the environmental variable in other policies'. This was further specified into six goals and nine commitments, including ideas such as the approval of environmental strategies for various policy sectors, and the introduction of integrated environmental policy appraisal procedures. The Basque approach, then, would be one of giving at least equal weight to environmental concerns than to traditional economic and social worries.

Also in Catalonia the concept of SD has been strongly associated with environmental concerns. In fact, when one analyses the evolution of the administrative organization of the Generalitat (the Catalan government), it can be easily seen that sometime around the late 1990s, all aspects of government action and organization related to environmental policies were relabelled as sustainable development. The idea that this commitment requires the integration of environmental concerns in other policy areas has been presented repeatedly in declarations by government officials in Parliament and other settings, but in relation to the level of priority given to environmental matters *vis-à-vis* other governmental objectives it is important to note that the Nationalist and Conservative government in power until 2003 explicitly rejected a commitment to either a 'strong' or 'weak' interpretation of SD (which would correlate closely with a high or low priority for environmental concerns in EPI) when questioned on the matter in the Catalan Parliament by the Nationalist Left party, ERC. When the Socialists, former Communists and ERC formed a new government in 2003 they included SD and EPI in their coalition agreements and sent strong signals in Parliament that these would be among their priorities, including a quick approval of an SD strategy. EPI was even included in the new regional *Estatuto* (regional constitution) approved in 2006 (Cataluña, 2006), which declared that 'public authorities must promote the integration of environmental objectives in sectoral policies' (art. 46.3).

However, successive declarations in Parliament made references to the need of an SD strategy or to institutional arrangements for EPI more and more vague (and in fact no SD strategy has as yet been approved). All of this suggests that the promotion of SD and EPI can be classic cases of policies that are easily preached from opposition but much harder to implement than anticipated. Not surprisingly, when parties that are committed to them reach power, the realities confronted in office lead them to quickly downgrade their promises.

Finally, in Galicia, as in the other regions, we find that the understanding of SD is also strongly biased towards environmental concerns. As we will see below, the term sustainable development has been incorporated into the denomination of several governmental sections or departments related to the environment. More precisely, EPI has been a prominent part of the official discourse about SD. In fact, the last conservative government (2001–2005) prepared a draft strategy for SD (that was never officially adopted) with this revealing title: 'Towards a strategy for sustainable development for Galicia: Integration of the environmental variable in sectoral policies' (Consellería de Medio Ambiente, 2003), where it proposed a number of instruments to achieve this integration, such as fiscal policies, R&D measures, environmental pacts, education, information and awareness programmes.

All in all we can conclude that, despite generic declarations referring to the three pillars of the concept of SD, whenever the concept has been specified in more concrete detail, it has veered in all four regions towards a renewal, invigoration and upgrading of traditional environmental policies, combined with a new interest in the integration of environmental concerns in other policy areas. EPI is, therefore, in all four cases, a substantive part of the discourse about SD. But the fact that two of the regions were unable to pass their SD strategies, and that Andalusia very clearly opted for a weak version of EPI, explicitly subordinated to traditionally defined economic growth concerns, must be taken as clear indications that SD and EPI are not very high among the priorities of the governments of the autonomous communities. In the following sections we will verify this observation by examining how far the four regions have gone in translating this commitment into actual institutions and procedures.

10.3 INSTITUTIONALIZATION OF SUSTAINABLE DEVELOPMENT POLICY IN SPANISH AUTONOMOUS COMMUNITIES: THE PLACE OF EPI

10.3.1 The Pursuit of EPI within Environmental Departments

One of the main obstacles to achieving EPI highlighted in the literature is the difficulty encountered in overcoming sectoral compartmentalization and power struggles among competing interests, views and paradigms. Many authors have suggested that in order to produce the kinds of policies and actions necessary for achieving more sustainable paths of development and EPI it will be necessary to experiment with solutions based on changes in governmental architecture (that is integrating departments and functions, adapting the existing institutional arrangements or developing new ones).

The most far-reaching proposals in this regard involve the creation of some kind of new overarching authority (chief executive, planning agency, a body within the domain of the legislature or a last-resort judicial organ) with the specific mandate to promote and supervise the introduction of SD policies or the adoption of EPI by all public institutions. None of the communities in this study has adopted such a bold strategy. Instead they have entrusted the existing environmental departments with responsibilities for these tasks. This seems to support the scepticism expressed by some scholars regarding the difficulties encountered in attempting to change existing institutional arrangements (except under the 'favourable' conditions created by political crises,

Lenschow, 2002). Reorganizations, as is well known, disrupt existing patterns of interactions and procedures (indeed, that is the intention!) and, in any case, require a certain amount of time to become established and effective.

The institutional changes in our four regions have followed a double strategy. On the one hand, some division within the environmental department has been charged with reviewing other departments' activities and/or promoting the introduction of environmental or sustainability concerns on them. On the other hand, we find several attempts to create inter-departmental bodies with the same intention. In this section we will review the first route, and the second will be examined in the next section.

The main actor in environmental policy in Andalusia is the regional Ministry of the Environment, created in 1994. It is interesting to note that prior to this the Andalusian government experimented with a different type of organizational structure, the Andalusian Environmental Agency (AMA), which was attached directly to the President of the Region, and was expected to be less bureaucratic than a government department. However, the AMA was dissolved in 1996 and its competences were transferred to the Ministry. Within the Ministry the General Secretariat for Environmental Policies is in charge of overseeing and reporting on activities, plans and programmes by other departments in the government that may have potential environmental implications. When these programmes are legally obliged to undertake an integrated impact assessment, this report has to be approved by the Director General of Prevention and Environmental Quality, located in the office of the vice-minister. The vice-minister also has important responsibilities with regard to coordination with other departments, when necessary.

Since 2004, the Ministry of the Environment has a General Secretariat for Sustainability, which is nominally in charge of promotion and supervision of all actions related to the Andalusian Strategy for SD.[4] This mandate, if interpreted broadly, could cover almost all activities in the ministry. But in practice the interpretation has been quite narrow, focusing only on a few specific activities (the creation of the General Secretariat was the result of a coalition pact between the dominant Socialist party and a minor Green party, who put one of their members at its head, with the result that the GS is not well integrated in the overall activities of the ministry).

The promotion of sustainability and in particular EPI has not led to any related change in the institutional structure of the Basque Government. In fact, the powers over environmental issues have been fragmented for a long time among several different departments of government (combined, at various times, with Public Works, Transport, Land Planning, Urban Planning, Housing, and Agriculture and Fisheries). It is only since 2001 that the Ministry for Territorial Planning and the Environment has concentrated the powers in this sector. (In 2005 it was re-named as Ministry for the Environment and Territorial Planning, DMAOT). Within the ministry it is the vice-minister who has responsibility for the environment, and in particular it is the Directorate for Environmental Planning, Evaluation and Control, which is in charge of the elaboration, monitoring and reporting on the Environmental Strategy for SD and the Framework Programme. This requires quite an intense interaction with other departments. However, most of these functions are carried out through IHOBE, a private law company owned by the department, which in turns subcontracts many tasks, like the preparation of planning documents or writing of annual reports, to private consultants (IHOBE, 2006).

With regard to the evolution of the governmental structure of Catalonia on these matters, it is possible to distinguish three stages. The first one (1991–97) was characterized by efforts to institutionalize environmental policy in general. The Department of the Environment, created in 1991, took over a series of competences that until then had been spread over three sectoral departments (Territorial Policy and Public Works; Energy and Industry, and Agriculture and Fisheries). The intermediate stage, covering the period 1998–2003, consisted of introducing actions intended to translate the political commitment to SD into concrete – but, as it turned out, insufficient – measures. For example, the implementation of the EU Directive on integrated pollution prevention and control and the associated regulations, led to the restructuring of the Department and the creation of a new General Directorate for Environmental Planning responsible for SD. Later, at the end of 1998, the Advisory Council for Sustainable Development (CADS) was established with the main task of recommending general guidelines for policies with repercussion on the environment and SD.

The third stage, starting in 2004, has been characterized by unsuccessful attempts to create an institutional structure responsible for carrying out the process of transition to a more sustainable pattern of development. It began with the establishment of the General Directorate of Environmental Policies and Sustainability, which includes the General Sub-directorate for Sustainable Development, whose functions include analysing SD policies applied abroad or by other authorities, and promoting sustainability policies in the programmes of other departments of the Catalan government; and the General Sub-directorate of Environmental Evaluation, in charge of integrated environmental evaluation of plans and programmes. Additionally, an Office on Climate Change was established in 2006 within the same General Directorate.

In Galicia environmental political-administrative structures are relatively new since the Department of the Environment was only established in 1997. Later on, in 2002, a Centre for Sustainable Development was created within the same department to promote SD through citizens' participation, information and training. It is also in charge of fostering research and technological development to improve the environment. Finally, in 2006, with a new left-nationalist government, the Department of the Environment became the Department of the Environment and Sustainable Development, with coordination functions. In particular, the Office for the Promotion of Sustainable Development is in charge of the strategic environmental evaluation of plans and programmes. However, interviews and official documents show that the planning sections of the department have limited human resources to carry out the tasks of coordination and assessment.

The four regions have thus established quite similar arrangements. The promotion of environmental or sustainability concerns in the activities of other departments has been included among the tasks of some part of the environment department, which is also usually in charge of planning within the department of the environment itself. There is a more specific mandate for the same or another section of the department to carry out strategic environmental evaluations of plans and programmes. None of these sections is exclusively or even primarily concerned with EPI, and they are usually small parts of the overall structure and operations of their departments, with limited budgets and human resources.

10.3.2   Arrangements for EPI Through Inter-Institutional Coordination

Whether based on new or already existing arrangements (without changing hierarchical relationships or organizational mandates), coordination and communication are acknowledged to be a crucial organizational variable in achieving improvements in EPI.[5] Effective coordination serves to avoid problems like redundancy (two or more organizations dealing with the same problem), lacunae (no organization provides for the fulfilment of a service) and incoherence (the result of a policy dealt with by different organizations pursuing different goals and requirements). There is a wide range of coordination instruments designed to deal with these problems. These range from inter-ministerial committees and task forces to 'environmental correspondents' located in sectoral departments or a central unit with monitoring functions. Networking schemes can also be introduced, as well as regular circulation of staff between the several departments (Jordan and Schout, 2006). In this section we will examine the institutional arrangements for coordination among departments adopted by the four autonomous community in our study.

In 1966 Andalusia established an Integrated Actions Committee for Sustainable Development, to replace a previous Committee of Integrated Actions for Eco-development. This unit, with representatives of all departments in government, is supposed to concern itself with 'the promotion of activities that imply the integration of environmental considerations in all types of policies, plans and programmes carried out in Andalusia'. Once more, it can be seen, sustainability is narrowly interpreted as equal to 'environmentalism'. In practice the focus of this committee, which meets only sporadically, has been even narrower, concentrating on quite specific areas of its mandate, like those related to the evaluation of management plans for protected areas. Consequently, it has not acted as a central vehicle for EPI. To fill this gap with regard to especially important areas, the Ministry of Environment has, since 2004, created a number of mixed committees with other departments (like Agriculture, Tourism and Public Works), that meet regularly and serve as a strong vehicle for information exchange and cooperation. Finally, the Ministry of Environment has an important chance to influence and modify the policy proposals of other departments through a general mechanism of inter-ministerial coordination, the Vice-Minister's Committee.

This is a very important instrument for policy coordination. High-level representatives from each ministry meet weekly to inform their colleagues of the projects they are working on, and have an opportunity to exchange comments, worries, proposals for amendments or to resolve substantive discrepancies. However, the efficacy of this committee is variable, since there is no clear regulation specifying when each department should inform others about their projects, and how the differences should be resolved. Ultimately, the incorporation of the points of view of other departments depends on informal processes of mutual persuasion, the influence of external interests and the political influence that each Minister has in the negotiation process within the Committee.

A number of interdepartmental committees exist also in the Basque Country with regard to environmental or sustainability questions. The Basque Strategy for Environmental Sustainability created a framework for coordination in the form of an Inter-institutional Working Group, which included representatives from the regional government, the three provincial governments (which are quite powerful in the Basque case) and the municipalities. But the group had no clearly defined role, has met irregularly and plays no leading role in the implementation of the strategy. A few years earlier, an environmental protection law had created the Environmental Commission of the Basque Country, an instrument for consultation, participation, contact and coordination for different parts of the Basque administration, presided over by the Minister for Environment and Territorial Planning, and composed of vice-ministers from different departments, as well as representatives from the provincial and local authorities. Again, this body has had little practical impact, as it only meets when required by law to express its opinion on a project.

The most important coordination institution in the Basque government is in fact a small and little known Coordinating Direction, within the vice-presidency of the government. The Coordinating Direction performs coordination and control tasks with respect to all the plans, programmes and significant actions adopted by the government. It makes sure that the departments affected by a given plan will take part in its elaboration. It also watches over legal questions and competences, the coherence among different plans and their compatibility with the general programme of government, parliamentary initiatives, and other legislations and measures at both the Spanish and the EU levels. However, the amount of coordination achieved has generally not been satisfactorily. For instance the new Environmental Programme 2007–10 stresses the need to improve coordination among departments and policies, in particular with regard to the Climate Change policy.

In the Catalan case, there are also several institutions that attempt to integrate environmental and sustainability concerns across several departments. One of them is the Advisory Council for Sustainable Development (CADS), created in 1998 and composed of 15 experts, chosen by the government for their personal merits, or as distinguished members of academic and scientific bodies. The CADS is asked to express its opinion on the general direction of policies that may have an impact on SD, and also on specific draft bills, plans or programmes. It is also entitled to make its own proposals on measures to promote sustainability, on environmental information and education activities, and on research related to the environment. Additionally, in 2004, the Catalan government created a Coordination Commission for Sustainable Development, which is chaired by the vice-president of the government, and is composed of the ministers of Territorial Policy and Public Works and of Environment and Housing, one representative from the rest of departments, and the director of the CADS. Its functions include the preliminary examination and review of proposals for bills, plans and programmes concerning SD, the monitoring of governmental activities towards SD, and the coordination of activities against climate change. Unfortunately, information about its meetings and reports is not available. Therefore, it is impossible to evaluate its performance to date, although there are reasons to believe that it has not really had any major impact. Furthermore, some of its functions overlap with those of the Catalan Commission for Climate Change, established in 2003, as well as the Interdepartmental Committee on Climate Change, created in 2007 and chaired by the Minister of the Environment. There have been, thus, several attempts to institutionalize the coordination of departments on environmental and sustainability issues, but little evidence that they have made great progress.

As early as 1984 Galicia created a Delegate Commission for the Environment, a subset of the council of ministers to deal with issues related to the environment (the delegate commissions on various issues are responsible for preparing the work of the council of ministers). We have only indirect evidence of its lack of impact, in that in 1998 the Galician government created a new institution, the Galician Committee for Environmental Integration and Coordination, chaired by the Minister of the Environment, with representatives from several other departments (at the directorate general level). It was renamed after the change of government in 2005, as the Inter-departmental Committee on Sustainable Development. Its functions were defined quite vaguely (elaborate proposals, make suggestions, write reports, promote coordination), and it was not given any strong power to amend policy proposals.

We see again, then, common themes surfacing from the analysis of the four regions. All of them have established bodies with representation from different departments to study draft bills, policy plans and action programmes for different sectors in relation to environmental and sustainability issues. In all cases their formal powers are weak, since they are only consultative bodies, and they cannot veto or even amend projects if the department in charge of them is not willing to do so voluntarily. In the cases where we have information, it appears that their meetings are brief and not very frequent, and that they act mostly when their non-binding opinions are legally required.

10.4   PROCEDURES FOR EPI

10.4.1   SD Strategies and Environmental Plans

One of the most obvious ways to promote environmental policy integration is to adopt and support a high-level strategy or plan, which on the one hand declares and embodies the commitment of the government to SD and, as part of it, to EPI, and on the other hand specifies the steps to be taken to achieve that result (Jacob et al., 2008; Jordan and Schout, 2006). In fact the four regions in our study did start a process to approve such a plan, but only two of them approved it, and only one has publicly monitored the implementation of the strategy.

Andalusia approved a strategy for sustainable development (EADS) in 2003, after a long, four-year period of debate and deliberation. Three of its 24 chapters dealt with issues related to governance, and of the remaining 21 chapters, 17 were concerned with environmental issues, either dealing with classic environmental policies like nature conservation, or waste management (7) or with the greening of other policies (10 chapters), like agriculture, territory and town planning, tourism, and so on. The strategy made broad declarations of intent in all those areas, but included few specific targets or instruments, and in fact its implementation has not been publicly monitored or assessed.

The Basque Country approved in 2002 its 'Basque Environmental Strategy for Sustainable Development' which from its own title reveals the decision to concentrate efforts in the environmental dimension of SD.

The strategy contained a long list of goals and 185 specific commitments with a deadline for taking some action (most of them to approve a law, pass a plan, or a similar regulation, and about 40 to achieve a measurable outcome). The government made a yearly report which included an estimation on how many commitments had been achieved, were on track or likely not to be on time.

Unlike Andalusia, or the Basque Country, Catalonia has not yet approved a regional strategy for SD, despite a mandate in 1997 from the Catalan Parliament (resolution 409/V) to adopt one before the Johannesburg Summit of 2002 (the similar timing of all these efforts was related to the Johannesburg summit, where all countries were expected to present their national strategies, and many European regions intended also to present their own documents). The Nationalist government then in power did in fact set in motion a complex and ambitious process of consultation among departments, with external experts and local authorities and sectoral interest groups.

However, it took longer than expected to produce a document, and after missing the 2002 deadline it was decided that the results were too sensitive to be discussed during the 2003 pre-election period. Consequently further dissemination of the draft was postponed. The new coalition government formed in 2003 decided to rethink the whole process and start anew, but it has yet to produce any substantive result.

We cannot analyse here in full detail the reasons for this failure, but part of it can no doubt be attributed precisely to the difficulty of integrating in one document the environmental, economic and social goals of different social groups, political actors and governmental departments.

Finally, in Galicia there was also a project to produce a strategy for SD, although in this case the discussion was basically done within the Ministry of the Environment. The document was finished, but not officially published, just before the last election of 2005. It has never been endorsed by the new nationalist-left government.

10.4.2 Monitoring SD and Environment Quality as an Accountability Mechanism

Improving public information has been considered to be a functional prerequisite to achieve efficient governance for SD. Periodic evaluation of governmental activities provides important sources of feedback regarding the results of public programmes, focuses the attention of policy makers on results, and mobilizes citizens' understanding of and support for the necessary measures for changing prevailing patterns of development.

There is a growing consensus on the benefits of a system of quantitative indicators of sustainability. If they are well designed, they can summarize in a few numbers a good deal of information about the environmental aspects of any policy, and thus they can be a key part of the process of EPI.

All the regions included in this study have shown their interest in the idea of establishing some system of periodical evaluation of environmental and sustainability issues. However, there are wide differences in the way the have gone about this. Some started producing reports in the mid 1980s while others have not yet started; some have published broad, long, reports, with a coverage of a wide range of issues, while others have focused more on a relatively brief report, concentrated on a short list of key indicators. All regions are clearly attempting to create a system of environmental or sustainability indicators, but with one possible exception, they have not settled yet on one such system. In fact, some of the regions have produced several systems of indicators, which may defeat the whole purpose of the exercise.

Andalusia has a long tradition of publishing a yearly report on the state of the environment, which goes back to 1987.[6] This is a rigorous and extensive document, which in the last years has included references at some points to 'environmental indicators', using *emoticons* (smiles or frowns) to portray the positive, negative or neutral evolution. But the figures supporting the *emoticons* have not been published. Meanwhile, several internal documents related to the yearly evaluation of the Environmental Plan for Andalusia have included lists of quantitative indicators. And finally the General Secretariat for Sustainability made an important effort to prepare its own system of indicators, which was published in 2006 (Fernández Latorre, 2006), but has not yet been applied to a regular evaluation of the Andalusian situation.

In the Basque Country, transparency and accountability in relation with sustainable matters have been made a priority by the regional administration. Several publications and periodical reports assess the activities of the government and their impacts. The most important is probably the Report on Environmental Sustainability (Gobierno Vasco, 2006), an annual publication which monitors the degree of fulfilment of the Basque strategy, and quantifies the percentage of goals and commitments that are achieved, on track, initiated, or not initiated.

Another publication – Environmental Indicators – checks the evolution of a selected group of indicators aimed at providing information about the evolution of some key aspects of sustainability (DMAOT, 2006). Finally, there is the triennial Environment in the Basque Country Report, which reviews the environmental situation in a more extensive way.

In Catalonia, the government publishes two periodic reports on the environmental situation. One is a booklet called *Environmental Data in Catalonia*, which is a compilation of statistics on the most relevant environmental issues, and has been published since the mid 1990s (Generalitat de Cataluña, 2008). However, the publication has not consistently presented long-term trends, and has made no attempt to evaluate whether data on the different issues were moving in the right direction or at an acceptable speed. Thus, a new yearly publication, *The Environment in Catalonia*, was started in 2007 (Generalitat de Cataluña, 2007), with more statistics and some text that attempted to offer an interpretation of the situation, but did not summarize information through a system of indicators. This was done, however, for the first time in the *Catalonia 2005 Report on Environment and Sustainable Development* (Generalitat de Cataluña, 2005), a publication structured around 163 indicators of economic, social and environmental sustainability.

Finally, in the case of Galicia, despite several proposals and discussions about the development of a system of indicators, and the publication of some periodic evaluation of the state of the environment in the region, none of them has appeared yet.

With the possible exception of the Basque Country, then, the communities have not yet achieved a simple, comprehensible system of indicators to monitor the evolution of the state of environment, or the results of regional policies oriented towards the environment. In particular it is worth noting that no region has even attempted to measure EPI itself, although the government of the Basque Country announced that it intended to produce a set of 'integration indicators', which has not yet materialized.

10.4.3 Intergovernmental Relations

Institutional capacities are related to the way in which the levels of government interact, along both horizontal and vertical lines. It is generally assumed that EPI, in addition to the horizontal inter-sectoral integration, also requires the management of multilevel inter-governmental networks of cooperation (that is in fact the whole topic of Jordan and Schout, 2006). Since the environment may be affected by policies from different levels of government, a fully integrated environmental policy should be coordinated with governments below or above the level of the region (that is, with

European and Spanish institutions, and with local ones). Additionally, since the environment knows few boundaries, environmental policies should be coordinated with those of other regions, within Spain or in other countries. In this regard, we can look at the activities of Spanish regions in relation to three other types of governments.

First, in relation with other regions at the UE/international level, we can mention that Catalonia and the Basque Country are active participants in ENCORE and NRG4SD, two networks of regional governments focused on SD and environmental policies, where there are opportunities for exchanges of information, diffusion of best practices, and cooperation of different types. Since the four communities in our study have some international border it is worth noticing that all of them are also engaged in some type of trans-border cooperation, although this tends to be channelled through cooperation between local authorities, with the support of the regional government.

The most important case is probably the network of local authorities created by Galicia and the North of Portugal in the *Eixo Atlántico*, but there are other cases of cooperation between the Algarve and Andalusia, and the municipalities at both sides of the Spanish–French border around the Bidasoa river. Catalonia is part of the Euroregion Pyrenees-Mediterranean which is expected to facilitate cooperation on both sides of the border regarding environmental matters, among others, but no important activity has happened yet in this respect.

Secondly, with regard to the relations with the central state, we must point out that the central government has only very recently approved a SD strategy, so it has not had a leadership role in establishing a frame of reference for regional and local governments. The autonomous communities do participate in two formal mechanisms of intergovernmental coordination. The first one is the Conference on the Environment, which reunites representatives both at ministerial and technical level of the central government and the regions. The second one is the Network of Environmental Authorities, a forum of cooperation and coordination between environmental officials and those responsible for programming and managing Structural and Cohesion Funds. They seem to play a useful role mostly for diffusion of information. All this has left the autonomous communities with a great deal of discretion and leeway in formulating their own strategies, guided more by what happens at the EU – and international – level.

Finally, the most important inter-governmental activities have been directed towards the sub-regional and the local level, promoting the adoption of Local Agenda 21 plans by municipalities or counties. This is of course a process that has been taking place world wide since the Rio Summit and particularly in Europe since the Aalborg declaration of 1994, with the support of the European Commission, started vigorous movements of towns and cities committed to SD. In Andalusia, this has been done through the Program City21, implemented in 2002, with the objective of promoting SD in the Andalusian municipalities. Within the Urban Environmental Plan (1997–2002), the regional Ministry of the Environment signed an agreement with the Andalusian Federation of Municipalities and Provinces in order to carry out a Program on Environmental Sustainability that brings support to the Local Agenda 21 and to strengthen the Andalusia's Network of Sustainable Cities (Consejería de Medio Ambiente, 2005: 268–9).

The Basque Government has promoted the adoption of the Local Agenda 21 with the aim that by the end of 2006 all the municipalities larger than 5,000 inhabitants (more than 98 per cent of the total population) would have their own Agenda 21 approved (individually or in clusters of neighbouring localities). The policy included funds for the hiring of at least one environmental officer in most of municipalities with more than 10,000 inhabitants. This was considered to be an important institutional improvement at the local level that guarantees the continuity of SD policies.

In Catalonia, a programme designed in 1996 to support Local Actions for SD included collaboration between the Department of the Environment, the Catalan Association of Municipalities, and the *Diputaciós* (provincial authorities) of three of the four provinces in the region. The programme had four main objectives: a) to provide information about sustainable policies at the local level; b) to define the rules of procedures for local actions on sustainable development; c) to offer financial incentives to local authorities already acting on issues of SD; and d) to provide technical assistance to local initiatives.

More important for the success in implementing Local Agenda 21 in Catalonia has been the role played by the *Diputació* of Barcelona, the provincial government of the by far most populated province in the region, which was precisely the one not involved in the previous initiative. These activities have been carried out without any support from or coordination with the Generalitat (the regional government). The Diputació provided financial and technical assistance to municipalities in the province. A particular important instrument in this regard was the Network of Cities and Municipalities for Sustainability that was established by the province in July of 1997. At present 220 local governments from the province of Barcelona – and outside – are members of this network. These municipalities represent roughly 78 per cent of the total population of Catalonia.

In the case of Galicia, support from the regional government to Local Agenda 21 programmes has been quite limited. In 2002 it signed six agreements with local councils in rural areas to support their efforts, but it did not support the activities of important industrial and urban municipalities. After the 2005 change of government, new programmes of support were announced for counties, rather than municipalities.

What we see, then, is that despite the declarations about the global dimensions of environmental worries, and the need to produce policies that respond adequately to that character, the level of coordination among regions, even within Spain, is rather low (although, of course, coordination through rules and regulations is very important). It seems that all our regions are more interested in and capable of promoting SD and EPI top-down, on the local authorities, than in coordinating with central government and other Spanish or European regions.

10.4.4 Social Participation in Decision Making

It is commonly agreed that governance for SD requires changes in administrative and political processes that render the policy-making process more open to social participation. These new mechanisms of social participation that allow interest groups, associations, unions, companies, local authorities, scientists and others to bring their points of view, concerns, interests and expertise to the elaboration of new plans and programmes can be expected also to be favourable to EPI, since it is precisely the environmental aspects and concerns that will be among those neglected by traditional policy making and brought to the table by innovative participation instruments. All four regions have established similar bodies that are intended to promote this kind of participation on decisions related to the environment and/or sustainability. However, their impact has been limited.

In Andalusia, the Andalusian Council for the Environment, created in 1995, is a consultative institution, formed with representatives from unions, business associations, farmers, environmental groups, youth and citizen groups, scientists, experts and local governments, together with some members of the Ministry of the Environment. It is by law required to report on some plans and programmes, but its role is rarely relevant, since it receives information quite late in the deliberation process, and it usually reviews several decisions in the same one-day meeting (of which there are two or three a year) (Consejería de Medio Ambiente, 2005).

There are two similar participatory bodies in the Basque Country. One is the Advisory Council on Nature Conservation, which reports yearly on the management of protected areas, and advises on all the planning decisions for them. The second is the more general Advisory Council on the Environment, established in 1998, that may advise on all policies with an environmental content, but is not usually required to do so by law.

In Catalonia, the Social Council for Sustainable Development was established by law in 2004, but two years later its members had not yet been appointed. Finally, in Galicia, a Galician Council for the Environment was established in 1995 and transformed, in 2006, into the Galician Council for the Environment and Sustainable Development. It has not been a very active body, and in fact environmental organizations have complained that it does not meet as regularly as its own rules prescribe (three times a year), and that too many of its members are representatives of the administration.

Strategic environmental assessments

The integration of environmental concerns in non-environmental policies traditionally has taken place through environmental impact procedures. The instrument of environmental impact assessment (EIA) was initially introduced in Spain in the late 1980s, at the time it joined the European Union, and the regions have been applying it since the early 1990s. The more ambitious strategic environmental assessment (SEA), to be applied to plans and programmes, rather than individual projects, was adopted by an EU directive in 2001, but Spain only transposed this directive with national legislation in April 2006. Technically, then, there has been no legal obligation to submit plans and programmes to an SEA until quite recently, although all regions claimed to be aware that EPI was necessary and they were committed to integrate environmental concerns in their planning activities well before this procedure was approved.

Thus, in Andalusia, several plans related to industry, energy, agriculture or tourism have declared that the protection of the environment was one of their main goals, and have included some measures directed to that purpose. But the first plan submitted to a strategic environmental assessment was the Territorial Plan of Andalusia, adopted at the end of 2006.

In the Basque Country the environmental impact assessment embraces all plans and programmes with potential impact on the environment (territory and urban areas, agriculture, energy, transport, tourism, telecommunications), but it has yet to be applied to a major plan.

Turning to Catalonia, the strategic impact assessment has been implemented by the Department of Territorial Policies and Public Works since 2005 to approve urban and territorial plans, before it was legally required. Meanwhile, the elaboration of the Strategic Energy Plan of Catalonia (2006–2015), was a cooperative effort of the ministries of Environment and Housing, Industry and Public Works, and the Catalan Institute of Energy.

Finally, in Galicia the procedure of Strategic Environmental Assessment has been started on dozens of local urban plans, and also on a number of plans for the whole region, like the Road Plan, the Hydroelectric Sector Plan, the Municipal Waste Management Plan, the Wind Plan, the Energy Plan, a Plan of

Action against Climate Change, and several others. However, all these plans are still being discussed, and thus is still not possible to make an 'assessment of the assessment' process.

10.5   CONCLUSIONS

In this chapter, we have described how the idea of environmental policy integration has been included in the system of governance for sustainable development in a selected number of Autonomous Communities in Spain. We have described these processes from three perspectives: the public discourse about SD and EPI; the institutions in charge of pushing for EPI; and some SD governance innovations that are particularly relevant for EPI. The ultimate objective of the project from which the examples discussed above have been taken is to evaluate the institutional capacity of the emerging system of regional governance in terms of its ability to perform a set of functions that, it is argued, need to be performed if sustainable development is to be promoted effectively. Before we draw some preliminary conclusions in this regard, it will be useful to review briefly the main findings that we have made.

In all regions, we found declarations accepting a broad concept of SD, following international discourse, and including a variety of elements such as the distinction between environmental policy and an integrated policy of SD, the fundamental importance of social participation, the cross-cutting nature of environmental protection as a vertebral axis of public policy, and the necessary integration of economic development, social progress and environmental protection as the basis for generating a new model of development.

However, more often than not, when the concept of SD had to be transformed into more specific commitments it took the form of a re-labelling of the set of pre-existing environmental polices as being 'sustainable'. In fact, one of the main additions that the concept of SD brought to traditional environmental policies was precisely the need to green other policy sectors, that is, to promote environmental policy integration.

With regard to the institutional arrangements, we have seen quite similar developments in the four regions. None has created a separate authority or body in charge of promoting EPI across the government. Instead, some division within the ministry for the environment has been put in charge of that commitment. However, those divisions tend to be understaffed, have relatively low political standing and are also in charge of several other matters (like planning) within the department. As for interdepartmental bodies, the four regions again show a willingness to create such institutions but a lack of strong commitment to empower them, as they are usually requested to give opinions only when legally necessary, and they rarely have a real chance to affect the outcome of the policy process.

Finally, in relation to some procedures to enhance the policy process, we have observed similar patterns: the idea is embraced theoretically, some regulations are passed, policy initiatives are started, but the process is slow, the attempts half-hearted and the results quite meagre.

For example, the formulation of strategic plans for sustainable development can serve as an especially important instrument for EPI, as they should integrate social, economic and environmental goals in a coherent manner. However, the decision process with respect to such strategic plans does not always run smoothly and the road to this goal is long and difficult. In the case of Catalonia, the first attempt to develop an Agenda 21 for the region was abandoned and then lost in the shuffle of the different priorities of the new coalition government. In Galicia, the leftist coalition in power since 2005 abandoned the previous strategy and has never produced a substitute document.

Another aspect where innovation has been slow involves the mechanisms of coordination with other regional governments as well as with local and provincial levels of government. Beyond participation in international networks of governments, such as NRG4SD and ENCORE, no concrete and coordinated measures of this kind have been identified among Spanish regions. Coordination with the Spanish government is also poor. As for local authorities, we see an irregular pattern, with apparently success stories in the Basque Country and Catalonia (thanks to the provincial government of Barcelona, rather than the regional government), but much less intense coordination in Andalusia and Galicia.

At the moment the decision and management systems with regard to SD at the regional level in Spain have not yet been opened to effective participation by citizens, although important steps have been taken to improve the situation. Access of local and supra-local actors to decision makers at this level remains limited as well. Responsibility for decisions on SD remains concentrated in the hands of a small group of experts, the department of the environment and limited inter-departmental exchanges realized through interdepartmental commissions or through informal channels.

The primary mechanisms for consultation and participation on the part of the diversity of non-governmental actors continues to be the traditional channels such as the obligatory phase of public participation with regard to legislative initiatives and specific projects or the right to environmental information guaranteed by the current norms. While these channels can also be used by individual citizens, collective actors have additional points of access at their disposal, such as representation in different administrative councils and advisory boards within public enterprises.

Strategic environmental assessment is also expected to play an important role in forcing non-environmental sectors to pay much more attention to environmental questions, but it has been adopted only recently and has yet to show its potential. Finally, there seem to be advances in the content and quality of the environmental reports prepared by the responsible authorities, but again progress is far from uniform and a clear, stable system of reporting and monitoring has not been firmly established.

All in all, it is possible to describe the search for appropriate institutional responses to the challenges of sustainable development as one of path dependence. This means the institutional 'logic' of sustainable development is 'filtered' through the pre-existing institutional arrangements designed to process other types of policies. The resulting changes in the traditional way of 'doing policy' tend to be incremental or marginal.[7]

Thus, we have seen several examples of institutions nominally in charge or promoting sustainability across the government, but whose main activity at the end of the day consists of managing traditional environmental policies. Equally, advisory councils or participatory bodies confront great difficulties in establishing themselves *vis-à-vis* the pre-existing array of governmental institutions, even though they represent no real danger to the position and interests of other political actors.

Given this weak position, their fortunes are sometimes linked to very contingent and transient political factors, like the pressure to prepare an SD strategy for a given internationally fixed deadline, like the Johannesburg 2002 summit (this explains the creation of the Advisory Council on Sustainable Development in Catalonia), or the electoral successes or failures of different parties (the change of government in Galicia in 2005 and in Catalonia in 2003 meant a 'revision' of previous processes which in practice slowed down considerably the adoption of new procedures).

On the basis of this overview we can, in conclusion, affirm that in our case studies there has been only a partial and incomplete transformation of governance for SD and in particular for EPI.

The transition to sustainable patterns of development is a long and difficult journey, with many, often contradictory, twists and turns. The societies and governments of the regions we have examined have just begun to take the first steps along this path.

NOTES

1. The work is part of two research projects funded by the Spanish National Programme of R&D at the Institut Universitari d'Estudis Europeus, Universidad de Barcelona: 'Governanza para el Desarrollo Sostenible: Requisitos Institucionales' (Ref.SEC2003-06918) and 'Integración de Políticas Ambientales y Gobernanza Multinivel' (Ref. SEJ2006-12137), We are grateful to Francesc Morata, Víctor Torres and Andrea Lanaia for their contributions.
2. Scholars like Collier (1994) and Liberatore (1997) have proposed normative conceptualizations of EPI. The first one underlines how the entire policy cycle must be informed by decisions aimed at achieving sustainable development and preventing environmental damage, and stresses the wide scope that exists to remove contradictions between policies as well as to pick the low hanging fruits of realizing mutual benefits. The second one refers to the principle of reciprocity, warning that if the balance among the three dimensions is not stricken by assigning at least equal weight to each, the resulting outcome will not be integration but rather dilution of the weaker dimension within the stronger.
3. It must be noticed that these authors add some caveats to their view by pointing that the environmental concern will not always prevail over other issues. For them, an ultimate tradeoff exists between a strong presupposition for the environmental mandate on one hand and exiting democratic norms and decision making rules on the other, with the latter determining, at the end, the context where the decision on the trade-off must be made. In their most recent work, they give a practical guidance on how to operationalize the principled priority on the suggestion of using a 'canon for practical judgment' leading to judicious decisions on trade-offs over the application of science, assessment and the precautionary principle as well as the securing of political will to support EPI in practice.
4. The autonomous communities differ slightly in the terminology they apply to their government departments and units within them. The ministries (*consejerías* or *departamentos*) are usually organized in several general directorates (*direcciones generales*) or simply directorates. In some cases, but not always, these are grouped and coordinated within intermediate institutions, which may be called vice-ministries (*viceconsejerías*), secretariats or general secretariats (*secretaría* or *secretaría general*). The units under the general directorate level may be called general sub-directorate, services or simply offices.
5. Some coordination tools are: inter-ministerial committees and task forces, 'environmental correspondents' can be sent to sector departments, and a central unit responsible for overview can be installed. At the level of individual officials, networking schemes can be introduced, as well as regular circulation of staff between sector departments. The budgetary process can be an important tool for promoting EPI in a given organizational structure. Training and awareness programmes are often used in sector organizations in order to achieve EPI.
6. They are all available at http://www.juntadeandalucia.es/medioambiente.
7. A further illustration of this point can be made with the story of the so-called strategic Plan Cat21, adopted by the Government of Catalonia in 2000, to improve the quality of policy making through interdepartmental coordination. The Plan was presented as a set of concrete measures to move ahead on the modernization of public administration in Catalonia. However, it was quietly abandoned before the parties in government changed in 2003, and forgotten since then, showing once again the difficulty of this type of exercise.

REFERENCES

Cataluña (2006), *Estatuto de Autonomía de Cataluña*, Barcelona: Generalitat de Cataluña.
Collier, Ute (1994), *Energy and Environment in the European Union*, Aldershot: Avesbury.
Consejería de Medio Ambiente (2005), *Medio Ambiente en Andalucía, Informe 2005*, Sevilla: Junta de Andalucía.

Consellería de Medio Ambiente (2003), 'Cara a unha estrategia para o desenvolvemento sostible de Galicia: Integración da variable ambiental nas políticas sectoriais' (Unpublished).

DMAOT (2006), *Medio Ambiente en la Comunidad Autónoma del País Vasco. Indicadores ambientales 2006*, Bilbao: IHOBE.

European Environmental Agency (EEA) (2005), 'Environmental Policy Integration in Europe. State of Play and an Evaluation Framework', EEA Technical Report No. 2/2005, Copenhagen: EEA.

Fernández Latorre, F. (2007), *Indicadores de Sostenibilidad y Medio Ambiente: Métodos y Escala*, Sevilla: Junta de Andalucía.

Generalitat de Cataluña (2005), *Cataluña 2005. Informe sobre Medio Ambiente y Desarrollo Sostenible*, Barcelona: Generalitat de Cataluña.

Generalitat de Cataluña (2007), *Medio Ambiente en Cataluña, Informe 2007*, Barcelona: Generalitat de Cataluña.

Generalitat de Cataluña (2008), *Datos del Medio Ambiente en Cataluña 2008*, Barcelona: Generalitat de Cataluña.

Gobierno Vasco (2002), *Programa Marco Ambiental de la Comunidad Autónoma del País Vasco (2002–2006). Estrategia Ambiental Vasca de Desarrollo Sostenible (2002–2020)*, Bilbao: IHOBE

Gobierno Vasco (2001), *Compromiso por la Sostenibilidad del País Vasco*, Bilbao: Gobierno Vasco.

IHOBE (2006), *IHOBE Sociedad Pública de Gestión Ambiental. Informe de actividades 2005*, Bilbao: IHOBE.

Jacob, K., A. Volkery and A. Lenschow (2008), 'Instruments for environmental policy integration in 30 OECD-Countries', in A. Jordan and A. Lenschow (eds), *Innovation in Environmental Policy? Integrating the Environment for Sustainability*, Cheltenham, UK and Northampton, MA, USA, Edward Elgar.

Jordan, A. (2002), 'Efficient hardware and light green software: Environmental policy integration in the UK', in Andrea Lenschow (ed.), *Environmental Policy Integration*, London: Earthscan.

Jordan, A. and A. Schout (2006), *The Co-ordination of European Governance: Exploring the Capacities for Networked Governance*, Oxford: Oxford University Press.

Junta de Andalucía (2002), *Estrategia Andaluza de Desarrollo Sostenible*, Sevilla: Junta de Andalucía.

Lafferty, W. (2004), 'From environmental protection to sustainable development: The challenge of decoupling through sectoral integration', in William M. Lafferty (ed.), *Governance for Sustainable Development: The Challenge of Adapting Form to Function*, Cheltenham, UK and Northampton, MA, USA: Edward Elgar.

Lafferty, W. (2002), *Adapting Government Practice to the Goals of Sustainable Development*, Paris: OECD.

Lafferty, W. and E. Hoven (2002), *Environmental Policy Integration: Towards an Analytical Framework?* Oslo: ProSus Report Ro. 7/02.

Lafferty, W. and J. Knudsen (2007), 'The issue of "balance" and trade-offs in environmental policy integration: How will we know EPI when we see it?' EPIGOV Working Paper. Berlin, Germany: Ecologic – Institute for International and European Environmental Policy.

Lafferty, W.M. and E. Hovden (2003), 'Environmental policy integration: towards an analytical framework', *Environmental Politics*, **12**(3), 1–22.

Lenschow, A. (2002), *Environmental Policy Integration*, London: Earthscan.

Liberatore, A. (1997), 'The integration of sustainable development objectives into EU policy-making: Barriers and prospects', in Susan Baker et al. (eds), *The Politics of Sustainable Development: Theory, Policy and Practice within the European Union*, London: Routledge, pp. 108–26.

Nilsson, M. and Å. Persson (2003), 'Framework for analysing environmental policy integration', *Journal of Environmental Policy and Planning*, **5**(4), 333–59.

OECD (2002), 'Improving policy coherence and integration for sustainable development: A checklist', OECD Policy Brief, PUMA, October, Paris.

Persson, Å. (2004), *Environmental Policy Integration: An Introduction*, Stockholm: Stockholm Environment Institute.

Peters, G. (1998), 'Managing horizontal government. The politics of coordination', Research Paper No. 21, Ottawa,: Canadian Centre for Management Development.

Underdal, A. (1980), 'Integrated marine policy: What? Why? How?', *Marine Policy*, **4**(3), 159–69.

Index